Nostalgia

A Psychoanalytic Study of Marcel Proust

Nostalgia

A Psychoanalytic Study of Marcel Proust

BY MILTON L. MILLER, M.D.

HOUGHTON MIFFLIN COMPANY BOSTON

The Riverside Press Cambridge

1956

From Remembrance of Things Past by Marcel Proust, copyright 1927, 1929, 1930, 1932 and renewed 1951, 1952, 1955 by Random House, Inc.; copyright 1934 by The Modern Library, Inc.

From Letters of Marcel Proust translated and edited by Mina Curtiss, copyright 1949 by Random House, Inc.

From The Basic Writings of Sigmund Freud copyright 1938 by Random House, Inc.; copyright 1938 by The Modern Library, Inc.

The Riverside Press
Cambridge, Massachusetts
Printed in the U.S.A.

Acknowledgments

Grateful acknowledgment is due to Random House, publishers of the American edition of Proust's *Remembrance of Things Past*, including the Modern Library Edition, translated by C. K. Scott Moncrieff (except for *The Past Recaptured*, translated by Frederick A. Blossom). I also wish to thank Random House for permission to quote from *Letters of Marcel Proust*, translated and edited with Notes by Mina Curtiss, with an Introduction by Harry Levin, and *The Basic Writings of Sigmund Freud*, translated by A. A. Brill.

Thanks are due to Harper and Brothers, publishers of *Proust: Portrait of a Genius*, by André Maurois, translated by Gerard Hopkins. To The Hogarth Press, Ltd., for permission to quote from Freud's *Collected Papers* and *Civilization and Its Discontents*. To the Librairie Gallimard (*Nouvelle Revue Française*) of Paris whose *Jean Santeuil* and *Contre Sainte-Beuve*, edited by Bernard de Fallois, are of inestimable value to Proust scholars, I am greatly indebted. To Lear Publishers Inc., of New York, a debt is acknowledged for making available interesting and pertinent material in the

volume entitled *Stavrogin's Confession,* which is comprised
of suppressed chapters from *The Possessed,* translated by
Virginia Woolf and S. S. Koteliansky, and also includes
"Dostoevsky and Parricide," a psychoanalytic study of the
author by Sigmund Freud, translated by D. F. Tait, copyright 1947 by Lear Publishers Inc., and used by permission
of Crown Publishers, Inc. Basic Books, Inc., are the source
of invaluable letters from Freud, in *The Origins of Psychoanalysis, Letters to Wilhelm Fliess, Drafts and Notes: 1887–
1902,* edited by Marie Bonaparte, Anna Freud, Ernst Kris,
translated by Eric Mosbacher and James Strachey, New
York, 1954.

The University of Chicago Press have made it possible to
utilize the research by Dr. Thomas M. French, two volumes
of which have been published under the title of *The Integration of Behavior,* copyright 1952, 1954 by the University of
Chicago. To Dr. Thomas M. French and to Dr. Helen V.
McLean, personally, I wish to express thanks for allowing
me to quote from their psychoanalytic research material.

My wife, Bernice, collaborated in all phases of the work
of bringing this manuscript to fruition.

M. L. M.

Foreword

In this study, Proust's keen conscious insight will be contrasted with his even more remarkable unconscious insight, and some mechanisms of the latter investigated. Proust's imagery will be compared with dream imagery in a psychoanalytic patient who became the subject of Thomas M. French's five-volume study (now in the process of being completed), *The Integration of Behavior*.[1] Proust as a psychological novelist, revealing his own emotional life, is discussed from a psychoanalytic point of view, and an attempt is made to show how he may have been influenced by Freud, but how he also prognosticated some of the findings later made by Freud and his followers, doing so consciously at times, at other times writing with unconscious or preconscious insight. Some discussion of how memory functions during the psychoanalytic process is intended to throw light on Proust's own special pursuit of involuntary memories.

This essay is not one of literary criticism. It is a compilation of notes which grew to book length because the investigation of Proust became increasingly interesting as a

[1] *The Integration of Behavior*, Chicago, Vol. I, 1952; Vol. II, 1954.

study in intuition. Proust's pursuits revolved around his impressions of the functioning of the unconscious. Thus we are led naturally to a comparison with Freud's beliefs, and with some very recent research into the nature of behavior patterns. The compelling nature of those patterns that seem to have determined Proust's subject matter and the precise way he dealt with what he had to say seem to require some comment from psychoanalytic as well as literary experts. It is not surprising that two men of genius explored the unconscious within the same generation, the one aesthetically, the other scientifically. Proust developed his aesthetic approach to the unconscious in a country which was, in subtle artistry, a leader among nations; his predecessor, Anatole France, helped introduce a tradition of delicate introspective analysis, which was later enhanced by André Gide, a great critic and writer who looked deeply into the unconscious. Meanwhile, from among the Austrians, Hungarians, Germans, English and the Swiss came most of the outstanding pioneers in psychoanalysis. In France, Janet's followers at first accepted psychoanalysis somewhat reluctantly, omitting theories of symbolism; and the earliest psychoanalysts came from the provinces, not Paris. Yet Paris provided the atmosphere in which the great impressionist painters and symbolist poets introduced their theories to the world. The aesthetic rather than the medical approach to the unconscious predominated in France.

In order to bridge the gap between the aesthetic and scientific attitudes which so often seem to conflict with each other, we will find ourselves employing the language of psychiatry and of aesthetics, but often departing from both, in order to make use of Proust's vocabulary of special images. No attempt has been made to be conservative, or to hold back any theories that might conceivably prove fruitful or stimulating. Proust's status as one of the greatest writers of all times is so well established that we may impose upon him in this way, for, as he indicates in *Within a Budding Grove*, the second volume of *Remembrance of Things Past*, the forms of familiarity taken with the really great are a mark of true respect.

We must agree with Freud, who, in *Civilization and Its Discontents*,[2] expressed his admiration for those to whom "it is vouchsafed with hardly an effort to salve from the whirlpool of their own emotions the deepest truths, to which we others have to force our way ceaselessly groping amid torturing uncertainties."

Parts of Proust's notebooks now being made available to the public as *Contre Sainte-Beuve*[3] are a precursor of psychoanalytic findings which deal with problems of ego related to the demands of civilized existence, the inconsistency between instincts and the ego which deals with external reality — as related to literary creativity. The endeavor to express human conflicts in art, Proust found, inevitably led one into problems of criticism, as a primary step. *Contre Sainte-Beuve*, an essay of literary criticism, inquires into the nature of sincerity. Because man is not harmonious within himself, his idolatries and paradoxes create barriers to self-expression in words. We hope that a psychoanalytic study of Proust, undertaken not as an attempt to "answer" all his enigmas, may lead closer to an understanding of the nature of the intuitive processes as they are related to art, to psychoanalytic method, and to instinctual expression.

The references for the individual volumes of *Remembrance of Things Past* are to the Modern Library Edition published in New York by Random House. For the date of each volume see Bibliography.

[2] Sigmund Freud, *Civilization and Its Discontents*, London and New York, 1930.   [3] Published in Paris, 1954.

Contents

Nostalgia

A Psychoanalytic Study of Marcel Proust

I

Biographical Data

IF THE CONTENT of our minds for an entire day could be automatically tape-recorded, and played back to us, we would each be astonished at the evidence of inhibition of our intellectual capacity. Yet our random thoughts, so many of them nonsensical, petty and repetitive, are to a large extent necessary to impede the stream of other thoughts welling up from the unconscious, which are unacceptable to us. Into this netherworld of unconscious emotion, Proust plunged deeply, uncovering blocked memories to garner the content and coloration of the fantasies he wove into *Remembrance of Things Past*. As Joseph Wood Krutch has pointed out,[1] Proust emphasized factors which are usually ignored, and overlooked what is conventionally emphasized in descriptive and narrative writing. To the psychoanalyst, accustomed to discover motivations in free associations and dreams, and behavior, much of the unusual manner of Proust's narrative seems quite logical.

Proust, himself, had a gift for conveying rather technical psychological comments by means of imagery rather than

[1] *Five Masters, A Study in the Mutation of the Novel*, New York, 1930.

psychiatric terms, for example in *The Guermantes Way*,[2] something similar to Freud's concept of "denial" is conveyed by the analogy of a silent beat in music, and in *The Past Recaptured* [3] he likens to tangled bookkeeping the truly estimated value of possessing that which one fantasies, in contrast with the price at which one's desires appraise it.

Marcel Proust's intellectual struggles had many parallels with those of Sigmund Freud, whose work was commenced within the same generation, with no early, direct linkage except that the two men, both avid readers, probably had essential stimuli in common (such as Havelock Ellis, Bergson, and so on; and later both were fascinated by Albert Einstein's discoveries). We know more about Freud's development since the publication of his letters,[4] and Ernest Jones's biography.[5] Freud published his studies in hysteria with Breuer in 1895, and Freud referred to his first exploration of the Oedipus complex in 1897, in a letter to Fliess. At the latter time, Proust was twenty-six years old. *The Interpretation of Dreams*, which contained Freud's first published description of the Oedipus complex, was printed in 1900, in German. Both Freud and Proust felt impelled to seek answers to ultimate questions regarding the nature of man and the purpose of life. Neither was religious in a conventional sense. Proust was able to articulate in aesthetic form the subjective, emotional basis of his own unconscious development, whereas Freud arrived at the technique and methods for an objective, scientific exploration of the unconscious. Later in his development, we shall see that Proust eventually had a good

[2] Pt. I, p. 357.

[3] P. 320.

[4] Sigmund Freud, *The Origins of Psycho-Analysis* (see Bibliography for full title), ed. Maria Bonaparte, Anna Freud, Ernst Kris, Transl. Eric Mosbacher and James Strachey, New York, 1954.

[5] Ernest Jones, *The Life and Work of Sigmund Freud*, New York, Vol. I, 1953; Vol. II, 1955.

deal of acquaintance with psychiatry, probably Freudian.

Is it possible that there are fresh and constructive comments still left to be made, where so many specialists in Proust have already attempted to disclose all the ramifications of this great and fascinating human being and his lasting work?

This essay will focus upon a number of themes which dominated much of Marcel Proust's paradoxical personality and writings, and which are all related to his need for protection. The "silent beat" which he himself left out of most of the music of his writing was his need for his father's protection and love, at the price of pain.

Proust's genius was related to his illness and his emotional sufferings. His homosexuality, which was his escape from his basic conflicts, was at the same time the trap that drove him back into them.

Bisexuality, to a varying degree, is universal. The conflict over an infantile cry for a mother's protection, which has been suggested as typical of asthmatics, is latent or stifled within us all. But it is not accidental that the creation of *Remembrance of Things Past*, and all the earlier writings that led up to it, in the smallest detail, were tied up with the anguish of homosexuality and asthma. The artistic presentation of certain specific basic conflicts which are extraordinarily strong in Proust, yet are present in all human beings, has created enemies as well as friends for Proust as a writer. For some, he is too disturbing.

Marcel Proust, in his earliest years, underwent a high concentration of all that destiny could provide in inheritance and circumstance to further artistic endowment. He was born July 10, 1871, at Auteuil, where his mother, Jeanne Weil Proust, was staying at her uncle's estate, in order to avoid the turmoil of the Siege of Paris and the Commune. Her pregnancy was a difficult one. Marcel's father, Dr.

Adrien Proust, was an eminent Catholic doctor, considered "radical" by the anti-Republican aristocracy. Marcel was raised a Catholic, with a strong sense of the beauty of churches, although he could not submit to conventional religious feelings. His father, who was Minister of Public Health in the Republic, was away a good deal on government business. (Thiers was elected in 1871 and fell in 1873. The Constitution of France was built up in the ensuing period.) It was Dr. Adrien Proust who originated the term "cordon sanitaire" during his campaign against plague and cholera. The boy was left to the care of his mother and grandmother, who were sensitive, aesthetic, highly cultured women from a wealthy Jewish family. They quoted Racine and the emphatically matriarchal Madame de Sévigné to the boy, and read him only literary masterpieces, with the love scenes deleted. Music, art, and the cadences of beautiful phrases which were written down and quoted by his mother and grandmother were among the earliest influences upon him. A younger brother, Robert, was born when Marcel was two. In *The Two Worlds of Marcel Proust* by Harold March, we are told that Robert later recalled that when Marcel was five, Marcel watched over him with a gentleness that was "infinite, enveloping and almost maternal." [6] Robert was robust, resembled his father, and later became a successful physician. Their friend Paul Morand [7] mentions that Marcel adored Robert.

At the age of nine, after a springtime walk in the Champs-Elyseés with his family and some of their friends, Marcel suffered an almost fatal attack of asthma. His mother moved into his room for a month, to care for him. After that, every spring he was forced to retreat from outdoor activities because

[6] Philadelphia, 1948, p. 20.
[7] *Le Visiteur du Soir*, Geneva, 1929.

of asthma. As time went on, he found he was allergic to flowers, ladies' perfume, cold, dust and a variety of emotional stimuli, so that he himself admitted his illness was psychoneurotic, but he said he preferred it to unknown evils that might replace it, were he to relinquish it.

He resembled his mother in appearance, with olive complexion, black hair, slender frame and expressive dark eyes. Like his mother, he was particularly sensitive to words, and to genuine feelings in contrast to pretentiousness, vulgarity or meanness. But a less apparent trait was to develop within him, as his biographer, André Maurois,[8] points out — an organizational ability akin to his father's — which was manifested at last in the beautifully integrated form of his mature work.

During his early years he was openly dependent upon his mother and grandmother, and made little effort to hide his physical frailty. At the age of thirteen, he gave the following answer to a questionnaire: "What is, for you, the peak of misery?" . . . "To be separated from Mamma."

Illness interfered with his studies at the Condorcet Lyceum, but he belonged to a clique of erudite young men there who read and discussed what was then the avante garde of literature. Anatole France, Lemaître, Maeterlinck, Barrès, Leconte de L'isle, Saint-Simon, LaBruyère, Madame de Sévigné, Baudelaire, Musset, George Sand — translations of Dickens and Thomas Hardy, Stevenson and George Eliot were among their "discoveries" and masters; Saint-Simon, who wrote of court intrigues with great distinction of style in certain portions of his memoirs, remained Proust's lifelong favorite, along with Galland's *Thousand and One Nights* (*The Arabian Nights' Entertainment*).

Reading the correspondence of his late adolescent period,

[8] *Portrait of a Genius* (transl. by Gerard Hopkins), New York, 1950.

one notes not only the serious interest he had in literary technique and style (which he later defined as "vision"), but the mature critical sense he displayed in his teens. His friends, impressed by his intellect, were bothered by his exaggerated need for affection, his readiness to take offense, his undue humility combined with a suppressed tendency toward biting sarcasm, his archaic qualities, affectation, and yearning for acceptance in aristocratic society. Later, a phrase, "to Proustify," was used by his friends, connoting overobservance of social amenities.

(We can more easily surmise his relationships to members of his family and his friends at this time from the original draft of his novel, which has been published under the title of *Jean Santeuil* and describes in detail the conflicts of adolescence.[9] At the very beginning of *Jean Santeuil*, we see enormous intellectual ambition instilled by the parents, and this is pitted against a desire to defeat them by intellectual failure. There is a strong urge for flight into the solace of close fraternal friendships, which are suspect and forbidden by the parents — particularly after the boy's precocious passion for a little girl named Marie is cut short. In the course of *Jean Santeuil*, we are given portraits of a handsome, well-intentioned, but inaccessible father, and an overwhelmingly affectionate, domineering, restrictive mother; other relatives and family friends are described, but no brother.)

In 1889, Proust's friendships and studies were interrupted by service in the Army, in the infantry at Orléans, which he was able to accomplish despite his fragile health. Then he studied law at the Sorbonne, in deference to his father's ambition for him to enter diplomatic service. But he did poorly in his legal studies, and turned away from them to philosophy. Like many students at that time, he fell under

[9] Paris, 1952.

the spell of the anti-mechanistic, highly subjective philosopher, Henri Bergson, who later became a cousin of his by marriage. Bergson's concept of "creative time" had a lasting effect upon the main theme of Proust's writing.[10] But in Proust's approach to all thinking and writing, Bergson's philosophy was overlaid upon the primary search for essential truths in a universe of constant flux, which Plato established. Proust was an avid reader of philosophy from the classical Greeks to Gobineau, with his racial theories, whom Proust termed an "old fool," but admired for a time.

Nearing the end of his adolescence, Marcel Proust exhibited such strong attachments to the mothers of some of his friends as to cause comment when he sat at their feet in the salons. He delighted in surprising them with overly elaborate gifts of flowers and sweets.

At the age of twenty, answering the same questionnaire [11] as he had at thirteen, when asked the principal trait of his character, he answered: "The need to be loved, and more precisely, to be caressed and spoiled more than the need to be admired."

When asked his preferred occupation, he answered: "To love."

"What would be your greatest unhappiness?"

10 Bergson, it will be recalled, says that "in our conscious state all our memories form at a given moment a solid unity, a pyramid as it were, whose apex coincides with our present which is ceaselessly plunging forward into the future. Although only the memories which interest our actual preoccupations are admitted by the brain, there are images retained by the subconscious memory, not dormant, but very alert, waiting for the first opportunity to insert themselves into the apex of the pyramid. Such is surely the process that Proust is trying to interpret." Quoted from page 403 of *The Mind of Proust* by F. C. Green (Fellow of Magdalene College, and Drapers Professor of French at the University of Cambridge), published 1949, Cambridge University Press, England.

This is similar to Freud's famous iceberg analogy: that most of the personality is submerged in the unconscious like an iceberg.

11 André Maurois, *ibid.*

"Not to have known my mother or my grandmother."

His worst fault he considered was lack of will; his favorite fictional character, Hamlet; his favorite heroine in history, Cleopatra; the quality he most preferred in men, feminine charm — and in women the virtues of a man, such as frankness and comradery.

The first four or five years after his Army service, he studied the paintings at the Louvre, music, genealogy, history, and the ways of aristocratic social life. It was the time of symbolism [12] in France. Paul Verlaine's *Poètes Maudits: Rimbaud, Corbière et Mallarmé*," was published in 1888. Proust founded a literary review, *Le Banquet*, along with Fernand Gregh, Daniel Halévy, Léon Blum, and others who were also to gain illustrious reputations. One of the basic editorial tenets of *Le Banquet* was to combine the essential depth of viewpoint of the great classics of the past with typically French roots and traditions as a foundation for French literature. This type of approach was enhanced by Proust's admiration for Ruskin's writings. Through his boyhood friend, Robert de Flers, and a friend from his regiment, G. A. de Caillavet, Proust had opportunities to write for *Figaro* about society, and for four years he wrote social notes. By the end of the nineteenth century, his articles in *Figaro*, mainly on the salons of the period, were known to the élite of France. He wrote portraits of fashionable women and celebrated courtesans, as well as literary criticism, articles about historic churches and famous families of old France, with what seemed the superficial finesse of a Georges Ohnet, whom he feared he resembled. Actually, a great deal of profoundly original development was in progress and he was, with intermittent diligence, filling his notebooks, as we know from correspondence and papers, and even small scraps of his writings, which his

[12] "Pas de couleur, rien que la nuance."

friend Robert Dreyfus preserved.[13]

From 1892 to 1900 his asthma attacks were more severe and frequent, but in between attacks he led an almost normal existence, except that because he felt better at night, he adapted his hours of work and social life to night hours. His brother, Robert, was becoming a successful doctor. Marcel maintained abnormally close ties to his mother, still; and at night, when he had insomnia, he wrote her long, endearing letters and left them for her in the vestibule so she would see them in the morning.

In 1895, to satisfy his father, he became what his biographer, André Maurois, called "a most detached of attachés, always on leave." [14] He had passed third in a competitive examination for attaché to the Bibliothèque Mazarine, a job which paid nothing and called for five hours a day of attendance — in his case not at the library but at the Ministry of Public Instruction for the legal deposit service. He applied for, and received, almost continuous leave — until in February, 1900, his work-record irregularity was looked into and he was given an ultimatum to return to his post or give it up. He did not return. His connection with all employment ended.

The death of his grandmother was a great blow, not only to his mother but to himself, and he noted sympathetically how his mother became more and more like his grandmother in appearance and actions after the latter's death. A great writer in the sphere of mourning, his observations were not dissimilar to Freud's [15] and Karl Abraham's [16] on the process of mourning (especially the identification with the deceased,

---

[13] *Souvenirs sur Marcel Proust,* Paris, 1926.

[14] *Portrait of a Genius.*

[15] Sigmund Freud, "Mourning and Melancholia" (1917), *Collected Papers,* Vol. IV, London, 1925.

[16] *A Short Study of the Development of the Libido* (1924), London, 1927. Selected papers.

the gradual evolution of comparative indifference through eradication of the beloved image from within oneself, and the mechanisms of delayed mourning reactions in memories, dreams, and symptoms.)

In 1896 Marcel Proust announced publication of his first book, *Les Plaisirs et Les Jours*,[17] with a preface by Anatole France and musical text by Reynaldo Hahn, a musician whose fame at that time far outshone Proust's. There were illustrations by the well-known Madeleine Lemaire. This book, heralded with much fanfare, was not very successful. Later it was to become vastly more interesting, as an indication of Proust's incipient genius and a revelation of the earlier, less subtle ramifications of the author's personality. These uneven, and at times somewhat puerile stories (although Proust later considered them better written than *Swann's Way*), are comparable in their candor with a series of childhood photographs or the early dreams in a psychoanalysis. The very first story deals with the theme of death, a motif which Proust later said was a constant part of himself. Those stories which are about love already indicate that love is a "transference" phenomenon (to borrow a term from Freud), that it comes from within, as a sort of inner compulsion, deriving from the unconscious, sometimes even originating from a dream, and like a dream, capable of fixing upon the most mediocre of objects — a force that is not governed by laws of intellectual logic or conscious good taste. Interspersed with frothy, eulogistic verses to outstanding artists and musicians and descriptions of aristocratic society, there are notes that later became the foundation of *Remembrance of Things Past*. We see, revolving nebulously, the substance that was to appear in *Swann's Way* and other sections of the great novel, sometimes to be turned to diametrically opposite uses, the sexes reversed,

[17] Paris, 1924.

loves and hates interchanged, until the author evolved the
form of fantasy he finally intended.

Love, as Proust conceived of it, was essentially connected
with anguish. Jealousy and the fear of separation were so
integral a part of love that he called jealousy "the best Procurer," and reiterated that only death could end jealousy.
This death-and-love theme was most prominent in his literary
work from first to last.

It might be worth while to digress, in order to set down a
summary of one of these early stories, a crudely naïve fantasy
called "The Confession of a Young Girl." [18] It actually tells
us more about Proust than do some of the data of his early
biography.

In this unadorned tale, we are told about a girl who has
just shot herself and has eight days left to live. She confesses
the crime that has led to her suicide. Lack of will was the
cause of her deterioration. She loved her mother dearly, idolized her, demonstrating her excessively strong affection by
constant kisses and gifts of flowers. But this girl mortally
offended her mother by succumbing to habits of sexual sin:
she was seduced by a mediocre boy and could not give up
her sensual habits. The girl's mother had heart disease, and
a doctor had warned her that excitement might be fatal.
Finally, at church, the girl confessed her sexual guilt to her
confessor, re-established her good character, and renounced
her current affair. To please her mother, she became engaged
to an eligible young man of whom the mother approved. The
mother had only a few more weeks to guard her health, and
would have been cured. But unfortunately the girl drank
champagne to celebrate the engagement, in the fiancé's absence, and then, intoxicated by the champagne, went off with

[18] *Les Plaisirs et les Jours.* Also see Edmund Wilson, *Axel's Castle*, New
York, 1931.

her latest seducer to see some verses he had written. Her consent to go off with him meant assent to a renewal of their relationship. They locked themselves in a room and had intercourse, and then she looked in a mirror and saw the ruthless, bestial joy on her own face, with his face next to hers. In this mirror she then beheld the reflection of her mother looking at the two of them from a balcony across the way. The mother, shocked, fell dead. The girl said she wished her mother had witnessed the preceding love scene, or any other crime being committed by her, but not that bestial expression on her face. She hoped God had not permitted it, and that her mother had died of apoplexy first. "What desolated my mother was my lack of will.[19] I did everything by the impulse of the moment," the girl lamented.

Never again was Proust to express so clearly the peril that might be implicit in all sexual temptation, and his impression of the destructiveness of sexuality. Here we have a blunt fantasy: to succumb to physical (sexual) temptation, with a mediocre individual (ultimately the one who must most strongly evoke it), to debase one's will, to give in to destructive habit, and to kill — thus to lose — the beloved mother — this is potentially the worst crime. Confession of such impulses is a literary way to express a need for forgiveness and reassurance, but only death seems a suitable punishment.

Later, we see how the sexual (homosexual) sin of Mademoiselle Vinteuil killed her father, in *Remembrance of Things*

[19] This conflict over moral issues, as well as over habit and lack of will power, were typical of Proust, and were probably connected on a less profound level with precepts he received, based on the Aristotelian philosophy of habit formation, and stress upon the concept of will power which his reading of Schopenhauer, and his parents', especially his father's, attitudes must have enhanced. In addition to the philosophical connotations of his preoccupation with habit and will, in relation to morality, his deepest conflicts were concerned with habit formation and will power in relation to sexual temptation. How this is related to his unconscious, oedipal conflict, will be elaborated in Chapter XII.

Past; and in the section entitled *Cities of the Plain* there is a description of how the homosexual's sense of guilt forever stands between himself and his parents, how his whole life is filled with deceit even when he shuts their eyes in death. At the same time, the need to confess, to exhibit sexual guilt and habitually to spy on it, is a theme that recurs insistently. For example, the two homosexual girls in the hotel at Balbec, Mademoiselle Vinteuil and her friend, Charlus and his partners, Odette and Albertine and their partners at various times, are just a few of the objects of spying and investigation in the novel.

During the writing of the preliminary stories, published in *Les Plaisirs et les Jours,* and then after they appeared in 1896, Marcel Proust lived with his parents and used to write in the dining room of their apartment. He translated Ruskin, whose long, rather dull sentences he enjoyed and whose enchantment with earlier religious art and architecture fascinated him. In beauty, he learned to look for something beyond mere pleasure. In an article on Ruskin written later on, he commented on a fundamental conflict, an insincerity in Ruskin, common to everyone — because Ruskin was idolatrous toward art in choosing moral values for their beauty and presenting them as true rather than as beautiful. Proust considered aesthetic beauty precisely that which accompanied the discovery of a truth.[20]

Proust's mother knew English well, and assisted him in his translation of Ruskin. He had begun to entertain such notable guests as Hervieu, Paul Bourget, Calmette (editor of *Figaro*), Madame de Noailles, and Anatole France at dinners served with old-fashioned formality. He presided at the head of the table while his mother or father sat at the other end; but he partook of almost none of the food, because of his digestive

[20] Proust, *Pastiches et Mélanges,* Paris, 1949.

difficulties. Unpublished letters furnish records of the quarrels
he had with his parents about some of these dinners, and his
sensitivity about remarks he feared his father might exchange
with his guests.[21]

One gathers from *Jean Santeuil* that as a child he had a
tendency to stuff sweets, but that these readily upset his
stomach. In one chapter he describes the tempting lobster he
had to renounce the morning he went to see the giant storm
that became a symbolic model for his later concepts of artistic
creation. In *Remembrance of Things Past,* the final version
of the novel, just as in his real life, pleasure in food was usually
forbidden because of medical necessity, and drinking wine
liberally caused him nightmares.

In 1903 his brother, Robert, married as most of his friends
were doing. His father died suddenly of a stroke that year on
November 26, after becoming ill two days before, while
working. His mother never recovered from the shock, and
she died in 1905. In the summer of 1898, his mother had
undergone a serious operation. After his father's death, his
mother, in addition to her own poor health and grief, was
burdened by worries about Marcel's illness. For several
months Marcel looked for a suitable sanitarium for himself,
and after his mother's death he went ahead with his plan to
seek treatment. She died September 23, 1905, and in January,
1906, he entered Sollier's, to stay about six weeks. He was
dismayed at first, because Sollier was depreciatory of Bergson's philosophy, and he did not seem to improve very much.

After his parents' deaths, Proust gave the impression of
taking his work far more earnestly, and of becoming gradually so absorbed in it that it was the greater reality for him.
He remained fifteen months in the apartment he had inhabited
with his parents, and then, after seeking endless advice from

[21] See André Maurois, *Portrait of a Genius.*

his friends, he finally went to live where he had formerly lived with his mother, in his uncle's apartment at 102 Boulevard Haussmann, where he had seen his uncle die in the room that he now used as his own. The many idiosyncrasies of his life there are too well known to require description. He stayed in a sound-proof, dust-proof room and worked at night, receiving friends at very late hours. His room was littered with objects he wanted to study, such as half-filled glasses, in different sorts of light. Sometimes he went out at 2 A.M., to see if anyone was still attending a dinner party he had ordered to be given at the Ritz.

As time went on, his somewhat dandified attire became more and more eccentric, so that he was overdressed and at the same time disheveled. The latter was due largely to his poor health and inability to groom himself, but it also displayed his infantile, frail aspect to the world, his need of special understanding and protection. His overcoat, in summertime, was one of the astonishing sights of Paris.

Playing the maternal role himself, he formed attachments to handsome adolescent boys, who came to inhabit his apartment like prisoners there, and these aberrant affairs caused him much remorse and anguish. He later confessed to André Gide that he never loved women except spiritually, and never experienced physical love except with men. Briand [22] tells us about Proust's escapades with a band of youths of low character. He had cruel streaks, but also could be exceedingly kind; in fact, kindness was his predominant characteristic. For example, he insisted on paying a large medical bill for a friend; and he delighted in giving pleasure to others through long-planned, thoughtful gifts. His tips were embarrassingly lavish, his letters affectionate, and his politeness punctilious. He was easily offended, and notoriously demand-

[22] Charles Briand, *Le Secret de Marcel Proust*, Paris, 1950.

ing in his friendships. As Robert Dreyfus tells us, Marcel Proust sometimes took umbrage at what he intuitively suspected his friends might be thinking, without their being aware of it themselves.[23]

He was curious to the point of spying upon strangers,[24] and kept all sorts of notebooks with phrases and reminders, some containing names of real persons later to be used in fiction. He looked upon the fashionable world much more as something to be studied objectively, sociologically as time went on. Yet his being accepted socially meant a great deal to him, always, because of the reassurance he derived from it, and proof that he amounted to something. It was also a release from family domination because the highest social circles represented a sphere beyond the upper middle-class "Republican" level on which his family moved. He was not completely passive, even outside of his writing. He took an active part in the Dreyfus case, and he also fought a duel (with pistols) on February 6, 1897, with "Jean Lorrain." Jean Lorrain was the pen name of Paul Duval, a Belgian poet and novelist who had written a scurrilous article about Robert de Montesquiou's influence on "pretty little society gentlemen in literary heat," naming Proust as one of them.

Proust interested himself in the Briand laws, taking the side of the clergy [25] in the separation of the Church from the State, as one may see from his warm, vibrant article, "En Mémoire des Églises Assassinées," especially the part of it entitled "La Mort des Cathédrales."

In general, Proust's ties to the real world were of an eccentric nature. He pursued people of his acquaintance with

[23] Dreyfus, *Souvenirs sur Marcel Proust.*

[24] Marie Scheikévitch, *Time Past: Memories of Proust and Others,* Boston, 1935.

[25] In his *Pastiches et Mélanges,* Paris, 1919. Proust felt that if France's churches were turned into museums the truth, the life, would depart from them and "a generation of infidel clericals would arise that would be far more anti-Semitic, anti-liberal, and 100 times worse altogether."

detailed inquiries and disturbed his friends at odd hours of the night to ask questions about their attire of twenty years before. All of this seeming madness was part of his perfectionistic approach to his *Remembrance of Things Past,* and an attempt to obtain some support from the current scene. He was trying to construct his book with the consummate form of a cathedral, to make it factual and yet thoroughly subjective, and to this day it is an almost incomparable work. It is in many respects a sociologically accurate study of French society from 1880 to 1919, the time of the interpenetration of the bourgeoisie into aristocratic circles in that country. It is also a first-person rendition of a text still full of psychiatric instruction.

On one occasion, Proust heard the noted violoncellist, Capet, play Beethoven quartets,[26] and was introduced to Capet. That evening he discussed the quartets with Capet so brilliantly that the great musician later said it was as if the music had been subtly re-echoed and enriched by the sensitivity of a remarkable listener. Some time later, Proust telephoned Capet at about three o'clock in the morning and said it was essential that he hear Debussy's quartet immediately — could Capet arouse the others from their sleep and come to play it for him? Capet complied with this request and the musical theme was later used, in composite form, with other themes, such as Saint-Saëns' Piano and Violin Sonata, the Good Friday Spell from *Parsifal,* Franck's Violin and Piano Sonata, the Prelude to *Lohengrin,* and a Fauré piano piece — for Vinteuil's music. Thus, Proust's idiosyncrasies and genius supplemented each other.

Although he was secretive about his manuscript, he did send parts of it to Georges de Lauris, a close friend of his,[27] whose

[26] See p. 271 and footnote.
[27] Mina Curtiss: *Letters of Marcel Proust,* transl. and ed. with notes by Mina Curtiss, New York, 1949.

literary talents he respected highly, for criticism. He was aware of the difficulties he would encounter in seeking a publisher for a work so extraordinary in subject, treatment, and physical proportions. In 1909, when he sent Georges de Lauris the first part of *Swann's Way* to read, he cautioned him not to tell a soul about it because he did not wish it to be discussed, commented upon, or imitated.

It was in 1907, when this friend, Georges,[28] lost his mother through a protracted illness, that Marcel wrote to Georges, "Il me semble que je perds une seconde fois Maman . . ." At this time more than seven hundred pages of *Swann's Way* were written and corrected.

In the same year, a newspaper article which Marcel Proust wrote by request brought attention and notoriety to him with explosive suddenness.

On February 1, 1907, Paris had been stunned by the murder of a society woman by her own son, who then killed himself. Gaston Calmette, editor of *Figaro*, having learned of the existence of some correspondence between this young man and Marcel Proust, asked Proust for an article about him, to be written immediately. Proust stayed up all night to work on it. He thought poorly of the result, except for an ending which the night editor, Cardane, threw into the wastebasket and destroyed because he considered it an encomium of homicide. No copy of this ending, which was the only part that Proust himself admired, has ever been found. The article, as it appeared, shocked many subscribers to *Figaro*, but impressed certain others so favorably, including Ludovic Halévy,[29] with its spark of genius that from then on, Proust received much more serious attention. The article, which reads like a story, and recalls in some ways "The Confession

---

[28] Proust's *A un Ami* (Préface de Georges de Lauris), Paris, 1948.
[29] Robert Dreyfus, *Souvenirs sur Marcel Proust*, p. 199.

of a Young Girl," may be summarized as follows:

A young man, "Marcel" — the author — sends a card of condolence to a friend upon the death of the latter's father. Marcel has recently lost his parents, and is aware of playing their role in sending this card. He receives a meticulously gracious reply. He scarcely knows the young man, Henri van Blarenberghe, and remembers him as quite ordinary; but then he reflects that he has met him at dinner, in discriminating company. Later he receives another ultra-polite letter from this same Henri van B., in which Henri says he is sorry to hear that Marcel has been ill and that he, also, has been ill physically and mentally and does not know what the coming year (1907) has in store for him. Marcel is about to reply to the letter, but sees in the morning paper an account of how this youth has gone mad. The boy murdered his mother by stabbing her and then fell on his sword to commit suicide — making his final atrocity the eradication of his own left eye with a pistol shot. The dying mother had screamed, "What have you done to me?"

Proust quotes at length from *Oedipus Rex*, and refers to other tragedies, including the equally appropriate story of Ajax (who was betrayed by the goddess, Athena, and in his madness slaughtered the sheep left in his charge); Tolstoy's Prince Andrey, King Lear clasping the dead Cordelia, and the sadistic police superintendent's scene with the murderer in *The Brothers Karamazov* also come to his mind. He comments that some basic relationship must have existed between his friend's overly polite personality when sane and his later maniacal one, and then he goes into a long, eloquent statement of how we all kill those we love by our demands upon them. In this article, Proust also quotes H. G. Wells, in regard to time, one of his earlier references to a subject which preoccupied him intensely; here he quotes Wells as saying the eye can penetrate time like a telescope. Gregory Zilboorg has pointed out how Proust universalized the theme of the Oedipus complex [30] in this article, having arrived at an intuition about its positive and negative phases independently of Freud, at about the same time. (As already noted, Freud wrote about his discovery of the Oedipus complex to his friend Fliess in 1897, and published his first demonstration of it in German, in 1900.)

The "parricide" article in *Figaro* and "The Confession of a Young Girl" are in apparent contrast to Proust's major work, the novel, in which love of Marcel's mother and dependence upon her are ostensibly unmarred by any outburst of aggression. In *Remembrance of Things Past* it is a father figure, quite removed from Marcel, who confesses intentions to murder a younger man toward whom he has actually shown love and forbearance. It was characteristic of Proust to describe diametrically opposed sides of every personality, and to confront love with hate, sublimity with degradation. Therefore, his description of the girl as loving her mother particularly deeply and then causing her death in the Confession story, and his description of the politeness and kindness of Henri van B. before he went mad, are in line with Proust's characteristic approach. He believed that the whole personality could be found refracted in any one intense feeling if only we know how to select it — that the true history of the self is reflected in a sudden passion, such as violent anger — as indicated where Bergson speaks of the "masse compacte" of the fundamental, real self.[31] This Bergsonian viewpoint, in addition to Proust's concept of using contrasts to create a three-dimensional exposition of human nature, is

---

[30] "The Discovery of the Oedipus Complex," *Psychoanalytic Quarterly*, Vol. VIII (1939), pp. 279-302.
[31] F. C. Green, *The Mind of Proust*, Cambridge, England, 1949, p. 357.

only a partial indication of how Proust was experimenting all
the time, to achieve a gradual course from the earlier stories
and articles to the sort of descriptions he would develop and
interlock more subtly in the final novel.

In Henri van Blarenberghe's madness, Proust saw the beauty
of a Greek tragedy, because he felt he discovered a universal
truth. He was convinced that all truth is imbued with moral,
undefiled beauty.

Marcel Proust started to write *Remembrance of Things
Past* at around the age of thirty-four and had it published
when he was forty-eight. This delay was partly due to World
War I. In 1911, when he had begun to look seriously for a
publisher, he met with rejections, and in 1914 he had *Swann's
Way* printed at his own expense. André Gide confessed that
turning down this manuscript was his greatest literary mistake.
The critics, except for Paul Souday of *Le Temps*, were not
enthusiastic immediately, but were puzzled, noncommittal.
La Nouvelle Revue Française published *Within a Budding
Grove*, which won the Goncourt Prize in 1919. Even then, a
bitter controversy arose. Proust was considered by many to
be nothing more than a dilettante and snob. It is now easier to
see, beneath the cloak of his dilettantism, a vivid portrayal of
profound universal conflicts. The most varied of readers may
respond to this living textbook, which delineates possessive,
jealous love, bisexuality, ambivalence, and the nostalgic return
to past memories for a solution of current conflicts. Proust's
wealth of social observations, philosophical subtleties, and
human compassion, conveyed in a style akin to music, still
enchants us. But his approach has always been disconcerting.
Disguised under dilettantism, and even under the ultimate in
aestheticism, is an attitude that is clinical. He struggled to
unearth from himself, as if scientifically, and to integrate, the
most anxiety-provoking emotions. He lived out his somewhat

schizoid characteristics superficially, but was at work on one
of the most highly integrated artistic works ever produced.
He literally killed himself with overwork and self-neglect, at
the same time as he wished for so much life and love.

He had planned three volumes, but expanded the work to
nine, and finally to sixteen volumes. The last three were published posthumously. Proust still remains enigmatic. His
letters, at first published by his brother, were eagerly read,
but they disclosed little about his personality and were unlike
his books in style. The first draft of the novel, published very
recently as *Jean Santeuil,* is written "at a gallop," to use the
author's phrase (and does not resemble *Remembrance of
Things Past* in certain essential respects).

At the time of publishing *Sodome et Gomorrhe,* translated
as *Cities of the Plain,* which deals extensively with homosexuality, he stopped having young men come to live with
him. He then (in 1913) had a sincere and charming woman
servant, Céleste — a fine-looking blond woman, the wife of
his chauffeur — come to take care of him like an infant. She
dressed him, combed his hair, prepared his meals and medicines, guarded his manuscripts, and was with him until he
died. He gave her name to a minor, very likable character in
his novel.

While engaged in correcting the proofs of *The Captive,*
he caught his last bronchitis. Although very ill, he refused
to consume anything except cold beer, or to rest from his
work. His brother, Robert, summoned by Dr. Bize, his
physician, ordered him to a hospital, but Marcel became
enraged and would not allow anyone at all to see him or
prevent him from working. One of his last acts was to have
a basket of flowers sent to Dr. Bize, in apology for the defiance
he had been showing. He saw his brother again when he felt
better. But he insisted upon going out while still ill, and soon
became extremely debilitated. He hallucinated a frightening

fat woman in black, in his room, like a woman symbolizing death whom he had previously described in a letter to Paul Morand.[32] He knew he was dying, and he begged Céleste to protect him from the pain of further injections. The doctor and his brother were summoned. His brother cared for him for three days. Marcel was given the unwanted injections, and showed his great annoyance at the medication. When Robert apologized for moving him around and asked if he hurt him, Marcel answered, "Oh yes, my dear Robert," and he died.

It was on the morning after November 17, when he believed himself much better, and kept his brother near him a long while, that, at about 3 A.M., he called Céleste, and although choking and feeling worse again, he dictated supplementary notes about Bergotte's death. At this time, the doctor later figured, an abscess must have broken in his lung. At about 6 A.M. he had asked for a cup of milk; at 10 A.M. he asked for iced beer; his difficulty in breathing increased. It was then that he stretched out his arm and said, "Céleste, Céleste, she is so fat and so black. She is entirely black. She frightens me." Céleste promised to chase her away.

"You must not touch her, Céleste, she is implacable, but more and more horrible."

Céleste's verbal account of Proust's death, given to Marie Scheikévitch, may be read in the latter's book, *Time Past*.[33] At the very last, there were indecipherable scribblings, in which he tried to write something about Forcheville.

It is of interest that in his article on Ruskin, in *Pastiches et Mélanges*, Proust said he imagined Ruskin, as an old man, might have hallucinated [34] the Golden Virgin (La Vierge Dorée) before his death.

[32] See Harold March, *The Two Worlds of Marcel Proust*, p. 129.
[33] Boston, 1935.
[34] "En Mémoire des Églises Assassinées," *Pastiches et Mélanges*, Paris, 1919, p. 119.

Swann's Way

Although *Remembrance of Things Past*, Proust's complete novel, is widely known, probably only a small fraction of those influenced by reading his work can remember the proliferating intricacies of his plot, book by book, for years afterward. The famous incident of the madeleine dipped in the cup of tea, evoking memories of Combray, has become a universally accepted symbol of the screen memory and how it may be evoked by a sudden, somewhat trivial sensation. The great length of Proust's books, their endless detail, and the hypnotic spell they cast upon modern readers has prevented many of us, especially outside of France, from reading the entire series, or remembering more than portions. Only a comparatively brief résumé of this very long work can be given here.

It is an account of the life and artistic development of a fictitious individual, Marcel, who is in many respects a replica of the author. But some notable contrasts become apparent; there is no brother. And the fictitious Marcel's love life is exclusively heterosexual, unlike the author's, and unlike that of most of the other characters in the book. Procreation and the raising of children are topics that are scarcely mentioned at all in his writing. Most of the leading characters other than Marcel and Swann are flagrantly bisexual. Although a real brother is absent, an idealized brotherly figure with the same first name, Robert de Saint-Loup, is almost always connected with Marcel's activities, especially his loves. Robert is accorded preferential treatment in most situations, because of his nobler birth. But Robert becomes degraded in character and an overt homosexual, although he regains honor in death by his bravery at war. Men who might be considered connected with Proust's father because of their prominence in the government, in psychiatry or medicine, receive critical treatment. Ambivalence toward these men, however, is less disturbing than the dichotomy of the feelings expressed toward the leading female characters, who tend to be either debased or idolized, or both at once.

The first volume, *Swann's Way*, opens with an Overture which is best understood in retrospect, after a knowledge of all that follows it, and quite a bit of rereading, in order to grasp the richness of its detail. At the beginning there is a discourse on sleep, and the merging of the dreamer with the books over which he sometimes nods. We are soon led into the famous description of little Marcel's inability to fall asleep without the ritual of a goodnight kiss from his mamma, and the incidents of the night when he cried so hard because this kiss was withheld, owing to the presence of a dinner guest, Swann. Marcel's father later that evening insisted that his wife spend the remainder of the night in the sobbing boy's bedroom. She read Marcel a novel of George Sand's, *François le Champi*, until late in the night. From then on, Marcel felt that this never-to-be-repeated night was a turning point in his life, because the entire family gave in to his nervousness and weakness. (Although it was through his asthma and his childish weakness that he felt he had won his mother away from his father that night, he seemed to have presentiments of a special sort of potency greater than his father's: this was the ability to share deeply the enjoyment of literature and all aesthetic things with his mother, and even the ability to create such things, for her admiration.)

Another outstanding passage of the Overture is concerned with a long train of vivid memories, reproducing the beloved past of Combray, with its dominating female figures, their all-enveloping warmth, and their emphasis on culture. Exploration of the process of evoking memories by association sets the tone for all that follows, and especially for the rest of the first volume: Swann's great love affair.

There were two main directions to take from Combray for walks. One was the Méséglise Way where Marcel, as a child, fell in love with little Gilberte Swann, and wanted to shock her to gain her attention and make an impression, even if not a favorable one. Perhaps the chief attraction of Gilberte was the fact that she was Swann's daughter, and often helped to entertain the renowned writer, Bergotte (a composite of Anatole France, Renan, and others), at her home.

Along this same Méséglise Way lived the widower, Vinteuil, celebrated musician and composer. This man died of a broken heart when he discovered, as everyone else already knew, that his beloved daughter was carrying on a homosexual affair. Not only was Vinteuil linked to Gilberte and the Swann family by geographical proximity, but also by musical alliance. The theme song of Swann's love was a little phrase from Vinteuil's sonata. This melody, likened to "moonlight on the ocean," or "the blue tumult of the sea," grew to become the ultimate masterpiece of Vinteuil, his septet, which won him posthumous renown, and parallelled Marcel's literary awakening. The theme of homosexuality runs through Gilberte's, Marcel's, and Vinteuil's lives, mainly because all three are victims of the homosexual tendencies of those they love. In the first volume we are told how the lewd antics of Vinteuil's daughter with her friend were observed through a window, accidentally, by Marcel. The girls carried on their affair ritually with the father's photograph facing them, and Mademoiselle Vinteuil's homosexual partner always said she would like to spit on the photograph and did so. Vinteuil's daughter was both shocked and submissive; and Marcel remarked that she was really a person of high standards, since she could only vent her wickedness, her sinfulness, by being so very immoral. Good people have sudden, defiant outbursts, but for really evil people cruelty is just natural, he reasons.

The other walk from Combray described in the first volume, is the Guermantes Way. In this connection Marcel describes his feeling of the apparent omnipotence of his father, and his own lack of ability to achieve literary success of any sort without his father's assistance. He feels that it is only his father who can, by a miracle, make him a writer. These thoughts are tied up with the scenic beauties of the Guermantes Way. He greatly admires the Duchess de Guermantes' prestige as a social leader and is thrilled by her glance in the nave of the Combray church. Associated closely with his thoughts about the Duchess, there is an ephemerally lovely description which he jots down, while riding home from church with his parents in the carriage of the country doctor. This is Marcel's first real literary inspiration, one of the famous passages of the novel. It is a description of the illusion of movement of the three steeples of Martinville, seen from the carriage. (Really, it is a transposition of a description in "En Mémoire des Églises Assassinées.[1])

[1] *Pastiches et Mélanges*, Paris, 1919.

The actual story of *Swann's Way*, which is the history of
Swann's love affair, is approached by circumlocutions and
digressions, followed by detailed unburdening. At first it is
Swann's little daughter, Gilberte, who attracts and frustrates
the child Marcel. But then we are plunged back in time into
a moving account of how Charles Swann, a man of sophisticated taste and high social standing (a successful Jewish stock-
broker, beloved by the aristocracy), falls in love with Odette,
a courtesan, his inferior socially and intellectually. "To
cattleya," meaning to make love, a verb which Proust formed
from the name of an orchid, is added to our language by
Swann's story. Swann humiliates himself through participation in the meetings of the Verdurin clan, a group of bourgeois social climbers. Madame Verdurin utilizes her wealth
to insinuate herself and her adherents into the hub of the
fashionable art world and to manipulate whatever aristocratic
social "lions" she can attract; thus she exerts a real influence
on artistic fashions. Swann spends every evening with this
group, only because Odette is to be found in their company.
The more completely his passion for Odette absorbs him, the
less Odette responds to him. He goes through all the stages
of falling in love, from initial indifference to tantalizing rejections by Odette which make him increasingly anxious to
hold her affection. We experience his jealousy, his suspicions about being betrayed, his spying on her house at night,
and opening her mail — his acquiescence to the knowledge
that successful rivals exist, among women as well as men —
his abject acceptance of ostracism from the Verdurin clan and
his hopeless longing for a woman who is his inferior.

But Swann is a wealthy man, and apparently Odette has
decided to marry him for the sake of financial security and
social position. After he has outgrown his love he has married
her in order to legitimize his daughter; for, at the end of this

volume, we see him introduced as Odette's husband and the father of Gilberte Swann. Odette Swann's promenades in the Bois de Boulogne are made especially real for us, by the attractiveness of her person and garments. Children play games in the park, where Odette long ago was seduced by a woman. The men with whom Odette has had affairs watch her walk by, a showy, fascinating figure — for each of them she has a different sort of smile.

Comparing "Marcel" of the novel (and also many aspects of Swann and other characters) with Proust's actual life, we see that we have here a reconstructed self, such as each human being carries about within him to some extent, in which the romanticized notion of the varied facets of his real personality, and an awareness of the real life within him, is partly composed of drastic departures from fact. There are composites, rather than identical copies of persons and places, in all our inner, subjective lives. Proust's confessions convey emotional reality, one might say, in preference to factual reality. He had the capacity to create a variety of characters with an intimacy composed partly of similar experience and based on an exceptional ability to observe others — and to control feelings in the reader.

After reading *Swann's Way*, one is struck by the idea of sexual urges as the factor that separates one from protected situations. Starting at the beginning of *Swann's Way*, for example, we see that Swann is received into the household of Marcel at Combray only without his wife, who, having been notorious for her promiscuity, is beneath their station. Marcel's mother, grandmother, and great-aunt order Swann about, and do not even thank him directly for the case of Asti wine he has sent them. Françoise, the servant, is equally fastidious, in her way, and prefers to visit her daughter when her son-in law is absent. Exclusion is one of the main preoccupations of

the Verdurin clan, and it is Madame Verdurin who really
separates Swann and Odette when they are most in love.
Originally it is Swann, the dinner guest, who keeps Marcel's
mother away from him at the boy's bedtime. And it is Marcel,
sobbing and sick, who prevents his mother and father, the
latter already in nightshirt, from retiring together. Jealousy,
separating the beloved woman from all other loves — and
being separated — are repeated endlessly, but never monoto-
nously, so ingenious are the variations.

Proust's use of imagery never seems accidental. Therefore
we must pay attention, in the first pages, when Françoise, the
servant, is putting Marcel to bed and Marcel tells us, "For
things which might or might not be done she possessed a code
at once imperious, abundant, subtle and uncompromising on
points themselves imperceptible or irrevelant which gave it a
resemblance to those ancient laws which combine such cruel
ordinances as the massacre of infants at the breast with pro-
hibitions, of exaggerated refinement, against 'seething the kid
in his mother's milk' or 'eating of the sinew which is upon the
hollow of the thigh.' " This, in order to show Françoise's ob-
stinacy, is part of the explanation of how difficult it was to
get Françoise to summon Mamma, at night when she had
guests, to come upstairs to kiss Marcel goodnight. It is one
of the rare references to an infant, or nursing, in all the published work of Proust.[2] There is a sadistic connotation in each
of the rare instances where he mentions anything connected
with infants or birth. (It is always Marcel himself who must
be favored, as if in infantile omnipotence.)

Although it is through the taste of the madeleine dipped in
tea that Marcel remembers Combray, it is through odors that
he recaptures the past most realistically. His curiosity, turned
back in time, runs a gamut from the most primitive aspects of

[2] *Swann's Way*, p. 34.

his sense of smell to scientific curiosity, aesthetic analysis, and philosophical inquiry. Proust was master of the entire range of curiosity, perceptive even to the degree of trying to cultivate a new sense which might evoke repressed sensations. In *Swann's Way*, we see Marcel's curiosity as that of an eternal child. It was said of the author, when he was an adult, at the time his mother died, that he was still like a four-year-old. To the end of his life, Marcel Proust was referred to by his friends as "le petit Marcel." The power of his curiosity from primitive senses to his aesthetic and intellectual approach, which was the quest for truth, dominates the complete novel.

Typically boyish memories of play with other boys are not mentioned in this volume, which explores so vividly the charm of Combray, and the love affair of Swann, and Marcel's miniature love affair with his mother. It is as if the author were telling us how he found the one acceptable way to assimilate all the tormenting, forbidden loves and hates which beset his boyhood, his confusions in regard to human bodily relationships, masculine competition, and the helplessness that accompanies illness, and his uncertainties about religion and social castes. His solution was to follow the lines his mother laid down, in the direction of literature, and the manipulation of imaginary projections of himself, in beautiful language and artistic forms.

Within a Budding Grove

THE SECOND VOLUME, *Within a Budding Grove*, is about Marcel's unique adolescence, in which infantilism is merged with genius. It opens with a description of an ambassador who has befriended Marcel's father. The family is astir and a-flutter because the Marquis de Norpois is dining at their home for the first time. He is a politician who has concentrated every outward grace upon the purpose of self-advancement. Through consummate fraud, allied with perceptiveness that penetrates the shams of others, he has achieved worldly success and consequently he holds Marcel's family enthralled, without winning over Marcel who is merely confused by him. Norpois suggests that Marcel must see the incomparable actress, Berma, so for the first time the boy is permitted to attend a performance of *Phèdre*. The result is disappointing, since Marcel is carried away by the audience's enthusiasm but has no impressions of his own, and is unable to grasp the essential idea of what great acting really is. When he tries to explain his reactions to Norpois he falters idiotically.

Marcel has been attempting to gain an invitation to visit the Swanns' home, because of his love for their daughter, Gilberte, with whom he plays in the park. When Norpois indicates that he will speak well of Marcel to the Swanns, Marcel moves as if to kiss Norpois' hand. This foolish gesture later proves to be the very thing that makes Norpois ridicule Marcel to the Swanns instead of recommending him.

Marcel's games in the park are described only in connection with the attraction he feels toward Gilberte. After an amusing description of the details of the reign over the park lavatory of a decrepit, overly powdered elderly lady in a red wig, who is so pretentious that she is nicknamed by his mother and grandmother "the Marquise," he tells an incident of wrestling with Gilberte which arouses to a peak his sexual feelings. (This sort of wrestling is later used as an illustration of how homosexuality is stirred up among boys.)

In the earlier version of the novel *Jean Santeuil*, there is a little girl, Marie Kossichef, who plays in the Champs-Elyseés with Jean and excites his love, upsetting him so that his mother forbids him to see her. In Proust's own life, there really was a Marie Bernadaky, of a higher social class, with whom he fell in love as a child in the Champs-Elysées. The Marie of the first draft of the novel becomes an important source of family dissension, and then, long after Jean's mother has separated them, he does not care to see Marie when he has the opportunity to do so, with parental sanction that has come too late.

In *Within a Budding Grove*, the situation regarding the little girl is the reverse of that in *Jean Santeuil* because it is implied that Marcel's mother has overcome the Swanns' objections to Marcel and apparently has arranged for Marcel to be invited to their home to see Gilberte after his ill health prevents his playing in the park. Marcel's mother has maneuvered this because she wants him to take a keener interest in life, in order to improve his health. Here the fever thermometer has, so to speak, become the key: Marcel at last is invited to the Swanns'.

He visits Gilberte formally, and wins her parents' warm

approval. Odette Swann is not accepted in the most respectable social circles herself, and has an ex-courtesan's tastes, but to Marcel her home is enchanting. She plays her favorite phrase from Vinteuil's sonata, the theme song of Swann's love for her, on the piano for Marcel. He meets Bergotte, France's greatest living writer, at the Swanns', and observes some rather unexpected but characteristic qualities of literary genius, notably the relation of literary power to self-imposed limitations.[1] Marcel's parents, presumably because of his father's rigid social standards, derived from those of the Marquis de Norpois, do not approve of Bergotte any more than they do of Odette.

Gilberte's parents have now become devoted to Marcel, but apparently for this very reason Gilberte has tired of him. Marcel painfully tries to damp down his love for Gilberte, hoping she eventually will be more attracted to him if he is aloof and inaccessible. He calls only upon her mother, Odette, when Gilberte is out. He decides to sell a valuable Chinese porcelain bowl left him by his great-aunt, Léonie, and thus he acquires funds to provide for a long series of gifts, which he plans for Gilberte. But then he sees her walking with a young man, with an air of intimacy that immediately makes him feel his possessive love for her is hopeless. He then has a dream of an unidentified boy friend's treachery and, using a process of association, analyzes his dream and interprets it, concluding it is really a dream about Gilberte. Thus, on the basis of a dream, he makes his final decision to give up seeing her.[2]

After Marcel instigates his own separation from Gilberte,

[1] *Within a Budding Grove*, Pt. I, p. 188: Bergotte "loved nothing really except certain images and . . . the composing and painting of them in words."
[2] Proust was probably familiar at least secondhand with Freud's *Interpretation of Dreams*, which appeared in 1900, by the time he wrote about the dream of Gilberte. Previously, two dreams (p. 490 of *Swann's Way*,) have also given evidence of his knowledge of some of the technique of dream analysis.

having in a way assimilated into his person the restrictive standards of his parents, we see the renunciation of his strong ties to his mother as the next theme. He is so nervous and ill that he must, upon medical orders, go to Balbec, a beach resort, with his grandmother. His mother remains behind with his father, because the latter cannot stand to be with Marcel when he suffers from nervous illness. Parting from the Chinese bowl which was an inheritance from the authoritative, cultured women of Combray, then giving up Gilberte, and finally separating from his mother, which forecasts in his own mind his eventually growing completely apart from his mother and losing her in death, are like a dirge, which anticipates the mourning process as it becomes a dominating theme of the novel. The most real separation from his mother occurs at the train, when he says goodbye on his way to Balbec, although she remains in the book as a shadowy figure.

At Balbec his grandmother is a revised image of his mother, loving, desexualized, completely self-sacrificing, entirely his own. He feels he is hastening her death by the worry he causes her, and his constant demands.

He is particularly unnerved by the strangeness of the hotel room at Balbec. It is of enormous size, and yet he feels as if he were in the cage of Cardinal la Balue, in which Balue could neither stand up nor lie down. He is disturbed by a feeling of isolation amidst the host of strangers at Balbec, whom he really wants so very much to impress, from the lift boys to the most distinguished guests. But happiness finally comes to him through the arrival of an eccentric old lady, Madame de Villeparisis, who is a member of the most antiquated aristocracy, so

---

See Chapter XVI for discussion of Proust's use of dreams in his writing. Probably Marcel's love for Gilberte was too close to the author's unconscious homosexual love for Robert, and the brother image had not yet appeared in the narrative. For a fuller discussion of Marcel Proust's relation to his brother, see pp. 37, 141, 160, 170.

highly distilled in her culture as to be misunderstood by most people but delighted to see Marcel's grandmother, with whom she can talk about the writers she has known in her youth: Beyle, Balzac, Hugo, and so forth. Marcel's prestige has been presented to him, full-blown, in a matter of moments, and he feels more at ease at Balbec. But he soon grows restless with these two elderly ladies. When he goes driving with them in Madame de Villeparisis' carriage he turns aside long-ingly to the attractive girls on the road, the milk girl, a delightful girl on a bicycle, and other possible partners for romance.

Marcel's Jewish friend, Bloch, whom he knew at Combray, who initiated him to the local house of prostitution, had assured him of the pleasures to be experienced with casually encountered girls. But with his grandmother and Madame de Villeparisis now guarding him, Marcel cannot yield to such temptations at Balbec, although he considers the roads and thoroughfares full of possibilities for pleasure. It is in this connection that he has a second profound literary inspiration, reminiscent of his ecstatic description of the three steeples. This time three ancient trees which he sees while his grandmother and Madame de Villeparisis are riding beside him, in the latter's carriage, appear, in their immobility, to move upon the landscape as he rides. Their position seems to alter as he changes his own status in time and space. First the three trees are like witches, then vanished friends of childhood, or beloved ghosts eager to return to life and regain the power of speech. Marcel feels the carriage bearing him away from what would have made him truly happy — *his life*. He feels great sadness as if he has lost a friend, died, broken faith, or denied his God. (Through this exceedingly simple image, we have, as if in an impressionistic painting, a visual synopsis of his basic attitude toward time, and this is connected, in a way, with his quotation in the "parricide" article from H. G. Wells about time as a telescope. Proust later describes his own use of the telescope in regard to time as a telescope turned the wrong way.)

Nostalgia and artistic preoccupation well up just when the temptations of the street are about to overwhelm him. But he is soon to find in brotherly love his first attempt at a solution to the quest for renewed love of his mother, a substitute for the affection of mother and grandmother.

It is Madame de Villeparisis who introduces him to her nephew, Robert de Saint-Loup, a handsome, gifted boy, outstanding at sports, physically robust, attractive in every way. Robert is pursued by all the girls at Balbec. Although Robert has a mistress, one of a long series, he is interested only in books, philosophy, art, and things of the spirit. He is anxious to become the closest friend of Marcel.

The name given to Robert de Saint-Loup is interesting, since Robert was the name of Marcel Proust's brother, and Loup (wolf) was a pet name by which his mother actually used to call the real Marcel, in her letters. In the first draft of the novel *Jean Santeuil*, there is a similar brotherly figure, Henri, with almost identical characteristics, to whom Jean wishes to flee, in refuge from his domineering parents, although he dares not do so.

Robert de Saint-Loup, like Henri in *Jean Santeuil*, is of noble birth, has every possible asset, and yet it is he who really appreciates Marcel, and loves him best of all his friends. It is through Robert that Marcel is eventually to meet a band of exclusive young aristocrats, who will love him in brotherly fashion and accept him in their regimental life at Doncières, which is not very far from Balbec. (This turning from the mother's love to the love of a brother was also the theme of one of Freud's most important papers, first published in Ger-

man in 1922 and later translated into other languages.[3] Not
only did Freud consider this erotized method of solving the
problem of avoiding hatred of the brother as rival for the
mother, most apt to occur in adolescence, as a homosexual solution to the unbearable jealousy occasioned by too deep a love
for the mother, but he also observed this mechanism to be a
basis for social feelings, in so far as such brotherly love is sublimated, and a more or less universal tendency.)

Love for Robert, pure and platonic, is not a stable solution.
Marcel finds competitors among women and is forced to yield
the first place in Robert's affections to Zézette, Robert's present mistress. Robert is succumbing completely to her domination, and thus scandalizes his family.

Robert's uncle, the Baron de Charlus, arrives at Balbec. He
is one of the great "gods and monsters" who persist vividly,
for all of Proust's readers. (Proust's friends, in real life, felt
that his mimicry made those he imitated seem colorless and
unreal, themselves, compared with Proust's imitations of them.
The haunting reality of Charlus indicates how this may well
have been so.) Charlus is a large, handsome man with black
mustaches. He is impeccably dressed in somber hues, punctilious in manner, and equipped with education in the arts and
classics, befitting his aristocratic standards. Descended from
Princes of Sicily, representing the utmost in "civilized" culture, he betrays the madness that somehow seems inherent in
overbred individualism. With two other men, almost as
distinguished as himself, he has had, in his younger days, an
apartment in Paris where they invited their women and where
they were known as the Three Graces. On one occasion, in
winter, a man who came there, seeking not any of the women

[3] See page 170 and footnote. Sigmund Freud, "Certain Neurotic Mechanisms in Jealousy, Paranoia and Homosexuality" (1922), *Collected Papers*,
Vol. II, London, 1924, p. 232.

but Charlus himself, was set upon by the three of them and beaten almost to death, then cast out into the snow. There is no particular reason for Charlus to become fond of Marcel, and yet he does so, and goes through contradictory steps of courtship, insulting him as often as he makes overtures to him. It seems that he is trying to seduce him when he comes to his room to present to him a specially bound book by Bergotte. Later, at the beach, he pinches Marcel's neck vulgarly, calls him a rascal, and says the boy doesn't give a damn for his grandmother. (We are reminded of Mademoiselle Vinteuil's compulsive disrespect for her father.) Charlus's sadism, his perverted way of loving, is gradually discernible to the reader. Apparently Marcel, innocent and youthful, lags behind the reader in becoming aware of what makes Charlus enigmatic until much later.

While at tea with Marcel, his grandmother, and Madame de Villeparisis, Charlus complains that his former estate, one of his many large mansions, is now owned by Jews by the name of Israel, one of the leading Jewish families of Europe.

After Charlus's anti-Semitic remarks, Marcel overhears at the beach a diatribe against the Jews by Bloch, his Jewish friend. This is apt to be perplexing to the reader, since it is well known that Marcel Proust's mother was a Jewess, but the reader soon becomes habituated to a tendency on the part of Proust to exhibit not only his best side, but also all that can conceivably be interpreted as depreciatory about himself, to confess and to shock by his confession — as if he felt the need to blurt everything out defiantly before possibly being accused or ridiculed. (Excellent traits of Jews as sincere friends and as individuals of real character and spirit are later delineated by Marcel, in the *Guermantes Way*, where the Jews are favorably contrasted with the Guermantes.)

Now we are told a great deal about Bloch, Marcel's osten-

tatiously intellectual Jewish friend, and about how Bloch's
father's personality, lagging forty years behind, is imbedded in
his son. Bloch's misplaced deep admiration for his father is
one of the few descriptions of anything resembling submissive
reverence for a father by a son, in the entire work, with the
notable exception of Marcel's deep respect for the painter,
Elstir, who really represented a composite of the great impressionist painter, Claude Monet, in real life, with several
others, such as Manet, Degas, and Paul Helleu, Proust's close
friend. (Monet's paintings are described in *Jean Santeuil,*
naming the painter.)

Swann's great love for Gilberte, a counterpart to love for
a father, in Bloch is more sympathetically treated.

Marcel takes Robert de Saint-Loup to Bloch's for dinner,
and young Bloch sarcastically expresses the keenest interest
in the Baron de Charlus, not realizing Charlus is Robert's
uncle. Bloch asks for details about him, saying he is eager to
meet him, to write about him, because he is comical, but has
great style. Robert, infuriated, is too well bred to show his
feelings. Bloch then brags that he has had an affair with a
woman on a train who turns out to be Odette; he adds that
he wishes Robert would tell him her name and address, so that
he can see her regularly. Bloch's tongue wags on and on, dis-
playing his learning, his uncouth manners, his eccentricities
and vulgarity, in embarrassing conversations with Robert and
Marcel, who nevertheless continue to be his intimate friends,
with that forgiving quality Proust always tends both to de-
mand and to exhibit.

Robert's mistress is gaining increasing success as a new sort
of actress and holds Robert as enslaved as Odette once held
Swann. Robert's family are grieved, but cannot separate them.
Robert's love gradually makes him more kind and understanding. It turns out that he has learned much from a less-than-

mediocre girl's discipline of him. Because of what she has taught him, Robert grows more understanding of Marcel, also — and a finer person.

Marcel and Robert dine at Rivebelle, the fashionable restaurant near Balbec, where every attractive woman seems to be falling in love with Robert, or else to be his past mistress. It is there that Robert and Marcel first see one of the great living artists, Elstir. They are still young enough to have faith in such an act as to send him a note, in the restaurant, saying they are great admirers of his work and wish to make his acquaintance. Although Elstir does not invite Robert, he gives Marcel permission to visit him at his studio, after convincing himself, from a conversation with the two boys, that Marcel's interest in art is genuine and vital. (This meeting of Elstir and the two admiring boys is a second rendition of a theme introduced at the beginning of *Jean Santeuil*, in which the teller of the story and his youthful friend meet the greatest living writer of France, C., at a similar beach resort, in the same manner. The manuscript of *Jean Santeuil* is bequeathed to the two boys, Marcel and S., when the renowned writer dies, soon thereafter.) In *Remembrance of Things Past*, the final version of the novel, we receive the impression that Marcel's actual debt to Elstir is greater than his debt to Vinteuil or Bergotte. (Proust's deepest originality must indeed have taken inspiration from Monet's attempt to look within himself for a fresh view of the world, to re-create nature, and to make of art something greater than life.)

Robert is summoned back to duty with his regiment, toward the end of this volume, and Marcel, deprived of Robert's brotherly affection, becomes enchanted by watching on the beach a frieze of six or eight girls, with whom he falls in love as a group. They are physical rather than spiritual beings, and he considers them unchaste, coarse, cruel, semi-barbaric.

Although they vary in their emotional and physical types, they are all extremely attractive to him, mostly on the basis of being dissimilar to himself, lacking his fastidiousness.

It is in Elstir's studio that Marcel sees for the first time the impressionistic paintings he has only heard about, but which have already been an inspiration to him. He finds Elstir very anxious to give of himself, but not able to find many people who can perceive what he really has to offer artistically.

Alone in the studio for a few minutes, Marcel happens to unearth a painting of Odette hidden there. She is wearing a disguise, a costume for a musical comedy, in which she is Miss Sacripant, but Marcel recognizes her and suddenly realizes that Elstir, now a mature, renowned painter, was once the foolish, corrupt little painter called Master Tiche by the Verdurins, who used to go there to pursue Odette. Elstir admits this and gives Marcel reassurance, by indicating to him that great men commit errors in their youth and then, through understanding these errors, may grow to be truly mature.

Elstir, now elderly and happily married to a stout woman in whom he still sees great beauty, is acquainted with some of the young girls of the Balbec beach. He tells Marcel the name of the one who is to become Marcel's greatest love: Albertine Simonet. Although Albertine is the one to whom Marcel is bursting with eagerness for an introduction, when Marcel and Elstir happen to meet her at the beach, the painter neglects to introduce Marcel to her, and Marcel does nothing about it. But later Elstir gives a tea where they are to meet. When Elstir summons Marcel to be introduced to her, Marcel hesitates, finishes his éclair first — then presents a rose to an old man, as a boutonnière, and finally comes to be presented. He gradually becomes an intimate of the entire group of Albertine's friends, and they play games and indulge in sports together, but Marcel has no great success at their games of skill. He is made clumsy by being overly sensitive to possible rejections by Albertine. Having been disappointed in love by Gilberte, he sets out to control the situation with Albertine by practicing deceptions upon her. To incite her jealousy, he pretends to be in love with Andrée. Albertine, apparently jealous, invites Marcel to her room when she is in bed, but checks his advances, and tells him that only a pure friendship must exist between them. He later considers that this chaste and moral attitude of hers has led to his downfall.

Albertine is very much like Norpois, Marcel's father's friend, in that she is scheming, resourceful in her duplicity. The technique of Norpois' opportunism is something Marcel now understands well, and imitates himself. He is learning worldliness, cheating, lying and conniving toward self-advancement. Perhaps in stressing all this deception, he intends to give us a clue. Some critics have thought that the names of the girls he loved: Gilberte, Albertine, Andrée — and in *Jean Santeuil*, Françoise, Charlotte — were the transcribed names of boys. It has been suggested that Proust originally created them as boys and merely used female names for purposes of publication. But he was sensitive and recondite in his pursuit of names suitable for his characters. He went to a great deal of trouble to find the name of Guermantes, for example. It is more likely that in selecting bisexual names for his loves, he had, intuitively at least, an idea of the importance of such equivocal names in the fantasy he was so painstakingly creating. In his early notes the principal Balbec girls, for instance, had more feminine names.

In Freud's original papers on the development of male homosexuality,[4] we also find indications of the origin of the bisexual idealized image — such as Gilberte and then Albertine represented to Marcel. Such a typically bisexual being

[4] Sigmund Freud, *loc. cit.*

is described as an idealized self, a transition between self and loved object.

Within a Budding Grove, which deals with adolescence, is a confession of the various facets developing in Marcel's youthful personality: shame over what he considers his weaknesses and his "Jewish" traits, the deceptiveness and opportunism implied in his loves and in his techniques of social climbing, his awareness of clique psychology in social groups, his conscious and preconscious grasp of the problems of homosexuality, his struggle with lack of frankness in friendship and yet his all-forgiving qualities. The interplay of physical frailty and childish dependence with his determination to conquer the long road of artistic development which seems, for himself, so hopeless have prepared the way for an attempt to do what the author once described crudely in an early story in *Les Plaisirs et les Jours*, entitled "Violante" — that is to rise higher and higher socially in order to solve an inner problem. The way to elevate oneself socially, as Norpois has demonstrated, is through observation of others. The way to progress artistically, is through self-analysis, as Marcel sees from Elstir. At both forms of observation, Marcel is growing adept.

The Guermantes Way

Proust seems to have been intuitively aware of how the factor of hope operates in goal-directed behavior. When Marcel was overenthusiastic about meeting Albertine the first day he found out, on the beach, that Elstir was acquainted with her, he did not manage to obtain an introduction. Hope had come so suddenly that it created a sort of paralysis. When he first saw the Duchess de Guermantes in the nave of the Combray church, he felt no hope at all and did not even smile to her. But just the right degree of hope began to operate now in regard to the Duchess, and it fitted his geographical as well as social needs.

In *The Guermantes Way*, Marcel is back in Paris, living with his family in an apartment owned by the Duchess de Guermantes, who is his neighbor as well as his landlady. Although they live in proximity, socially they are far apart. The Guermantes salon is the most exclusive in Paris, and even a nodding acquaintance with the Guermantes is just a stretch beyond Marcel's expectations. Yet it is the Duchess de Guermantes who makes a sign to him.

He goes to the theatre to see the great actress, Berma, once

more, in *Phèdre*. This time he understands her acting and appreciates the fact that she is "a window opening on a great work
of art." He esteems the lack of personality and individuality
in a great actor or actress, where the artistic work itself is
more important than the interpreter of it.

At the theatre he sees the exquisite Princess de Guermantes,
like a "mighty goddess," with downy plumage, and a veil on
her head studded with innumerable pearls, as if from the sea.
Her cousin, the Duchess de Guermantes, is beside her, dressed
more simply, in a style that might give the Princess a lesson
in good taste, in clever competition. Marcel's passionate love
for the Duchess de Guermantes is ignited because the Duchess
catches sight of him and nods to him from her box. After
that, he roams the streets daily in the hope of meeting her and
causing her to nod to him again in greeting. Her varied cos-
tumes are a source of delight to him. This wandering on the
streets in order to meet her continues until he finds out that
he is making a nuisance of himself. His reaction is to leave
Paris, and to turn his affection back to Robert de Saint-Loup,
who is her nephew.

He visits Robert at his garrison at Doncières. At the pala-
tial, eighteenth century Hôtel de Flandre, with its ancient
tapestries, where Robert has reserved a room for him, Marcel
experiences love for a room the first time he inhabits it.
Usually he spends a sleepless first night in any new room, sens-
ing hostility in all the inanimate objects, and an unbreathable
aroma. But not here, in this spacious, antique place with its
familiar feeling and secret passageways which give him a
sense of great privacy. (It is like the room, in *Jean Santeuil*,
at the Hôtel Angleterre, where Jean visits Henri, and where
he feels it is possible, even, to commit a crime within its recess-
es without being discovered, so great is its solitude.) Marcel
enjoys his stay at the inn and spends much time with Robert,

learning about military history, technique and strategy, and
merging himself with a group of young men of topmost aristocratic background, who are Robert's closest friends, and
who look upon Marcel as a great conversationalist. The only
time that Robert is invited to dinner at the home of the commanding officer, the remote, aristocratic Captain de Borodino,
Marcel is invited there also, and treated with equal courtesy.

He becomes acquainted with Robert's mistress, Zézette,
who turns out to be Rachel, the very same prostitute whom
Marcel himself once turned down. (He had been frigid toward Rachel, at Combray, partly because her establishment
had received from him the sofa he had inherited from his
Great-aunt Léonie, and this piece of furniture seemed to in-
trude its austere disapproval.) Marcel has always thought sarcastically of this girl as "Rachel-when-from-the-Lord," after
the tender love song in Halévy's opera.

Marcel's main purpose, with Robert, is to try to get Robert
to intercede with Robert's aunt, the Duchess de Guermantes,
with whom he is still hopelessly in love. His excuse is his wish
to view the Elstir paintings she has in her home. Such an invitation actually does not materialize, because Robert goes off
with Rachel and does not contact his aunt. But Robert later
introduces Marcel to the Duchess de Guermantes at the home
of Madame de Villeparisis, who is the Duchess's aunt. At this
same reception, Robert brings the Baron de Charlus and Marcel together again. Charlus is the brother of the Duke de
Guermantes; the circle of relationships is a closed one, in the
book.

The Guermantes family slowly begin to take more notice
of Marcel. He is on the verge of becoming a sought-after social figure, and (owing mainly to his poor health) is very difficult to obtain as a guest. Here again, we have a repetition of
the social pattern established with the Swanns: first Marcel is

ignored, rejected, then admitted to the salon and made much
of, and in the end even keenly pursued — his invalidism serving to win him favor.

Although we are told of the Duchess's famous wit and gift
for mimicry, we are not told in complete detail about how
Marcel's own charm and attractiveness were developing, along
with his erudition. Proust, the author, according to the written comments of friends, such as Paul Morand, was a remarkable companion. His wit, his uncanny understanding of people, his aesthetic genius, and his encyclopedic knowledge of
all types of matters, particularly topics which interested those
in the topmost social circles, including scandals, bon mots, and
the borderline between genealogy and gossip, made the actual
author an incomparable guest. His manners were more than
perfect, and his reputation as a promising literary man, even
long before he had published very much, enhanced his value.
Still he did not so easily achieve the social heights attained by
"Marcel" of the book. He tried to be part of every group at
once, at social gatherings, was quick to make friends, but
then dropped people with equal ease. The real Marcel Proust's
need to be loved and admired, of which he was always so conscious, was reflected in the Marcel of the story, who was universally loved and petted, and succeeded inevitably in becoming everyone's acknowledged favorite. (In Proust's
early story, "Violante," where the young girl deliberately
concocts a career of social climbing, she does so in order to
win the man with whom she is in love. She finds social climbing a simple process for anyone who is clever, but the consequences are tragic.)

While the groundwork for his social elevation was being
accomplished, in this part of the novel which deals with young
manhood, Marcel's constant fear of social ostracism (perhaps
in real life it was based on the author's homosexuality) was

split off and sequestered, and dealt with separately. For instance, in his many derogatory references to the Bloch family, and to Rachel, and at times even to Swann, he reminds us of how each of these were excluded, how they did and said the wrong thing, and placed themselves in embarrassing positions with regard to many who were their intellectual and artistic inferiors. The varied characters in the book very often felt contempt for each other. It is as if one part was attacking another part of the author's personality.

Frequent references to the Dreyfus case begin to focus on the pro- and anti-Semitism of the characters. Robert, the aristocratic "good brother" of the book, is Dreyfusard. Odette, with her typical combination of social climbing and questionable tactics, makes a point of being against Dreyfus, in spite of the fact that her husband, Charles Swann, is Jewish. It is through her anti-Semitism that Odette is later to be admitted, suddenly, to salons where her husband is no longer quite so warmly included, for example among the friends of the Duke de Guermantes.

We soon find out that the Duke de Guermantes is habitually unfaithful to his wife, and not burdened with very much intelligence. He is little more than a distinguished foil for his wife's social leadership. His many mistresses, exquisite, but of inferior social status, are rewarded when he is finished with them by his interceding for their admission to his wife's salon. The Duchess does not object because their great beauty serves to grace her drawing room, and is of use to her. She has a genius for manipulating others, and is always calculating; toward accomplishing her own ends, she is inclined to do and say the unexpected. Sympathy with the Duchess's innate understanding of human weaknesses and the functioning of social orbits, as well as her wit and charm, convincingly reflect the growing sophistication of Marcel.

The Guermantes are of the loftiest, most inaccessible aristocracy in France, and the Duchess is in a perfect position to exercise her chief talent, to maneuver socially, to exclude undesirable elements, to admit only those who suit her purposes. Intelligence or worldly success are not the keys to her drawing room. In order to become part of her salon one has to be subtle as a chameleon, one must take on the protective coloration of the other members of her select group. In *Jean Santeuil*, the operation of such salons and the art of social climbing are described with humor, but more crudely. In *The Guermantes Way*, Proust tries to show us the ineffable glamour of a great salon through the eyes of an enchanted stripling who is too intent upon forcing his entrance to be humorous about it, and who labors seriously at his goal of penetration into the most exclusive groups in Paris. Marcel's acceptance by the Guermantes set is a convincing reality.

The Baron de Charlus, the Duchess de Guermantes' omnipresent brother-in-law, is a figure with enormous prestige, and ability to make or break the status of others. Several times he and Marcel converse and go for walks together, during which Charlus offers Marcel his protection, making suggestions of devotion expected in return; but Marcel completely misunderstands Charlus's homosexual interest in him, and they always part on uncertain terms.

A moving description of Marcel's grandmother's illness and her death end Part I of *The Guermantes Way*. Oddly enough, we are introduced to this most pathetic episode of the novel by a second description of the comfort station in the Bois, and the "Marquise" who runs it. The agony of Marcel's bereavement, and his sensitive grandmother's suffering, are so great that the ugly setting of her stroke in no way detracts from the moving effect, but is a weird concomitant of it. We are also afforded an unsympathetic account of the various doctors' coolness, inefficiency, and self-interest. (Guilt is apparently projected to the doctors, here.) Dr. du Boulbon, who has tried to treat the grandmother psychologically when she needed medical care, is described as the man Charcot predicted would become the most brilliant neurologist and psychiatrist of his day. The author states the case for the psychosomatic viewpoint, but immediately shows how it has miscarried, on more than one critical occasion, in relation to his grandmother.

The scene of his grandmother's death is followed by a new section of the novel, opening with the announcement that Marcel feels as if he were reborn. Actually, he has foregone, along with his grandmother, some of the restraints of his conscience. He is now in his Paris room, ill in bed, and Albertine comes to visit him there. (As usual, invalidism helps bring him love.) They exchange kisses and she offers no resistance to his physical advances. She willingly becomes his mistress, eager to return to him whenever he wants her. But an inner restriction is set up; he has little urge to send for her again. At this time he finds he is falling madly in love with the idea of a woman, a vague, beautiful Madame de Stermaria whom he has not yet actually met, but with whom he has an assignation arranged, upon Robert de Saint-Loup's enthusiastic recommendation. He looks forward to this encounter with all his being, to the eclipse of Albertine. But Madame de Stermaria cancels the engagement at the last minute, and they never meet.

Marcel is invited to dine with a small, intimate group for the first time, at the home of the Duchess de Guermantes, instead of being part of a large reception. He finds himself treated with the utmost affection and respect there, even by the Duke de Guermantes, his host. The initiated in the Guermantes' home feel a strong sense of importance and fellowship, only because of the many who are excluded; it is really the excluded who make the salon desirable.

Section II of *The Guermantes Way* nears its end, with Marcel paying his first actual visit to Charlus, late at night. His mind is filled with well-rehearsed monologues, with which he intends to make a brilliant impression on Charlus. Instead, a humiliating scene occurs, quite the opposite of what Marcel has planned. Charlus, the embodiment of aristocratic breeding, has a verbose temper tantrum, accusing Marcel of having said something insulting about him. Marcel does not understand what could have provoked such behavior. Charlus unreasonably shifts to a wooing attitude. Marcel becomes panicky, and so infuriated that he stamps upon Charlus's hat. The hat is replaced by a servant who does not seem upset by the proceedings. Charlus crudely expostulates that he will never see Marcel again, but once more he reverses his attitude, and quite tenderly sees Marcel home, says a few things to make amends, and treats him paternally. At the end, in a calm conversation, Charlus explains to Marcel that the Princess de Guermantes is far more exclusive socially, and more utterly inaccessible, than the Duchess de Guermantes. Only through Charlus can one be invited to the Princess's home at all, and this will forever be impossible because Marcel will never be Charlus's friend, after this night. Then, with inconsistent reluctance, he leaves Marcel.

To Marcel's amazement, he receives an invitation to the Princess's home, shortly after, and does not know whether or not it is a hoax. He goes to call on the Duke and Duchess de Guermantes, to obtain assistance in verifying the invitation. The Duke flatly refuses to be of any service in this regard. He will not even mention it to his wife. Real friendliness and aid, even in trifles, are not forthcoming from men like the Duke, Norpois, or the Baron de Charlus. Doctors are necessary, so are politicians; and the Dukes and Barons and other nobility lend their encouragement and prestige at times. Marcel cannot quite do without them. Yet they fail him when he turns to them for true aid. The Duchess, so lavish in her praise and affection, is fundamentally self-centered, and not very intelligent. Marcel blames himself for always expecting too much of human generosity, which is subtle, never complete. He tries to give us, here, a three-dimensional view of the anatomy of human compassion.

The final pages of *The Guermantes Way* show us the Duchess de Guermantes in her famous red gown, on her way to an exclusive social function at the Saint-Euverte's. Just as she is departing, Charles Swann confides to her that he is fatally ill. He will soon die of the same illness that once afflicted his mother. But the Duchess's attire is far more important to her than her friend, Swann. She and her husband have no time to hear about his illness, although she does decide to wait while her husband, at the last minute, goes back to exchange her black slippers for red ones.

Now we have discovered, with Marcel, how death removes loving persons, how unreliable social prestige in the salons may be as a source of gratification or aid, how homosexuality and other personality traits may upset basic social relationships, and how physical love, as for Albertine, may waver irrationally. Most constant is his affection for Robert. Robert, without making too much effort to do so, has nevertheless provided Marcel's original introduction to the Duchess de Guermantes, and also his first encounter with Charlus. Even the room at the Hôtel de Flandre, which Robert has found for Marcel, seemed to abound with protective affection. It is Robert's group of young aristocrats who have first appreciated and loved Marcel as a companion. (In the original version, *Jean Santeuil*, it is Henri, full of brotherly affection, who, similarly, invites Jean to his family's exclusive estate at Réveillon, where Jean becomes a favorite of Henri's mother, and the lover of a handsome, twenty-four-year-old servant-girl.)

There is a connection between the need to be adored by such brother-figures as Robert and the winning of parental, particularly maternal, approval. At the same time, these brotherly figures (such as Robert or Henri) apparently control the directives toward Marcel's heterosexual affairs. With the exception of the artists, who are so sensitive, so human, and have many failings of their own, in the novel, fatherly types are usually aloof, awe-inspiring. The country's most famous doctors, the greatest politicians, the topmost aristocrats are disillusioning, often stultified by their own bombast, not sufficiently sensitive, not loving enough. Although needed, they are usually too frightening, inept. The brothers, the younger men, or artists, are those Marcel can really love.

V

Cities of the Plain

PUBLICATION of the next volume, *Cities of the Plain*, introduced to modern literature a less inhibited attitude toward homosexuality, opening the way for more frankness and courage in dealing with this topic. Intricacies with which the psychiatrist [1] deals in treating this widespread problem still remain enigmatic to most laymen. Many ramifications are subtly sketched, probably without even being consciously understood in their entirety, by Proust's images, his rather grotesque emphasis on unexpected facets, and the vagaries of his manner of exposition.

For example, Marcel goes to Balbec, to the Grand Hotel, hoping to have an affair with Madame Putbus's maid, whom Robert has described as particularly luscious. But just as Marcel stoops to tie his shoelace,[2] he is reminded, with a pang,

[1] See Part II, page 73. "When it is a Charlus, whether he be noble or plebeian, that is stirred by such a sentiment of instinctive and atavistic politeness to strangers, it is always the spirit of a relative of the female sex, attendant like a goddess, or incarnate as a double, that undertakes to introduce him into a strange drawing-room and to mould his attitude until he comes face to face with his hostess."

[2] Re curtailed walking and inhibited sexuality, see pages 182, 214, footnote pages 251, 270, footnote page 291.

of how his grandmother used to do this for him when they were at the Grand Hotel together. Marcel succumbs to a delayed mourning reaction which plunges him into a depression for weeks. Several dreams about his grandmother show us his sense of being abandoned. But this is directly connected with the sexual temptation which would have aroused conflict and torments of conscience. He no longer can externalize his conscience in the form of a loving, forgiving grandmother. He argues in his dreams about whether or not his grandmother is really dead, and how dead she is. Actually, she is alive within him, still forbidding the sexuality which would have shocked her. In this, of course, she represents also his mother. A punitive fate must always see to it that his love affairs are richer in suffering, which instructs him and inspires him to work, than they are in actual pleasure.

Omitting the last few pages of the preceding volume, *The Guermantes Way*, it is conceivable that quite a number of other novelists, Stendhal, for instance, would have continued the thread of the story with Marcel and the Duchess de Guermantes falling in love with each other. But as the French title of the next volume, *Sodome et Gomorrhe*, indicates, there is a flight from the passionate love Marcel once felt for the Duchess de Guermantes to the complications of homosexuality, studied by Marcel from afar. *Cities of the Plain* starts with Marcel still at the home of the Guermantes' where he has gone on his fruitless errand of seeking to verify the authenticity of the invitation from the Princess de Guermantes. While he stands in an obscure position, beside the staircase, he finds himself inadvertently spying upon Charlus who is coming down the stairs. Charlus, thinking himself unobserved, by a fast reflex action assumes a posture of feminine coquettishness when he sees and immediately recognizes in Jupien, an ex-tailor, the characteristics of a feminine man, an "aunt," as Proust prefers to call him. Charlus starts an acquaintance with Jupien and accompanies him to his shop, pursued by Marcel, whose curiosity forces him to eavesdrop.

In a long discourse on homosexuality, written with great distinction, the sociological and psychological position of the homosexual is described: his loneliness, his isolation in a small community, his constant search for companionship and for fulfillment of the drives within him, his amazement at the large number of confrères he eventually finds as he roams to larger communities, the types he seeks: strong pseudo-masculine individuals, or feminine ones like himself, as substitutes for the virile men he really desires. His contempt for his own kind, his constant fear of being found out for what he is, the social advancement that may result from the unusual ties he forges, and at the same time the danger of sudden exposure and ostracism, his constant sense of guilt, are movingly portrayed. The masculinization of the wife of the homosexual man, and the reasons for this — are gone into with minute sensitivity. Proust's dissertation constitutes a pioneering work, and has done much to liberate writers who, since then, continue to bring similar topics within the scope of literature.

The next part of *Cities of the Plain* takes us to the reception of the Princess de Guermantes. Marcel's invitation turns out to be genuine, and it has not come through Charlus. The Prince and Princess have brought together a select social gathering, on an even higher plane than any of the receptions given by the Duchess de Guermantes. In each volume, as we see, Marcel has risen to greater social heights, and Charlus's homosexuality has become more blatant. Many parallel themes are being delineated. The more familiarity with homosexuality the author frankly admits, the more reassurance we are given that Marcel, the "I" of the story, was accepted socially, at the highest levels. And besides, in the story it is always Charlus who is interested in Marcel; Marcel, disgusted with Charlus, loves only women.

Charlus, at the Princess's reception, is interested in two attractive young brothers, and flatters their mother, Madame de Surgis, only because he has designs on the boys. It is plain that Madame de Surgis will be helped along socially with little realization that it is due to Charlus's interest in her sons — just as Jupien, the ex-tailor, will rise financially, thanks to Charlus's recommendations.

Proust, like Freud, had a habit of making impact-laden statements in very brief allusions. In this volume, he reflects on a series of other sociological points besides those related to homosexuality. For example, his statements about the Dreyfus case, and at other times about the French Republicans versus the aristocracy, or pro- and anti-Germanism in France, contain implications regarding unconscious determinants of group opinions. He reflects on how nations as well as individuals make important decisions and later reverse them on purely emotional bases. This observation is articulated after reflecting on how the Duke de Guermantes, under the influence of some charming ladies, shifts from an anti-Dreyfus to a fanatically pro-Dreyfus position. In his philosophy of perpetual change, Proust is revolutionary, more than is generally suspected.

Change is constant, and yet, as symbolized by the image of the three steeples and the three trees, Marcel's inspiration requires a passivity that controls through cognition and perceptiveness rather than action. One notes how sensitivities and feelings are uppermost in all the characters of his novel, and the processes of looking and being looked at, rather than action, are skillfully interwoven in such a variety of ways that an appearance of action is always given, when it is mainly time that is moving.

Just as when Albertine first became his mistress immediately
after his grandmother's death, in the earlier volume, it is
when he is mourning his grandmother, in this volume, that
Albertine sends word that she is in a town near Balbec and
wants to come to see him (as if her love for him replaces some
of the lost grandmother's devotion to him).

Albertine continues to be Marcel's mistress and comes
frequently to visit him, whenever he sends for her. They
both attend the Verdurins' parties on Wednesdays, at Raspelière, an estate leased for the vacation season. They are
under Madame Verdurin's domination much as Swann and
Odette used to submit to the restrictions of the Verdurin
clan. Dr. Cottard, an habitué of this salon, and a friend of
Marcel, hints that Albertine's friend, Andrée, a girl who is
nervous, intellectual, highly sensitive, like Marcel, and even
looks like him, is Albertine's lover. Marcel watches them
together with great jealousy. He finally confronts Albertine
point-blank with the question of whether or not Andrée is
anything to her, and she denies this in an innocent manner
that utterly convinces him. But one night he sends for Albertine and she cannot be found. Like Swann, when he cannot find Odette on the night he searches for her through all
the restaurants of Paris, Marcel, tormented by jealous curiosity, falls deeply in love with Albertine. Here Marcel makes
the famous statement that personal characteristics are less frequently a cause of love than a phrase such as, "No, this evening I shall not be free." [3] From this time on, his jealous love

[3] *Cities of the Plain*, Pt. I, p. 276. "Certainly, personal charm is a less
frequent cause of love than a speech such as: 'No, this evening I shall not
be free.' We barely notice this speech if we are with friends: we are gay
all the evening, a certain image never enters our mind; during those hours
it remains dipped in the necessary solution; when we return home we find
the plate developed and perfectly clear. We become aware that life is no
longer the life which we would have surrendered for a trifle the day
before, because, even if we continue not to fear death, we no longer dare
think of a parting."

of Albertine is intense. All Proust's previous writing about the torment of possessive love has been but a rehearsal for this. Although Marcel has not felt that he was in love with Albertine at first, suddenly he is unbearably jealous of her in relation to all the girls they know. The thought of Albertine's having a homosexual affair is something he cannot stand. He has a compulsion to keep her away from other girls, and in order to do so, monopolizes all of her time so far as possible.

The exhibitionism of a Jewish girl, Bloch's sister, in love with an actress at the Balbec hotel, is described. These girls carry on their lesbian relations in the public rooms of the hotel. But they are not expelled from the hotel because the girl's uncle, Monsieur Nissim Bernard, is in love with a waiter there and has influence with the headwaiter and the hotel management. (We have here, in addition to the fear of homosexuality being discovered, its actual exhibition by two girls, and its confession to all; still there is no punishment, no expulsion from the hotel. Confession has led, as it were, to a forced demonstration of forgiveness.)

Marcel's intense jealousy of Albertine is focused on her homosexuality. But it is related to her heterosexuality, also, in regard to Robert de Saint-Loup; Marcel is consumed with jealousy on a train trip with Albertine because he has to leave her alone a short time with Robert.

Parallel to the love affair of Marcel and Albertine, we are told how Charlus falls deeply in love, practically at sight, with a handsome violinist, a young man of lowly origin, boorish tastes, base character, and crude manner. Charlus sees this man, Morel, at a railroad station and sends Marcel over to fetch him, pretending he is already acquainted with him. After that, Charlus causes Morel to become the most fashionable violinist in Paris, taken up as the chief attraction of the Verdurin group. Charlus goes to the Verdurins' regularly with Morel. Everyone at the Verdurins' is suspicious of their relationship, but accepts it. Just as the Grand Hotel at Balbec sheltered the flagrant behavior of the homosexual girls, we find the Verdurin salon countenancing the Charlus-Morel affair, affording protection such as Marcel Proust always seems to insist upon providing, for a time, for his characters' sexual aberrations.

The competition of Madame Verdurin and Madame Cambremer, who has leased her country estate, La Raspelière, to the Verdurins, and who is trying at the same time to operate a rival salon, is mercilessly drawn. The ladies of the upper bourgeoisie *versus* the impoverished aristocracy employ every conceivable trick to lure socially desirable people to their homes, using artistic and any other sort of attractions, as well as offering aristocratic prize morsels. This callous conniving, resorting to almost any tactics to build up a leading salon, in turn actually affects cultural trends as well as worldwide fads. Important political problems may approach solutions in these salons. The Verdurins, for example, are Dreyfusards. Robert de Saint-Loup is a Dreyfusard, in rebellion against most of the Guermantes set; so is Marcel. The majority of the other characters in the book, especially the aristocrats, are anti-Semitic, and therefore, of necessity, anti-Dreyfusard for a time. But the Duke de Guermantes, the most anti-Dreyfusard of them all, as we have noted before undergoes a complete reversal of opinion.

In the former draft of the novel, *Jean Santeuil*, the Dreyfus case is treated more journalistically, with a portrayal of the trial, and a convincing picture of Colonel Picquart's reactions to incarceration and to the temporary freedom of the trial itself. (Proust actually had met Picquart and had sent him a copy of *Les Plaisirs et les Jours*.) In *Remembrance of Things Past*, we see the trial only through the eyes of the characters of the story, as it gives us insight into their feelings.

The next section of *Cities of the Plain* recounts the pitiful struggles of Charlus, who has difficulty in retaining Morel's interest and affection. Charlus sits in a restaurant, suffering pathetically because he cannot hold Morel and concocting trickery which has no limits. He shams the threat of a duel which would scandalize Morel, in order to persuade Marcel to summon Morel back to him one night. On another occasion, Charlus pays a huge amount of money to the proprietress of a house of prostitution when he hears that Morel has gone there with the Prince de Guermantes, so that he may spy on Morel and the Prince there. But apparently they have been warned. After being kept waiting a long time, Charlus merely catches a glimpse of Morel, very nervous, talking to three ladies, and apparently Morel can see Charlus, secretly, also.

In this volume there has been an exhaustive general analysis, not only of homosexuality among men and among women, but of abject humiliation in love. Charlus is an example of this supine attitude, even more degrading than the submission of Swann to the sadistic control of the Verdurin clan, during his pursuit of Odette. Because Charlus's love is inverted, he suffers far more. Morel rises to fashionable success, and needs Charlus less. His aging protector becomes progressively less attractive than other protectors and lovers.

The volume ends with Marcel quite bored with Albertine, no longer in love with her, about to give her up — when he accidentally finds out, through her knowledge of the "little phrase" of music from Vinteuil's sonata, that she used to know Mademoiselle Vinteuil, and that Mademoiselle Vinteuil's friend, the notorious, professionally homosexual woman, was "mother and sister" to her. Albertine says she intends to go off to meet Mademoiselle Vinteuil's friend in another city.

This awakens Marcel's piercing jealousy. In order to keep her from any possible homosexual ties with Mademoiselle Vinteuil's friend, or Mademoiselle Vinteuil, Marcel decides to marry Albertine, and informs his mother he will do so. He makes Albertine go back to his home in Paris with him.

Why does this preposterous idea of marrying Albertine only in order to keep her from a homosexual attachment carry such conviction in the story? In the next two volumes, while Charlus struggles to hold on to Morel, we see how an attempt is made by Marcel to hold Albertine's affection without actively competing, and the consequences.

Albertine is never a clear individual. Her outstanding characteristic, apart from her youth and the absence of any unusual beauty, is her adaptability to Marcel's images of her, her malleability and indefinite outline. Marcel notes several times that the background of Balbec and the sea were essential to the charm she held for him, that she was "as much a part of the sea as the gulls." The most tangible characteristics she displays are her combination of boyish and feminine graces and her talent for deceitfulness which keeps Marcel guessing. Toward her he is even more conniving than she is toward him. He justifies his duplicity on the grounds that falsifying is the only way to hold her interest.

(In the short stories that preceded this novel, and in fact through all of Marcel Proust's writings, we see his conviction that to declare love is to lose the beloved, to admit love verbally is to demonstrate one's humiliation and to invite jealousy — which ends only with death. Open competitiveness with another man practically never enters the stories. For example, when Swann begins to lose Odette's interest, her turning toward another man is considered inevitable, owing to Madame Verdurin's control of everybody. The question of who the other man may be is secondary — there is no real use in Swann's competing.[4] In *Remembrance of Things Past*, the Duke de Guermantes is not at all interested amorously in his wife when Marcel is in love with her. Charlus, a homosexual, offers only feigned competition for women. So there is rarely a competitive situation among men, except briefly in Marcel's jealousy of Albertine's few words with Robert and his jealousy of his own grandmother's "coquettish" attitude toward Robert. Both jealousies, we later are assured, were completely unfounded.)

Marcel continues, well liked in a platonic way by almost all of the characters in his story, men and women alike, but his affair with Albertine is an enduring torment.

The noteworthy parallel between the Marcel-Albertine and the Charlus-Morel affairs, in *Remembrance of Things Past*, we shall see later is in harmony with a statement made by Freud in a letter to Fliess, in which he said: "I am accustoming myself to the idea of regarding every sexual act as a process in which four persons are involved." [5] Freud was referring here to universal bisexuality, and its effect upon every love.

---

[4] See page 233 for discussion of a dream of Swann, in which he yields Odette to another man.

[5] Sigmund Freud, *The Origins of Psycho-Analysis, Letters to Wilhelm Fliess, Drafts and Notes: 1887–1902* (see Bibliography for full title), ed. Marie Bonaparte, Anna Freud, Ernst Kris, transl. Eric Mosbacher and James Strachey, New York, 1954, Letter #113, p. 289.

V I

The Captive

THERE IS comprehensive unity in *The Captive,* as in all the volumes of *Remembrance of Things Past,* although upon first reading one might receive the impression that random imaginings lead the author to describe, just as it all occurs to him, two exotic love affairs, some inconsequential activities among the élite, and a series of highly symbolic, aesthetic impressions, including the description of a great piece of music.

In this fifth volume, Marcel, in an effort to control the activities of Albertine, has brought her to live in his apartment in Paris, the one owned by the Duchess de Guermantes. Marcel's mother is away at Combray, attending her sister in a serious illness, and there is only vague mention, at any time in this volume, of his father, who is presumably absent from the apartment most of the time. Françoise takes care of Marcel and, despite her shocked sense of propriety, her reiterated objections and jealousy, she has to accept the presence of Albertine, as Marcel's fianceé, quartered down the hall from his room. Marcel is rather ill and remains confined to his bedroom most of the time. He is malingering, mainly as an excuse to avoid going out. Although Albertine is his "captive," he feels even more imprisoned than she, because his jealousy paralyzes him, and he cannot bear to go out in public with her for fear that he may witness her interest in a strange girl or woman, or perhaps a man.

Nothing is said about his literary pursuits, except that he keeps looking each morning in *Figaro* for the article he wrote long ago about the three steeples of Martinville and is disappointed that it has not yet appeared in print. Most of his time is spent either amusing himself with Albertine or planning lavish gifts for her. He obtains advice from the Duchess de Guermantes, and sometimes Odette, or others, so that he may order for Albertine the most exquisite furs, jewelry, gowns, scarfs and gloves. He makes her one of the most desirable women of Paris, certainly one of the most expensively attired, and at the same time he is tormented by jealousy and sends either his chauffeur or Andrée to watch over her, to prevent her from having affairs, not knowing that Andrée herself is one of Albertine's lovers.

He pretends that the doctor has ordered him to remain in his room, but actually he cannot bear to go out with Albertine. His jealousy amounts to a "street phobia." He cannot tolerate going out in the public streets with her, but he sends her out as seductively dressed as possible. This fantasy of Albertine's possible interest in the attractive women on the streets will be discussed later. Proust, the author, actually did spend most of his time in his room, especially in the latter part of his life when he shut out all noises and dust from the streets, and only emerged late at night when streets and restaurants were depopulated.

In *The Captive*, we are given a dissertation on the streets, town, and world, as full of women whom Marcel himself might love if he could be rid of Albertine. Albertine causes him only pain, never positive joy — only the tortures of jealousy.

This possessive love is a repetition of the separation-fear described in *Swann's Way*. Marriage is a solution Marcel has not yet decided upon, although he is still considering marrying Albertine, whenever he is not certain of maintaining his exclusive possession of her. But when he is certain of his domination over her, he is depressed, bored, and enticed only by the prospect of other loves, and his longings to travel without her, especially to Venice. Never does he have fantasies of parenthood or the peacefulness of ordinary domesticity.

Charlus and Morel have tea every day at Jupien's (the homosexual ex-tailor's). Regarding this, Marcel remarks that "the regularity of a habit is generally in proportion to its absurdity." [1] Morel is in love with Jupien's delightful niece and plans to marry her. Charlus approves of this. When Charlus finds out she has been "in trouble" long ago, he does not tell Morel, but conserves this information as a weapon to hold over both of them in the future. Charlus favors the wedding, and plans to continue his relations with Morel, after Morel's prospective marriage. Instead of being jealous, he finds the girl's company refreshing. The intricate counterpoint of Morel and Charlus, and Jupien's niece — and of Albertine and Marcel — are so well fused that it is not always easy to tell where the roots of fantasy regarding these characters begin, leave off, and begin anew. The irrationality of the various forms which jealousy may take is illustrated here quite consciously, and therefore it is not an inconsistency in the writing to learn that Charlus approves of Morel's marrying, but Marcel deeply fears Albertine's unfaithfulness of any sort, with either girls or men.

The infinite repetition of the themes of love, jealousy, and separation-fear gives one the impression that the author was

[1] *The Captive*, p. 49.

aware of how he was driven by a "repetition compulsion" (to use Freud's later phrase for this sort of repetitive drive). It is as if Proust somehow hoped that by repeating the jealousy theme in every possible way, with every kind of reversal of roles, he might somehow arrive at a better solution of the dynamics of it for himself, in actuality.

One day when Marcel chances to see Albertine and himself in a mirror,[2] noting his expression of passion as he is with Albertine, he ponders on this aspect of himself. Some insight follows. He realizes that his relation to Albertine is like his relation to his mother, whose goodnight kiss used to be so necessary a sedative. Albertine's kisses upon his throat every night before he goes to sleep are similar. This ritual is still as essential as the goodnight kiss of Combray days. Marcel says his aim is always to keep the women he loves away from all others, and that this possession of them is necessary in order for him to sleep. Insomnia troubles him if he is jealous.

He realizes that the women he loves are phantoms. Gilberte by now is completely forgotten; it is Albertine at present, and conceivably another may follow.

Marcel describes how he converses with Albertine as if [3] he were a child once more, at Combray, talking to his mother — at other times he listens to Albertine as if his grandmother were talking to him. He observes how our past relatives are always present in our current loves. He tells us that he acts toward [4] Albertine as his father has acted toward him, with coldness, a coldness that is but the external aspect of sensibility. Albertine's resemblance to himself (his feminine aspect) in his mother's attitude toward his father is less directly implied, through his various identifications with Albertine.

2 Cf. "The Confession of a Young Girl" (his early story) re the mirror and sexuality.
3 *The Captive*, p. 97.
4 *Ibid.*, 141.

Reflecting on the past, he implies that he himself must have made life difficult for his father in the family circle, for [5] "who can be more nerve-wracking than a neurotic?" (In other words, he used to interplay tormentingly with his father, as he and Albertine now cause pain to each other.)

Freedom of transposition of one personality into another is, of course, typical of all who fantasy, but in Proust's work it is especially articulate. He not only instructs Albertine liberally, but he scolds her as his parents used to scold him, and he provides for her as they provided for him; yet he is dependent upon her, like a child. We see how he and Albertine have been molded, he as the product of his parents, Albertine largely the product of his own domination over her malleable personality.

The sketch of Monsieur Lepic and his wife, in *Jean Santeuil*, which seems by comparison a somewhat amateurish carica- ture, is nevertheless a forerunner of the portrayal, in the story of Albertine, of how possessive love creates submission-and- domination patterns. Marcel's avowed fear that he might lose the beloved, in the later novel, recalls [6] the sadistically dom- ineering love of Monsieur Lepic, ending in death. Marcel's love is at times almost indistinguishable from pure anxiety. Albertine, he admits, is unreliable, a consummate liar, full of duplicity. He shows himself equally deceptive. It is through deceptions that the characters later created by Proust always attempt to control the objects of their infatuation, rather than by direct, sadistic domination such as Monsieur Lepic's. Urges to confess and to deceive are exposed with equal frank- ness. *In Remembrance of Things Past*, we are constantly given the impression that naïveté, sophistication, and extensive learning are oddly assimilated. Confession piques and sup-

[5] *Ibid.*, p. 143.
[6] *Ibid.*, p. 124.

plements curiosity. Françoise spies upon Albertine; Charlus spies upon Morel; Marcel is consumed with such agonizing curiosity and jealousy regarding Albertine that he cannot bear to watch her, but hires a chauffeur to do so. His turmoil over her is the excuse for all his decisions and actions. His extension to time and space of all he feels so deeply of love and jealousy are the sources of his nostalgia and his psychological revelations.

Proust states that previous writers never wrote the truth about love. He does not refer, in his writing, to heterosexual love as the mainspring of procreation or domesticity, and the basis of family life, so much as he describes the passionate turbulence of "falling in love" and how it tends to recapitulate the child's anxious need for parental embraces, consolation and protection. He writes of possessiveness, jealousy, deception, leading to agonizing spying — confession — and ultimately to hating and destroying, but there is always an overtone of forgiveness. The abject suffering he describes is due to an impressive need for the exclusive affection of the beloved. It is the most important thing in life to him, and yet it is only superficially related to the actual personality of the beloved, who is but a phantom.

What was the original deception in Proust's own life, even before he had to hide his homosexual cravings from his family? Probably the original deception was a half-admitted collusion between his mother and himself to placate his father, who did not want Marcel to be so neurotic, and Marcel's use of illness to gain the mother so completely for himself. The boy was constantly winning away the mother, and she was forced to comply, just as in the book she gave reluctant consent to Marcel's involvement with Gilberte and Albertine. Proust and his mother shared their sensitivities and aesthetic pleasures, and paid the penalty in their mutual concern about his illness, like the mother and Marcel in the book. *Jean Santeuil* gives us a more candid picture of this relationship than does *Remembrance of Things Past.*

Apparently Madame Proust shared many of the subtlest aspects of life with her exceptionally perceptive boy more satisfactorily than with his father. Marcel's early identification with his mother was dominant in his development, but then her pregnancy and the birth of his brother, Robert, seems to have set a lasting pattern for Marcel Proust's neurosis. His unconscious rage at what he must have considered his mother's unfaithfulness to him apparently was never resolved. Both sides of his ambivalence are expressed clearly in *The Captive*. Marcel's maternal love for Albertine, combined with his dependence upon her coming to his room, especially at night, show how Marcel and Albertine play mother to each other, yet he also calls their love brotherly. In the accompanying themes of Charlus and Morel, the sado-masochistic older man, and his youthful dependent, we see how Charlus, in the novel, was like a fusion of Proust's mother and father, with his fussing, scolding femininity, insistence on the importance of art and fine taste, and also his masculine prestige as a handsome idol of society, admired by women. Interlocking themes which appear and reappear in the novel may at first seem confusing, but actually they convey decipherable patterns. The author confesses all he can about himself, with unexampled clarity, but still he tends to hide from himself and his readers the root of his deepest conflicts: probably he stresses bisexual love, the boyish immature love for an object resembling himself, to avoid conflicts connected with the relation of his mother and father, which excluded him, and which led to the birth of his brother, when he was two years old, an event he could never really assimilate. If he had some intuitive knowledge of the significance of these conflicts regarding his own oedipal situation and the brother's birth, at least he had no consciousness of their full ramifications or their strength, insofar as insight might have helped him control his own homosexual impulses or release his heterosexuality in real life. He merely knew that something still more unbearable than his asthma created a particular set of symptoms (he called homosexuality a "neurotic defect") in lieu of a variety of other possible symptoms.

Freud applied himself to a study of derivations, particularly those which originate during the first five years of life. But Proust's interest was in communication. Proust's desire was to inform the reader of every nuance of his feelings — beginning his narrative after the most formative years and asking the reader not to praise or condemn him, but only to tell him if he describes human nature correctly. In very few of his characters does Proust examine the infantile origins which Freud found most determining.

The entire novel, *Remembrance of Things Past,* belabors homosexuality and jealousy just as in psychoanalytic therapy certain topics are dealt with over and over again in each patient. Proust constantly repeats the patterns of loving a bisexual object as his mother loved him, and as he felt attracted to boys in his actual life. His identification with his own father was lacking; he offered no active rivalry toward his father or other men. Submission to all parental authority was the result of his extreme need for the approval of both parents, and their protection, in his illness. His acquiescence to their ambitious demands that he study and write kept him the more repressed, the more rebellious, in a vicious circle. The urge to conceal his aggression and his incestuous and homosexual urges, and then to make a sudden confession, hoping for forgiveness, largely on the basis of his deep suffering, also stemmed from this same need for support and protection.

When he remarks that his love for Albertine was "at once filial and maternal," [7] we have a volume of psychology condensed into a phrase. Proust's unsatisfying search for the relation of the child to the mother in his writing is turned around in many instances of infatuation, especially of an older person for a very youthful one; then we see the search for parental love turned into identification with the loving parent. In this parent-child attitude we usually have the domination which a parent exercises, actually, over a child. Such domination, combined with the provision of lavish gifts and protection, was what Proust substituted for active masculine competition, and conceived of as real love in contrast to the romantic love described by so many of his predecessors.

We are accustomed, especially in theatrical performances where censorship exists, when an unconventional love relationship like that to Albertine is portrayed, to be presented with an unhappy denouement in which we can almost hear the censor's scissors at work. Here the convention-defying elements stem from such profound personality characteristics in Marcel that the outcome seems preordained not from morality but from an impracticality in Marcel's trying to recapture what is really in the past. (In more "normal" life, we try to recapture vanished aspects of our past family existence by founding families anew.)

The aberrant nature of Marcel's actual love relationship with Albertine is hinted at. [8] Nowhere is there the thought of a possible pregnancy. None of this can be dismissed with the statement that Albertine was really a boy, superficially changed to a girl. To avoid any possibility of propagation is apt to be one of the roots of homosexuality, and probably

[7] *The Captive*, p. 98.
[8] *Ibid.*, p. 123.

was so in Proust's case. It is possible that Albertine was, in his mind, sometimes closest to being a boy, but a boy whom Marcel loved, with maternal or filial love, the roles being interchangeable. The author, in real life, could never enter into a love relationship which might produce a pregnancy, other than a sublimated, artistic one. In this volume, such creativeness is depicted by great music; and in every volume an outstanding representative of the arts appears. In the novel, Marcel's love relationship worked both ways, imprisoning and holding back both Albertine and himself. But within himself, Marcel did not see the acute hopelessness, and the desirability of a break, so clearly as he did in the Morel-Charlus relationship. There are hints that the Morel-Charlus affair may always have remained platonic; this is never stated clearly.

Since homosexual love for young boys and candidly bisexual figures like Albertine, Odette, Gilberte, and so on, are loves which are apt never to be wholly satisfactory,[9] it is this constant feeling of insufficiency which perhaps drives the author to break off ruminations about Albertine with a return to the Charlus-Morel theme every time, so that the two themes are thoroughly interwoven.

In this volume about Marcel's great love, we have the very moving account of Bergotte's decline in health, his use of drugs, and his demise in an art gallery where he has gone to look at Vermeer's "View of Delft," particularly that typical Vermeer yellow, upon a wall (wishing he could have created so successfully).

We may recall that after the two passages about Marcel's

[9] See Thomas M. French, *The Integration of Behavior,* Vol. II, Chicago, 1954, p. 22: "When compared with the gratification originally desired, the substitute always lacks something and tends to be supplemented by a craving for another substitute to supply what is lacking in the first one." Also see Volume I, Chapter XLVI.

Cf. *The Captive,* p. 244, where Proust indicates that dreams are formed by desire and the nature of their failure is instructive.

mourning for his grandmother, there was an immediate link between the idea of death and of rebirth, both in connection with Albertine (and sexuality). Now it is Albertine who claims to be the last person with Bergotte before his death, although she was not.

Proust emphasizes the fact that our lives follow a pattern, as if invested with obligations contracted in a former existence. (In Freud's terms, repressed conflicts of early childhood would be described as the source of those earlier contracts.)

When Marcel questions whether or not Bergotte is permanently dead, just as he previously questioned the permanence of his grandmother's death in two of his dreams, we find ourselves encountering Proust's philosophical speculations about a possible return to a more scrupulous, better existence after death, similar to the existence he surmised was experienced before birth. Emotionally true for him, the belief was of great significance for his patterns of feelings, rather than as part of any scientific deduction. Proust seems to have felt intuitively that there were profound connections between death, rebirth, and intactness, as if death were, for him, a possible first step toward a better beginning.

It is not accidental that in *The Captive* the death of Bergotte immediately precedes the apotheosis of artistic creation depicted by the flowering of Vinteuil's genius. (Proust originally worked out a version of this linkage between death, birth, and artistic creativity in *Jean Santeuil*, at the beginning, where writing a book was likened to bearing a child,[10] with much gratitude to the doctor, and Theodore, meaning "gift of God," suggested as an appropriate name for the illegitimate offspring. *Jean Santeuil*, the original novel, is then presented, as a posthumously published manuscript, after the original

[10] See Appendix A for summaries of parts of *Jean Santeuil* that are of special interest.

was given to Marcel and his friend by their country's greatest writer, a man whom they have met casually at a beach resort, just as Marcel and Robert meet Elstir in *Remembrance of Things Past.*)

It is at the Verdurins' that Marcel hears the great Vinteuil masterpiece. Mounting jealousy has brought him to the Verdurins' without Albertine, because he thinks Albertine has made plans to meet Mademoiselle Vinteuil there. We learn that Swann is deceased, and we have had another discourse on death. There is a lengthy description of the aging and senility of Charlus and his increasingly manifest homosexuality, his lack of restraint, and his pathetically transparent deceptiveness and lying. The repetition of these favorite themes which draw Proust like a magnet resembles more than ever the repetitions in free-association, where each individual is constantly drawn to his own characteristic topics.

Charlus, who sees Marcel enter the Verdurins' in the company of the highly moral Professor Brichot, makes flippant remarks to them both, accusing them of homosexuality.

Mademoiselle Vinteuil really was to have been present at this gathering, and perhaps did have an appointment there with Albertine, but she has stayed away, presumably having been warned at the last minute that Marcel, her rival for Albertine, would be there. The Vinteuil violin theme, taken from the sonata and including the "little phrase" which was the Swann-Odette love theme, likened to moonlight on the ocean, is played by Morel in this setting. The "little phrase" now appears with a seven-piece orchestral background (harp, violoncello, and others). It is a song on seven notes, apparently symbolic of — or at least parallel with — the fuller orchestration of Proust's own novel. The Vinteuil septet turns out to be convincing evidence of true genius. One recognizes beneath the apparent differences profound similarities to Vinteuil's other works. Vinteuil "reached his own essential nature . . . without being able to translate it into human speech . . . Each artist seems thus to be the native of an unknown country . . . The questioning phrases [become] more pressing, more uneasy, the answers more mysterious . . ." Vinteuil's masterpiece symbolizes to Marcel hope for actual recall of past beauties, along with increased maturity, and with the welding together of contrasting themes. Albertine is, for him, blended with the music, less than the music. It is universal and yet it is forever individual and "new."

Redness of the sky is suggested to Marcel, then cockcrow (reminiscent of the passage in *Swann's Way* where, after writing his description of the three steeples, Marcel felt like crowing, like a hen that has laid an egg.)

The music seems "blatant" and even ugly to Marcel, at first. He does not like it. But still this music awakens his overwhelming admiration for Vinteuil, and conveys his concept of a truly great artist. "When his vision of the universe is modified, purified, becomes more adapted to his memory of the country of his heart, it is only natural that this should be expressed by a general alteration of sounds in the musician . . ." A great work of art is, for Marcel, a subjective thing, never to be duplicated; it conveys to others a glimpse of one man's universe.[11]

Marcel reflects that in genius we see a capacity which is quite different from the concentrated diligence required to carry such genius to full expression; the latter is, after all, but a secondary factor. He thinks of how the public is blocked in grasping anything essentially novel, so that it takes about forty years for anything drastically new to penetrate to an audience, requiring a new generation. The public, established in set habits of values, finds it difficult to estimate or to under-

[11] *The Captive*, p. 347.

stand something fresh — humanity has been trained to fads and habits in thinking. The new at first seems ugly, difficult to comprehend or to classify. The new public has to be created along with the new work of art.

Ruminating thus, as he hears the great Vinteuil theme,[12] Marcel comes back to love, and realizes that his present love for Albertine is the greatest love of his life, for which other loves have been a preparation; but he has already hinted that the deepest things one feels in life are a recapitulation of something from the past. The greatest works of art do more than recapture the past, he concludes, because they also retain a quality of "permanent novelty." (This "permanent novelty," of course, suggests Proust's style, in the novel, which is like nothing else, not even his own published correspondence or previous writing.)

An important point which Marcel causes us to note, here, is how closely a "sheath of vice," in this case homosexuality, may be allied with a great work of art. Discovery of his daughter's homosexuality killed Vinteuil. But Vinteuil's daughter and her insolent girl friend, who spat on Vinteuil's photograph, really understood Vinteuil's greatness and admired his work, and in the end the "evil" girl friend turned out to be the one who transcribed Vinteuil's scrambled notes after his death — the notes of the great masterpiece now being heard are preserved for humanity, thanks to the "sinful" girl.

[12] *The Captive*, pp. 349–55: "I asked myself if music were not the unique example of what might have been — if there had not come the invention of language, the formation of words, the analysis of ideas — the means of communication between one spirit and another . . . this return to the unanalysed was so inebriating, that on emerging from that paradise, contact with people who were more or less intelligent seemed to me of an extraordinary insignificance . . . "
Marcel shows us here, in art, something greater than the "nullity" he has found in love. He thus implies that what is in the preverbal past, in other words, the relationship to his mother, is more attractive to him than the present.

(This was connected with the fate which Marcel Proust fore-
saw for himself, both because he hoped for forgiveness for
his homosexuality [13] and because his poor health and early
death forced him to leave his manuscripts not entirely per-
fected, in need of some unscrambling.)

Vinteuil's septet was well played (he emphasized the word
"blatantly" as a necessary quality of the playing) and introduced to society by Morel, through Charlus's influence. By
this mixture of good and evil, the author once more illustrates
his concept that art is greater than life. Combining opposite
forces, such as homosexual sterility and sublimated creativity,
the highest and lowest in human nature, brutality and godli-
ness, illustrates a favorite device of Proust's. He consciously
tried to make his psychological observations solid, "three-
dimensional," with all the contradictions, the good and evil
interpenetrating. So methodical was Proust in bringing out
this dialectic, in various parts of his long narrative, always
including the tangled threads of admirable and reprehensible
sides of everybody and everything, it is almost like solving a
riddle when one tries to piece together the complementary
characteristics in all the living beings he has created, with the
exception of his idealized mother and grandmother.

After successfully rendering Vinteuil's music, Morel feels
so firmly established in his career that he is induced by
Madame Verdurin to break off his relations with Charlus.
This is Madame Verdurin's revenge, because Madame Verdurin is offended. Charlus's aristocratic friends, invited to be

[13] The daughter's homosexuality killed Vinteuil. Marcel Proust's own
homosexuality symbolically was connected with the death of his mother.
It was perhaps most deeply connected with a reaction against a death-wish
toward her, the wish Marcel Proust must have felt toward mother and
baby at the birth of his younger sibling, and very deeply repressed, and
also the rivalrous feeling against his mother in regard to the father's love.
In very "harmonious" families, such as theirs was, such feelings can be
most deeply repressed.

present for the music, have ignored Madame Verdurin and clustered about Charlus. Madame Verdurin insists that Morel put himself completely under her social tutelage. She promises to introduce him, now, to the Queen of Naples, with the assurance that this contact will elevate him to the pinnacle of his success. Morel finds Madame Verdurin's arguments convincing and makes a shocking exhibition of his renunciation of Charlus before all the guests of Madame Verdurin. Charlus, stunned, completely deflated, loses all his famous power of declamation and is led off like a woebegone child by the Queen of Naples.

Marcel returns from the Verdurins' completely satisfied that he has forestalled the loss of Albertine through any possible encounter between Albertine and either Mademoiselle Vinteuil or Mademoiselle Vinteuil's woman friend. But still, he is uncertain of his hold over Albertine, so he pretends that he is about to break off with her — since it is only by threatening to leave people that he tries to hold on to them. He and Albertine have a quarrel which they finally make up. He questions her exactingly, and elicits from her still more information about her homosexual adventures. Marcel mentions here that his own father really had the courage to fulfill threats to people's security, but that he, Marcel, merely made such threats but could never carry them out. He then likens the very thought of separation from Albertine to the death of a loved one, which causes him to weep profusely. At the sight of his tears,[14] Albertine says she will never see him again if that is what he wishes of her, that she really loves him, but she would even be willing to leave him forever if he wishes her to go. They become reconciled. As proof of his affection, he

---

[14] See Appendix A: One of Proust's earliest stories was about drinking the beloved's tears as a decisive factor in falling in love. Tears and weeping often occur in his writings.

gives her his precious Bergotte manuscript, which she has always wanted. He feels comparatively secure now regarding Albertine.

This scene is followed by a lovely evening's companionship, and a conversation with Albertine in which Marcel goes into a critical analysis of various great writers, particularly Thomas Hardy and Dostoevsky. He is impressed with how frequently Dostoevsky wrote about murder (a topic Marcel considers alien to himself), and how consistently, in Dostoevsky's novels, personal pride and self-respect play a great role. Marcel recalls how, in *The Brothers Karamazov*, Karamazov impregnates the idiot, and then more than twenty years later the murder of Karamazov and the disgrace of his family are brought about by the son of this idiot. (Here again we have one of the very few references to birth in all of Proust's writing, and as usual, the reference is a destructive, gory one. Toward the end of *Within a Budding Grove*, however, there is a reference to a beautiful portrayal of the Immaculate Conception, but here, of course, no sexuality is connected with pregnancy.)

Marcel's longing for Venice is described at the end of this volume. It is the return of a longing, carried over from when he dreamed of it as a boy and was particularly fascinated with its Gothic qualities. He had been about to go there with his mother when he was very young, but developed a fever which prevented the trip. He thinks, now, of how pleasant it would be to be rid of Albertine and go off to Venice. He considers love Janus-faced; [15] the person he loves is ugly if perpetually at his disposal, beautiful when unattainable. Escape to Venice. That is what he really wants. It seems as if this circle must continue permanently: fear of the loss of Albertine and then rebellion at being tied to her, and an urge toward flight. But

[15] *The Captive*, p. 241.

quite unexpectedly, one morning when he is about to plan his trip to Venice, with travel folders, Françoise comes in and tells him that Albertine has taken her belongings and deserted him. His breath is cut short. He conceals from Françoise his feeling of complete despair (just as Swann, in his dream, pretended to approve of Odette's departure). Here the volume ends.

V I I

The Sweet Cheat Gone

ALBERTINE is a "phantom," not a well-defined person; she
is a composite from Marcel's past, and therefore the more real
to him through the indefiniteness of her outline. In a sense,
all the persons we attempt, subjectively, to know are composed of what we feel about them, based on previous feelings
toward others in earlier years. As Proust conveys reality, he
resembles not only a musician, but a painter like Monet, whose
approach to art he expounds so well in *Within a Budding
Grove*, in his description of the paintings of Elstir. Proust
at the same time forecast Freud's theories of "transference,"
especially in that Albertine is more than a simple image of a
"mother" or a "brother," but a composite of images that fuse
and separate again, embodying parts of many family figures
of long ago (as happens in real life and in dreams — with
paradoxes, contradictions, reversals, and turning around to
self-identifications). In losing Albertine, Marcel has felt a
part of himself severed. Her departure, which he accepts in
a rather paralyzed manner, is one of the turning points of the
novel.

When Marcel is told that Albertine has left him, his first

reaction is shortness of breath, clutching the region of his heart with perspiring hands, suppression of his tears out of shame before Françoise — and great incredulity. He tells us, "I was like a person who sees the same place in his room occupied by a sofa and by a grotto: nothing seeming to him more real, he collapses on the floor." [1] Marcel's incredulity sets the tone of this entire volume. Even at the very end we are temporarily given hope and the momentary impression that Albertine is not irretrievably gone.

Albertine's boxes had originally impressed him at Balbec as being shaped like coffins . . . again this thought recurs. Another image is that his love is like a lion in a cage [2] about to be swallowed by a python that will enter the cage — the python is forgetfulness. In the past he had referred many times to his love as a sleep-producing drug, and to the necessity for the sedative quality of love, like an addiction (reminding him of his mother's goodnight kiss, as a child).

He refers to Albertine as an urn [3] that has contained everything for him, also as an obstacle interposed between himself and everything else, so that he received everything from her. And later in the book, he says he himself contained Albertine, as if she were in a dungeon inside himself, in an internal Venice. [4] Still later he says that without Albertine he feels like an amputated cripple, [5] responding to changes in climate by painful longing for Albertine (like pain in a phantom limb).

Not long after Albertine's departure, he sends Robert de Saint-Loup as his emissary to Albertine's aunt with an offer of a large sum of money, to buy Albertine back. This mission

[1] *The Sweet Cheat Gone*, p. 84.
[2] *Ibid.*, p. 43.
[3] *Ibid.*, p. 92.
[4] *Ibid.*, p. 307.
[5] *Ibid.*, pp. 103-4.

is not successful, although the offer of money does not offend Albertine's aunt. Then, planning once more to arouse Albertine's jealousy, in order to bring her back to him, Marcel invites Andrée to come to live with him and writes Albertine that he plans to marry Andrée. Impulsively, he suddenly abandons his duplicity and sends a desperate telegram to Albertine, begging her to return on her own terms. This last frank appeal is crossed by a sad telegram from Albertine's aunt with whom Albertine has been staying, stating that Albertine was thrown from her horse against a tree and instantly killed by a head injury. After the telegram, Marcel receives a letter from Albertine written just before the accident, declaring complete submission and offering to return to him. The finality of the loss of Albertine as the loss of *the* woman of his life, whom he can never replace, the termination of all real happiness for him, makes it clear that the theme of *The Sweet Cheat Gone* is to be the mourning process.

The entire series of volumes comprising *Remembrance of Things Past* was begun after Proust's parents' death, but he had already been engaged in conceiving plans for the work and writing the first draft of it for a long time previously. However, he set to work far more earnestly after his parents' death, and his mourning for them is generally considered to have inspired the greatness of his literary achievement. It is interesting to note that Marcel's real union with Albertine, and their mutual declarations of love, occur practically simultaneously with her death, as if her complete submissiveness to him, and her death, were united by more than coincidence.

Jealous curiosity is the source of all of Marcel's activities, after the loss of Albertine. He has investigations made by Aimé, the headwaiter of the Grand Hotel at Balbec, to discover whether or not Albertine has led a secret homosexual existence at Balbec, and discovers many details proving that

Albertine had several female lovers in the bathhouse there. (The bathhouse superintendent who conveys this information, through Aimé, is a man who was described by Marcel, earlier in the story, as looking like a male Odette.)

Through his curiosity about Andrée, as one of the various girls Albertine has known, and his identification with Albertine's love for Andrée (the girl who is so much like himself), he gradually becomes Andrée's lover. (His grief is erotized, as his anxiety and grief tended always to be erotized in the past, but the erotization itself, as usual for him, becomes a source of new suffering. It is as if, after the loss of the beloved, he tries to recapture the capacity to love again, and to find a renewed love-object, whereupon new suffering returns and is even welcomed.)

Marcel questions Andrée about Albertine in the most intimate detail. He learns to his surprise that Albertine did not leave him for a woman — in fact she had given up homosexuality for him. She left him because of a young man who wanted to marry her. Financial security was her aim. (As Swann finally won Odette, Marcel finally lost Albertine, because of legitimacy and money.) Albertine's aunt had been convinced that Marcel never intended to marry her, and that by living with him she was jeopardizing her chances to marry well. The young man for whom she left Marcel had actually been at Madame Verdurin's party, where all the secrecy about Albertine's wish to go there had suggested to Marcel a plot on Albertine's part to meet Mademoiselle Vinteuil. Actually she had wanted to see Mademoiselle Vinteuil only to show that she, the little girl from an undistinguished family, was now received at the Verdurins'. The young man for whom Albertine actually left Marcel was one whom Marcel formerly had ridiculed at Balbec, with the nickname, "I-am-in-the-soup." But at the Verdurins' party, this fellow and Marcel had become more friendly. He had wanted to call on Marcel; and Marcel, now recognizing that his motive was mainly to see Albertine, still continued to credit him with sincerity. Not only did the young man really like Marcel, presumably, but Marcel continued to feel friendly toward him. (As in Swann's dream,[6] we again have the assurance that the man who takes away the beloved woman is the recipient of no ill will.)

Since Albertine is now dead, the two young men have in common their mourning, and perhaps some hidden resentments against her. (This theme is first worked out in *Jean Santeuil*, in a section called "La Religieuse Hollandaise," where Jean's friend Henri returns to the nun with whom he has once had an affair, and finds she is too busy with religious duties to continue their affair but tells him to return next year. A year later he sends his friend Jean to see her; Jean kisses her and thinks she is beautiful but he feels no desire for her. Some years later, both Jean and Henri come back together to Anvers, where the convent is, and now there is a different young nun there with the same name, Aline. The other Aline is dead. The Mother Superior takes the two boys to the first Aline's tomb. Her insatiable, sinful desires have ended in death. Since Proust expressed the conviction that a writer's entire life work is all one unit, it seems that he himself must have been aware of the connection between these earlier images and Albertine in the final novel.)

From Andrée, Marcel learns details about Albertine's seductions of many young virgin girls. Morel, a good friend of Albertine's, used to first seduce the girls and then pass them over to Albertine. Marcel's emotional vulnerability, after learning of all these things, is too keen to endure. A compassionate interest in human nature gradually helps him to

[6] See Chapter XVI on dreams in Proust's work.

learn to forgive. He himself feels the most guilty, and says
he feels as if he has committed a double murder [7] of his grandmother and Albertine, because possessive love, by its unending
demands, kills the loved one. Andrée tells him Albertine considered his treatment of her hostile and mean. He feels responsible for Albertine's accident because his funds enabled
her to have the horse that killed her.

Proust's aggression toward women, hitherto held back from
expression in the story, seems to have influenced the fantasy
of Marcel's whole affair with Albertine, which probably had
the double meaning of expressing the author's unconscious
attitude toward women as well as toward the various boys
with whom he fell in love in his real life. What breaks
through when Proust writes of heterosexual love is his ambivalence toward women, and this goes all the way back to the
attitude of Monsieur Lepic in *Jean Santeuil*.

Probably the root of the "double murder" idea is that the
mother and brother are both loved and killed, in Albertine.
This murderous drive Marcel has seen as typifying Dostoevsky's literary material, but alien to his own. In his own
personal life, Proust could rarely deal with overt aggression,
and this was probably one reason for his intense sufferings in
relation to people, and the necessity to remain isolated in his
room, ill or malingering, protected from life, always the love-
conscious, childish "petit Marcel," attempting to retreat to
a time when competition did not exist. His unresolved ambivalence is also one of the reasons he feared betrayal, separation,
and exclusion — and wrote repetitiously about the exclusion
of people from various social circles, cliques, and groups,

[7] On page iii of *The Sweet Cheat Gone* he refers to Albertine's and his
grandmother's deaths as "a double murder from which only the cowardice
of the world could absolve me."
   Cf. Oscar Wilde's "Ballad of Reading Gaol," also Proust's "parricide"
article in *Figaro*.

starting with the ostracism of Odette from his home at Combray and proceeding through the Swanns' and Verdurins' and Guermantes' types of exclusiveness, and that of Elstir and Borodino, even to the preferences of the "Marquise" of the comfort station. Stress is always laid upon Marcel's permeability into every sort of closed circle, owing, in part, to the illness that prevented his being active or physically at ease.

It was Marcel who felt cheated by Albertine, and later by Robert. He always was the one who suffered. The author, Proust, saw life so tragically, and hastened his death by his manner of overworking, probably because of the guilt feelings that were always with him.[8]

In *The Sweet Cheat Gone*, it is through Marcel's identification with Albertine's promiscuity and homosexual interest in girls that he begins to be interested in the girls on the streets, himself, once more.

He sees three girls on the street. One he thinks is Mademoiselle d'Éporcheville (but the name is really Mademoiselle de l'Orgeville, as he later corrects it), with whom Robert de Saint-Loup has told Marcel he had relations in a house of prostitution, although she is of noble family. She directs a suggestive glance at Marcel, whereupon he falls very much in love with her, expecting to have an affair with her, and he telegraphs Robert to see if she is really the one. He expects to meet her at the Duchess de Guermantes' where she goes to call.

It is in this phase that he realizes he never has conceived of

---

[8] At the time when Marcel is occupied with gaining information about Albertine from Andrée, who is now his mistress, he has a dream (p. 170 of *The Sweet Cheat Gone*) of Albertine. She is not quite dead, and also Marcel's grandmother, not really quite dead, is walking back and forth in the room. Albertine says she has kissed Mademoiselle Vinteuil, and is going to meet her now — Marcel is jealous. Marcel, it is indicated, will soon be where Albertine is. The grandmother's chin is somewhat corroded in the dream, like a statue's. See Chapter XVI of this book.

Albertine as a real human being. He did not value her kindness and intelligence sufficiently. He had been aware only of
his own feelings, and not of other people as individuals, as
persons.

Gradually Marcel is noticing a change in himself. He is
untangling himself from Albertine, eradicating her from
within his own personality. At the same time, in this volume,
he is becoming disillusioned about Robert de Saint-Loup,
whom he has overheard giving advice to the footman of the
Duchess de Guermantes on how to get rid of a fellow servant
by trickery and soiling methods, demonstrating a despicable
side of Robert he has never suspected; he also discovers how
stingy Robert is.

We see the gradual elimination of the image of the beloved,
mourned, and partly hated Albertine from within himself, and
recognition of her as a human being with a separate past existence, along with the gradual revival of Marcel's more kindly,
intelligent, and realistic self.

His mother suddenly appears in the book after a long
absence from its pages. She brings him a copy of *Figaro*
where his article about the three steeples, submitted so long
ago, has at last been published, just after Albertine's departure.
His mother is deeply gratified by Marcel's first literary success. The writing is an intimate bond with her, because as we
know, she admires this sort of achievement more than anything else. Françoise is outside the door complaining at not
being permitted entrance. Marcel, overjoyed to see his article
and his name in print, rushes to the Guermantes' to discover
their reaction. The Duchess and Duke de Guermantes have
not even noticed it in *Figaro*, but the Duke sits right down
and reads it, only to make adverse comments.

One reason the departure of Albertine is such a critical
point in *Remembrance of Things Past* is that Albertine's

desertion carries with it loss of esteem for the idealized brother-figure, Robert, and the beginning of determination to achieve literary success instead of being dependent upon friendships. Marcel abandons his illusions in regard to all the people he knows, with the exception of his mother. Men of genius are not as necessary to him as young, sensual companions. Particularly he changes his attitude toward erotic objects. From now on, they are nothing more than a necessary outlet for his physical urges, and are more depreciated than idealized; they are useful if they stir up the old torments that drive him to think, to write. And although he continues his social self-advancement, it is only for the purpose of gathering literary material.

His mother has returned, in the book, for a short time, as a pure, unsullied, beloved image.

At the end of *The Sweet Cheat Gone*, when Marcel is ready to feel some joy in life again, he takes a trip to Venice with his mother. He feels great ecstasy, exploring the beauty of the city and its art treasures. There is one consummately enchanting, secret part of Venice, lost in labyrinths,[9] where he feels like a character in the *Arabian Nights*, when he happens upon this place one day and explores it. But he can never find it again, and in his search for it, his nostalgia is typified.

Madame de Villeparisis and Monsieur de Norpois, erstwhile lovers and still excellent friends in their old age, are staying at a hotel in Venice. (Their description is somewhat remi-

[9] André Gide's *Thesée* is a short novel, completed in 1944, which offers an interesting comparison, because it deals with Theseus in the Labyrinths seeking the Minotaur, and discovering that the real lure of the Labyrinths is through the odor of opiates which inspire a return to the past through dreams that are more attractive than reality; people stay in the Labyrinths through lack of will rather than through difficulty in discovering the way out. This is related to the story of Phèdre, because Theseus becomes Phèdre's husband after killing the Minotaur.

See also Antoine Galland, *Mille et Une Nuits*, Paris, 1825. "Histoire du Premier Calender."

niscent of that of Jean's parents in their tranquil old age, toward the end of *Jean Santeuil*.) Madame de Villeparisis, the former beauty who has broken men's hearts and who was admired by great writers for her intellect, now has an eczematous blotch on her face, and is a desiccated, senile old lady — Norpois is quite deteriorated also. Marcel sees them when he is accompanied by a woman whose father was once madly in love with Madame de Villeparisis, long ago, and who still expects to see the ravishing beauty who wrecked her home. Monsieur de Norpois makes one more diplomatically strategic move which renews his fame. In a conversation in the Venetian hotel restaurant where he is overheard by Marcel, he suggests to Prince Foggi the name of Signor Giolitti as a candidate for head of the Italian Cabinet. This suggestion is subsequently carried out, with great publicity attached by the journals to the prestige of Monsieur de Norpois in the matter. (Age, the ravages of time, eternal transience, death's approach, as the themes of the final volume, along with the fatuity of success and fame, are presaged here.) Norpois' financial advice still is helpful to Marcel, whose funds have been seriously depleted by Albertine.

Venice is to Marcel a recaptured Combray, with streets paved with water. His mother lavishes all her affection on him here in Venice, "like rich food on a hopeless invalid, since it no longer can really hurt him." She makes no further effort to disguise her great love for him. In addition to the pure love he receives from his mother, he is erotically satisfied by a seventeen-year-old glass vender, in Venice, whom he wishes he could contrive to import back to Paris with him.

After he has eradicated from his inmost self the great part of him that was Albertine, he receives a communication, apparently from Albertine. It seems she is still alive and wants to talk marriage with him. He does not even reply to this, so

unreal has Albertine become to him, now. He remembers
her only as a plump, dark-haired, blue-eyed girl (Robert de
Saint-Loup had said she was not especially attractive).

Marcel's mother is anxious to go back to Paris, but Marcel
finds out that Madame Putbus's maid, whom he still hopes to
make his mistress, is due to arrive in Venice. He refuses to
return to Paris, because he wants to stay where he can have
an affair with this long-desired, unknown woman. His mother
starts out for the train without him. Marcel sits on the terrace
listening to a musician on a nearby boat sing "O Sole Mio,"
and feels paralyzed, unable to decide whether to join his
mother at the train or stay in Venice to pursue physical
pleasures. Suddenly all of Venice becomes unreal and ugly
to him, and he dashes desperately to meet his mother at the
train. (Proust's mother was really dead at the time this was
written; it was his concept of time, which he felt eventually
absorbed all of beauty and of grief, which was eventually to
make him feel reunited with his mother, typified by Marcel's
catching the train.)

On the train, Marcel's mother has two letters for him. The
first is from Gilberte, telling Marcel that she is planning to
marry Robert. Not Albertine, but Gilberte sent the telegram
which had been so garbled that Marcel had deciphered the
name incorrectly.

His mother reads the second letter to him. It is a gossipy
note, stating that the penniless, aristocratic Cambremer boy is
marrying Mademoiselle d'Oloron, Jupien's niece, who has
been given a noble title and large fortune by Charlus. Marcel's
mother refers to this as the "reward of vice," adding that she is
glad Marcel's grandmother is not alive to see such social up-
heavals taking place. (Marcel's own "reward of vice" is to
approach, perhaps with literary success, in the next volume.)

Robert de Saint-Loup expects to move into Swann's old

home, Tansonville, as Gilberte's husband. Marcel's mother considers this a shocking social decline, for a Saint-Loup to marry Gilberte.

Robert de Saint-Loup has never confided in Marcel his interest in Gilberte; he is no longer frank with Marcel, nor friendly (no longer the good brother, but a degraded sort of brotherly figure).

Robert and the Cambremer boy, as Marcel has now discovered, are both homosexuals. Marcel himself has no faith in such deep friendships as he has had with them. He is not interested in all the gossip about their marriages, no more than in "fashions in hats." (As if he unconsciously resents their heterosexuality and their receiving money from their wives, he prefers to console himself by feeling assured that they are getting nothing worth while, and are homosexuals, anyway.)

Back in Paris, Marcel later finds out that Jupien's niece, ill with typhoid the day of her marriage, died several weeks later. The Marquis de Cambremer, her widowed husband, has become the lover of Charlus. Jupien tells Marcel the details when they accidentally meet. He adds that Morel is now Robert de Saint-Loup's lover, and has written Robert love letters signed "Bobette." (The narcissistic element in love, especially homosexual love, is suggested by Robert's loving "Bobette," and Marcel's affair with Andrée who was so much like himself.)

At the end of *The Sweet Cheat Gone*, Marcel spends some time visiting Gilberte at Tansonville, once Swann's estate at Combray, now hers and Robert's. She confesses to Marcel that as a child she was madly in love with Marcel for many years. It was not a young man — but the actress, Léa, in male attire — with whom Gilberte was walking on the day Marcel became so stricken with jealousy that he gave up seeing her. And it was Gilberte whom he mistook for Mademoiselle d'Éporcheville (really de l'Orgeville) on the street. But he did not misinterpret the look of desire she flashed at him. He sees that he has habitually been wrong in his original psychological impressions of the people who mattered most to him, such as Gilberte, Albertine, and Robert. Just as people have their own individual ways of catching cold, he notes that people have their individual ways of falling in love. He sees that he ruined his relationship with both Albertine and Gilberte at the very start, by his profound misunderstanding of them. He even had a misconception of the geography of the Méséglise Way and the Guermantes Way when he took his childhood walks at Combray. They were really one walk. Thus, he reflects, we all have blind spots regarding people and places. But still, in his own mind he associates the Guermantes way with his inability to achieve greatness as a writer.

The episode of Albertine is ended. Oblivion has done its work, deliberately courted by Marcel in order to preserve the remainder of himself, after the part of him that was Albertine is deleted.

He has split up his ancient conflicts. His erotic life is now dissociated from idealized love. Physical satisfaction has become a trifling thing. He settles down to the habit of having a series of "captives" come to live with him. Brother-figures like Robert de Saint-Loup are far from idealized; Marcel sees base traits and blatant homosexuality in the young men he once admired the most. Robert and Morel are in practically the same category, now. (What Freud referred to as "the return of the repressed" [10] is illustrated in the return of the old, idealized love for the mother, and resentment of the brother. Guilt and homosexuality are projected to the brother-figures and the father-figure of Charlus.)

The reader is proceeding rapidly to an account of the final attempt at solution of the oedipal problems Marcel has always

[10] Sigmund Freud, "Further Remarks on the Defence Neuro-Psychoses" (1896), *Collected Papers*, London, 1924, Vol. I, p. 163.

faced. The last volume will describe his spiritual rebirth. *The Past Recaptured* is designed to tell us how the boy who lost the women he most loved through misunderstanding them, from his very first premises about them, once more tests his abilities as an intuitive psychologist in order to conquer his own increasing illness and disintegration, and to preserve a degree of immortality. His questioning the nature of reality,[11] typified by his wavering discernment of Albertine's (or his grandmother's) existence in death and life, and his general battle to find out what is real and what is unreal in human existence, will continue. The conflict between integration and disintegration, achievement and failure, self-realization and the complete waste of a life, will constitute his final battle.

As Charlus has to relinquish Morel, and remains only secretly faithful to him, preferring love-objects who resemble Morel, but whom he now also hates — Marcel, too, has given up Albertine and all "serious" loves, in favor of transient, purely physical ones and a clarified, unsullied "lost" love for his mother and the past of Combray. (Feelings of hatred for the unfaithfulness of a lover are projected to Charlus. Marcel forgets, excuses, analyzes, or sublimates his own hostilities.)

[11] One way Proust had for dealing with death was to pronounce life and death equally unreal. This feeling of unreality is probably related to infantile feelings of omnipotence. We shall see, when we discuss the dreams in the novel, several dreams in which the dead are semi-alive, and expressions of doubt about how permanently they are dead. At the same time the existence of the current world is questioned constantly. The source of Proust's exaggerated sense of unreality may have been partly in his inability to handle aggression against his mother, brother, and father. He dealt with this alien part of himself by erotization, attaching himself to reality wherever he could. The constant urge to be loved, petted, fussed over, and to form an erotic liaison, was a continuous attempt to hold on to some loving contact with people and with the world. We know that in Proust's real life, particularly the latter years, he had difficulty in partaking in the usual human activities, remained secluded, did not believe in friendship, but until publication of *Sodome et Gomorrhe* he did have affairs with young men.

V I I I

The Past Recaptured

THE MORE we have tried to explain Albertine, the more elusive she has become. Created as a "phantom," she is not really a boy; she is a large part of Marcel's self, and this includes an image of his mother. Eventually, he tells us, she vanishes into nonexistence. Another difficulty in our comprehension of Albertine has been the erotization of hostility which she represented, and the obsession about her which Marcel tried to cure within himself. After she is gone, Marcel feels hollow, his life has no future as a human life.

The author, quoting from La Bruyère, indicates that the core of *Remembrance of Things Past* is this: "Men often want to love and do not know how to succeed in so doing; they seek defeat, but are not able to find it, so that, if I may so express it, they are forced to remain free." [1] Proust prefers to substitute "You have tried to be loved" for "You have tried to love." *The Past Recaptured*, the final volume, deals also with the attempt to be defeated, which in Proust (who found it almost impossible to express or even to experience consciously his destructive, hostile feelings toward others) was

[1] *The Past Recaptured*, p. 224.

the only form of hate with which he could deal fluently in the novel. Ambivalence and passivity, in both loving and hating, are incomparably portrayed, not in clinical, psychological terms, and not in mere words, it seems, but in the feelings which make the novel so alive that one frequently has the sense, not of simply reading, but of having the inner life of another human being revealed. This is essentially the similarity of Proust's work to the revelation of unconscious conflicts in the psychoanalytic process; it is related also to the direct communication of feelings sometimes effected by music, painting, mythology, and other moving artistic works, where no interpretation is made, but where unconscious insight is conveyed, as if from the unconscious of the artist to the unconscious of the beholder.

At the opening of *The Past Recaptured*, Marcel is visiting Gilberte at her estate in Combray. He calls out for Albertine at night in his sleep because his flesh still remembers her, although consciously he has given up thinking about her. This is the last echo of his love for Albertine. Robert, now Gilberte's husband, visits there, absenting himself for a time from his mistresses and lovers. Robert is now very much altered in character although not in appearance. He still has his whirlwind manner, his attractive, youthful, noble appearance. He goes through the outer forms of devotion to Gilberte, although his notorious pursuit of women is breaking Gilberte's heart. Marcel observes that homosexuals, such as Robert, would make the best husbands in the world if they did not feel it necessary to flaunt their affairs with women.

Gilberte is reading Balzac's "The Girl with the Golden Eyes" (a story about female homosexuality). Marcel, meanwhile, is reading in the *Goncourt Journal* a fictitious article describing a dinner at Madame Verdurin's, and is impressed not only by the overly sonorous prose, but by the fact that the actual dinners at the Verdurins' cannot possibly equal the literature about them. He reflects that the most magnificent portraits are often of mediocre persons, and that great literature and art almost always present an exalted picture of quite ordinary living. Marcel regrets his inability to write as well as do the Goncourts and other great writers. He realizes he is too much of a psychologist. Instead of seeing people objectively, he scrutinizes them with X-ray eyes [2] and tends to create psychological generalizations, instead of real portraits of people. Marcel realizes that in daily life his wish to please others interferes with his ability to observe. He only listens attentively when personal curiosity based on jealousy or his interest in art causes him to cross-examine people. Fascinating, revealing anecdotes such as the Goncourts collected do not come his way because he is not the right sort of listener. His conclusion is that the great writer is not the cleverest, most learned, or most aristocratic of men but "the one who knows how to become a mirror and thus is able to reflect his life." [3]

A magical power in literature makes mediocre people and humdrum events of life glorious; this is his belief. But then he thinks that perhaps it is to console himself that he tells himself such things, because actually he now must spend some years in a sanitarium, away from the world, and give up the idea of writing.

Of his years in the sanitarium we are told nothing, except that in 1916, when the institution where he is under treat-

---

[2] *The Past Recaptured*, p. 25. Contrast Freud's apology to Fliess, in one of his letters, because his scientific material sounded like fiction.

[3] *Ibid.*, p. 29. The writer is also referred to as a mirror on pp. 180 and 191 of *Within a Budding Grove*, where genius is described as the reflective power of the writer. The image of the mirror is an interesting one, psychoanalytically, in that it is related to narcissism, insight, and also to an attempt to re-enforce the ego. See Miller, Milton L., "Ego Functioning in Two Types of Dreams: Mirror Dreams." *Psychoanalytic Quarterly*, Vol. 17, (Dec. 4, 1948), p. 346–55.

ment can no longer secure a medical staff because of World War I, Marcel has to return to Paris.

As it happens, he has been away during the period when his friends (and, in real life, his brother) have become parents of young children, a topic to which no reference is made in any of his writings.

When Marcel returns to Paris, Robert de Saint-Loup comes to chat with him in his room. Robert, truly patriotic, has requested front line duty. Still, Robert is able to appreciate German contributions to culture and quotes from German poets and musicians. By contrast, many of those men who have avoided combat are overly demonstrative of their patriotism. The popular pamphlets of Brichot, which have made him famous, and the monstrously successful salon of Madame Verdurin, as well as the electrifying phrases of Norpois, all ride on the crest of public enthusiasm about the war.

One night Marcel chances to meet Charlus on the street and they walk a few blocks together. Charlus is doubtful whether or not France can win the war, and cannot refrain from admiring the Germans in many respects. His masochism, which is really the basis for his fascination with the enemy, is perceptively described.

Observations about unconscious forces that predispose people to specific political and sociological attitudes prepare the way for a highly personal, dramatic event. Proust (as we stated previously) believed, with Bergson, that one searing and revealing moment [4] of a person's life, if properly understood, tells us more than a long biography. A study of the inner essence of Charlus's spirit is introduced by two statements: one is from Morel. After Marcel has tried to bring

---

[4] Similar to Freud's belief that the understanding of traumatic episodes in a person's life and the way they are later expressed in character formation and symptoms is the key to understanding a personality.

about a reconciliation between Charlus and Morel, at the former's insistence, Morel admits he would like to end the enmity, but he flatly refuses to go to see Charlus because he is physically afraid of what Charlus might do to him. Then a posthumous letter from Charlus to Marcel confesses that if Morel had come to his home, as he was beseeched to do, to reconcile with him, Charlus would unquestionably have murdered him. This is told to us out of context, looking ahead to the time of Charlus's decease.

We revert once more to the period during wartime when Charlus is still alive, walking with Marcel on the boulevards. Charlus reveals that his assignations with young men of the servant class are a little more difficult to obtain now; he must be less fastidious because the war has claimed the majority of able-bodied men, but still he manages to keep supplied with soldiers on leave. His eye is ever alert to the attractive figures in uniform on the streets. With advancing senility Charlus has descended to cruder depths. He is a more obvious prey to his homosexual drives. Although declining in character, he is still a perspicacious observer of individuals and of group psychology, an aesthete, a sensitive spirit full of rich tradition and historic information concerning his vanishing class. He is considered out of date by those who do not know the history of his title, stemming from the Princes of Sicily; he is openly rejected by the Verdurins and others among the wealthy bourgeoisie who have risen too recently to social prominence to appreciate the aristocracy he represents and the fine tastes he preserves in many respects, despite his streak of insanity.

After leaving Charlus, Marcel undergoes a strange experience. He is walking about like a character from the Arabian Nights in the deserted streets, which have an Oriental feeling about them. Very thirsty, he goes to a sinister, rundown hotel, where he thinks he may get a drink. He imagines he

sees, or does see, Robert de Saint-Loup's agile form darting
in the vicinity. Outside, the wartime terror of Paris which is
being raided from the air by the Germans suggests to Marcel
destructive lava flowing upon the streets of Pompeii, inundating the city. He thinks of the words *Sodoma Gomorra* written
on the walls of one of the houses of Pompeii. Now, in the atmosphere of a fantastic city, combining past and present, and
threatened with fearful punishment, Marcel enters the evil-
looking hotel, where he fears he may be robbed and murdered.
He sees disreputable, furtive figures there, and overhears something said about a victim in a room upstairs being beaten
bloody. This seems to be an establishment for spies. Apparently, "the boss" has had to go out to get chains to bind up
his victim sadistically for the night. Marcel remembers Robert had once been accused of spying but acquitted, and wonders if Robert is really here on some sort of evil business. He
feels he must, at all costs, find out what is going on, and he
manages to get upstairs and to peer through the transom into
the room where the victim is chained. To his astonishment, he
sees the victim is Charlus,[5] who has made a practice of hiring
men to beat and chain him there, late at night. Marcel later
overhears Charlus complain that the foul language used to him
by Maurice, the young man who did the beating, was not
sufficiently convincing, but was recited like a lesson. There is
a description of this degenerate male brothel in much detail;
certain of the most distinguished men of letters, science, poli-

[5] See Mina Curtiss, *Letters of Marcel Proust*, New York, 1949, p. 246.
In a letter to Louis de Robert, probably the summer of 1913, discussing
pederasts in his book, he makes it clear that homosexuality is a "neurotic
defect." In referring to a scene which is presumably Charlus's beating, he
says, "The idea of the scene was suggested to me by a number of different
things, but above all this: a very well-known man of great distinction was
the lover of a prostitute, although he was married and the father of a
family. But in order to achieve complete satisfaction, he felt impelled
when speaking of his own son to the prostitute to call him 'the little
monster.' At home, however, he was a very good father . . ."

tics, and the aristocracy — all walks of life — frequent it. It is run by Jupien, who derives enormous wealth from the establishment, but whose chief aim is to express, in this way, his protective devotion to Charlus, because Charlus would get into far more dangerous surroundings, otherwise. Here is a sort of motherliness that provides agony in a comparatively harmless way, and physical release with the utmost payment of conscience by suffering.

Marcel is only an onlooker, and nothing is too real or too unprotected, in Jupien's Temple of Dishonor. The employees who beat Charlus are innocent fellows, ashamed of working this way for their salaries. One pretends to have murdered a janitor's wife; but when these young men begin to confess to Charlus their heinous misdeeds, one of them can find nothing worse to say than that, as a child, he peeked into the room where his parents embraced each other. Charlus is disgusted with such naïveté and lack of real brutality.

The fascination which draws the frequenters of this male brothel toward contacts with strangers in the darkened underground railway where they cannot see their sexual partners, during air raids, is described. Amidst the horrible degradations of war, these perverse evils are comparatively childish. The denizens of Jupien's brothel feel safest from the police on the nights of the air raids. It is in this section of the novel that the guilt of children who masturbate is described, and their fear of being overwhelmed by sexual pleasure.

After this episode of spying on Charlus being beaten, Robert de Saint-Loup is discovered by Marcel, through tracing a medal which Robert lost, to be one of the frequenters of the brothel; Robert is killed next day, valiantly, in the war.

Later, Charlus, driveling, turned into an overgrown child, after having had a stroke, is watched over tenderly by Jupien in the park. Still unable to control his impulses toward homosexuality, Charlus cannot be trusted alone anywhere for a minute. Jupien confides to Marcel that Charlus seduced a young boy, under ten years of age, when left alone for a little while in a room at a hotel. Like a mother, Jupien guards Charlus affectionately.

Marcel spends a second period in a sanitarium. When he returns to Paris, he finds two invitations awaiting him. One is from the great actress, Berma. The other, conflicting with Berma's invitation, is to announce a reception at the home of the Princess de Guermantes. The latter's salon represents the peak of social distinction, a somewhat ironical fact, because it is Madame Verdurin, widowed and twice remarried, who is now Princess de Guermantes. Society does not mean very much to Marcel. He is preoccupied solely with combatting his artistic limitations, his inability to become a successful writer, the sterility of his mind. He goes to the Princess's reception, but does so mechanically.

He stumbles slightly on the uneven curbstone in front of the home of the Princess, and this small misstep recalls in a flash some mysterious, powerful happiness of the past. It is an ecstasy such as he felt upon seeing the three steeples of Martinville, or when tasting the madeleine dipped in herb tea which evoked the scenes of Combray, or upon hearing the last great work of Vinteuil: a feeling of great creativity and joy, based on something unconscious, out of the past. He thinks of Venice, and the uneven flagstones in the baptistry of St. Mark's there. Then, by a process of association, as he describes it, other images begin to recall the past vividly; and Marcel realizes how ordinary life can take on beauty because of mental images such as we all keep repressed within us, as in jars at various levels. This method of recapturing lost memories is the main revelation of the book. Marcel has developed insight into the fact that it is our innermost feelings (preconscious, or largely unconscious, although he does not use these terms) which impart emotional value to life. This is the beginning of his conviction that he *can* become a great writer, although but little time remains for him. (His insight into the unconscious derivation of the emotions which seem most real parallels Freud's discovery that unconscious feelings give the quality of living reality to experience.) Marcel, about to attend a social function at the apex of French society, tells us he is happy only because the breath of a lost paradise has caused happy memories to return to him involuntarily. He comments that "the only true paradise is always the paradise we have lost."

In the Princess de Guermantes' home, while he is attending the reception, Marcel has further mystical experiences of recollection of the past. The sound of the waiter's spoon against fine china and the feeling of a napkin against his lips afford further sensations of joyful recapture of the past which he cannot explain. (In *Jean Santeuil*, the napkin's pleasant touch is directly associated with Jean's mother's putting him into a clean white nightshirt as a child and tucking him between immaculate sheets.) The vividness and joy of his recapture of the past may seem unexpected, in the trail of the preceding narrative, and somewhat inexplicable to us.

Penfield's neurophysiological work [6] has shown that during brain operations, for example, stimulation of the temporal lobe of the brain may actually reproduce a sense of the full experience of a past memory, as if it were occurring again. This was discovered when epileptic patients were treated surgically. It is also of some interest that a Danish writer, a contemporary of Proust, with whose work Proust very possibly was

[6] Wilder Penfield, "Memory Mechanisms," *Archives of Neurology and Psychiatry*, Vol. 67 (Feb. 1952), pp. 178–91. (Whether or not the memories so stimulated by Penfield were of great emotional significance was not determined.)

never acquainted and who had not read Proust, hit upon this same preoccupation [7] with the vivid recapturing of moments out of the past and the great joy connected with such experiences. (Earlier, Proust's friend Fernand Gregh published a youthful story in which the sudden recapture of a memory was a hideous, fearful experience.)

Marcel gives us as the reason for his intense nostalgic gratification the following explanation: when he actually lived through important moments of his life, their reality was sullied by feelings of fatigue, sadness, anxiety, or lack of sufficient perspective to estimate their true meaning. Art, his own recreation of life, condenses past and present. He can live outside of time, now, in retrospect, and thus enjoy the true essences of life. He feels that death can be overcome by human beings only by escaping from time, both past and present, into a knowledge of essences. (This derives partially from Bergson's philosophy, and even more deeply from Plato's theories of the quest for essences, but it is also linked closely with Freud's parallel concepts. What Freud explained as the power of repressed emotions, keenly alive within us, linked directly to past events and to forgotten memories, creating the strength and reality of our feelings, Proust conceived of

[7] The Danish novelist, J. Anker Larsen, published an autobiographical record in 1926 which makes an important point of involuntary memory and its "lightning flashes of intense joy." When the joy became conscious the blissful moment of recall ended. "Meeting with Eternity," this author felt he learned to extract a mystic experience which he considered his actual meeting with Reality. See Harold March, *The Mind of Marcel Proust*, Philadelphia, 1948.

Also see Norbert Wiener, *The Human Use of Human Beings*, Boston, 1950. Applying the term Cybernetics (the steersman) to the field of research into human communication and its control, Wiener indicates that the recovery of repressed memories might be explained by the concept of "taping." "The change in the stimulus for which a given response takes place must have some such nervous correlate as the opening of a synaptic pathway leading to the response which would otherwise have been closed, or the closing of one which would otherwise have been open."

in a more poetic, philosophical or mystical way; but both Proust and Freud stressed the emotional impact of preconscious feelings summoned from our past involuntarily, by seemingly trivial stimuli.)

It is here that Proust gives us an analysis of his approach to artistic creation as a method of research into the past. He describes the recollection of a past self, blending with the present self and with present experience and arriving at a synthesis more meaningful, more aware, than any creature less than man could achieve. Here we have an attempt to describe the mind's integrative functions, the uniqueness of an individual's awareness of his own ego, which Proust considers necessary to the artist's emotional maturity, and to great art. To convey a purely political point, to communicate intellectual ideas, Marcel does not consider the function of art. Only to express the real inner self, the self that is not even conscious (and which includes, of course, the influence of environment, family and social forces, and cultural history) is, for him, art's function. What he seeks in art is synthesis of the emotional profundities of an individual, such as we sense in great music, great cathedrals — the depths of the sensitive individual relating himself to universality. It is interesting that the concept of art as embracing the relation between inner emotional reality and the outer world, the effort to draw more of the unconscious into awareness, of trying to communicate repressed or preconscious feelings, leads Proust into explorations which seem to parallel those of Freud, although the latter approaches human psychology from a medical, intellectual standpoint. Proust is searching for a stronger ego, not the transient ego of the here and now, nor the childhood ego of the past, but the more intrepid ego which is capable of integrating past and present experiences, and is able to exist "outside of time," an "immortal" ego. Freud, too, according to his self-analysis, which he describes in his letters to Fliess, was looking for a stronger, less neurotic self.

Not only Marcel of the book, but all of Proust's characters and even places and events, in his writings, as a whole, reflect his integrative process at work, combatting the fragmenting forces. In *The Past Recaptured* he reflects upon how imitativeness destroys creative art. Society, as the material of art, requires study; therefore social climbing may be a means to further one's observations. Yet he resents every social obligation which distracts him from his writing. His goal is to keep on working despite his illness, to present, while he still can, a lucid, candid mirror of all humanity. His sense of guilt is necessarily altered. He can no longer live according to the rigid standards of his parents: What is good for his writing is all that he can force himself to accept as moral. His struggles against his conscience have been relentless in the past, but he realizes, in his aging years, that, like a certain race horse that was fed on roses, the tastes of his genius might be unusual. Analyzing his true impressions to the depths, for the sake of his writing, has becomes his goal. But this is a race against death. He considers art "the most real of all things, the sternest school in life and truly the Last Judgment." [8] Ideas formed by pure intellect may abound in logical truth, but to Proust only subjective impressions are really true, however improbable in outline or inferior in material they seem. The self-sacrificing, creative process, by rigid standards that replace the ethics of Combray days, brings Marcel closer and closer to gratification of his literary ambition, and to death.

He is not afraid to call society folk the real illiterates, and he concludes that princes are as interested in reading about workmen as workmen are in reading about princes: to escape.

[8] *The Past Recaptured*, p. 206.

(Again, we think of Charlus, desiring to be beaten by workmen.) In art, Marcel feels that the true relationships of cause
and effect must be enclosed in "the necessary ring of a beautiful style." [9] Mere erudition regarding the arts and culture
he considers an escape from going deeply into personal reactions. "Celibates of art," he terms the arty dilettantes who
really feel nothing and therefore suffer a constant need, in
their daily lives, to surround themselves with artistic trap-
pings. The grandeur of real life is to rediscover, to grasp
again and lay bare before ourselves emotional reality, to know
ourselves and our lives as they really are, "the only life that
is really lived." This is his credo. He tells us that only
through the art of another person (as a form of communication) can we get outside ourselves and see the other person's
universe.

After a long digression, originally initiated by the sensation of the uneven flagstones outside the Princess's home, we
attend with Marcel a social event that emphasizes the deple-
tion and paucity of real life, compared with art. Here we experience what it is like to be no longer young, to perceive, as
in a masquerade, all the undeniable signs of aging in our ac-
quaintances, feeling none of these deteriorating processes subjectively, but being greeted at every turn by the indication, in
others — by their very assurance that we have not changed at
all — that we are aging. Time's hand is felt upon us as we
read. This is done subtly, and is probably as delicate an illustration of the process of "projection" as can be found in any
novel. Not only people but places have diametrically altered.
Combray, the peaceful scene of Marcel's past, has become a
battleground and has been destroyed; the Duchess de Guermantes, by her love of novelty which once made her so
attractive, has inevitably allowed bourgeois artistic elements to

[9] *The Past Recaptured*, pp. 217–18.

destroy her once rigidly aristocratic salon. The conniving, ruthless, thoroughly undistinguished Madame Verdurin now has the most exclusive title of Princess de Guermantes. All those whom Marcel once loved are dead, and his novel is a cemetery for past loves.

The narrative jumps ahead in time, for a glimpse of a brilliant reception given by Gilberte de Saint-Loup. Her mother, Odette, still superficially beautiful but frail in mind and body, is treated insolently by Gilberte's guests.

Time has revolutionized all relationships. Marcel's initial impressions were usually erroneous from the very start, owing, as he now realizes, to flaws in his own perceptions.

The Guermantes family have begun to receive intimately people whom they would have excluded from their drawing rooms in previous years. The Duchess de Guermantes, her husband, and Charlus, the three great aristocratic figures of Marcel's past, around whom his life has revolved, are far less influential. Morel, having become a distinguished citizen, has just served as character witness in an important trial; his words determined the outcome of the case. He is no longer a musician, having given up his violin when he stopped consorting with Charlus.

Robert de Saint-Loup is remembered kindly, after his death in the war. One of the guests remarks that it is well that Marcel had no sons, or they would have been of an age to be killed in the war, like Robert.

In the last scene of the story, many of the main characters are present with their daughters. But the daughters turn out to be a source of humiliation. For example, the actress, Berma, and Odette, are sacrificed and degraded, and their health endangered, by their daughters' social ambitions.

The guests of the Princess de Guermantes, including Marcel, have deserted the formerly great Berma in order to pay homage to the ex-prostitute, Rachel, Robert's ex-mistress, who was once disgraced years ago at the Duchess de Guermantes' home, when everyone made fun of her novel sort of acting. Now the Duchess de Guermantes falsely recollects that it was she who first appreciated Rachel's histrionic talent and introduced her successfully. (The coarsest, least aristocratic women in the cast of characters, Madame Verdurin and Rachel, are triumphant in the end. This is unlike the fate of some of the crudest social climbers in *Jean Santeuil*, who are ridiculed and do not succeed.)

The Duke de Guermantes is carrying on a love affair, in his eighties, with Odette. This alliance raises Odette's social prestige and lowers the Duke's. Private fortunes, social standing, empires, all have revolved, for unforeseen reasons. The Duchess, it is now disclosed, had actually behaved flirtatiously toward Marcel, when he was a young boy, gazing at her in the nave of the Combray church.

Gilberte de Saint-Loup has a sixteen-year-old daughter who later is to marry a literary man. Marcel states that in Gilberte's daughter the two "Ways" of the book came to an end: through Robert de Saint-Loup, the Guermantes Way — and through Gilberte, the Méséglise Way. We end with a recapitulation, a resynthesis of the opening of the book. Vinteuil's music, the love affair with Albertine, the Charlus-Morel affair, Swann and Odette, Madame Verdurin, Elstir, Bergotte, Marcel's beloved mother and grandmother, all slip into new relationships, new orbits, endlessly spinning out their elucidation of each other. Proust's "solid psychology," as he liked to call it, has given us contradictory sides of all his characters, and yet they are all facets of himself. Now Mademoiselle de Saint-Loup is a renewal of Marcel's own youth.

Marcel states that his goal is to extract the real essence of his life in his manuscript: he asks of the reader no moral judgment over him, but merely to tell him whether or not he has portrayed life as it is.

Death is drawing close to Marcel, now.[10] He fears an accident in the Champs-Elysées on his way home from the reception, or a stroke, which may prevent his writing. Life has suddenly become precious because he has something within him he wants to communicate. Formerly he would have thrown his life away, in favor of another. But now he says he is like a dying mother who still has the task of taking care of her son. The idea of death has been living with him "like love for a woman." He has always detested death, but still he has related every thought to it. In summing up his life, he confesses that all his work has been predetermined by that night his mother read to him and spent the night with him in his room.[11] And now that he is near to literary success, he feels like the aged Duke de Guermantes, who walks as if on dizzying steeples, with legs that are insecure, in the great expanse of time. He quotes:

> For, an the grain of wheat die not
> after it has been sown, it will abide
> alone; but if it die, it will bear much fruit [12]

Thus we see how closely productivity and death were allied in his essential attitudes.

Many readers feel, as they close the book, that they must ponder upon or reread this long set of volumes in order to understand their elusive implications.

On almost the last page there is a paragraph which might help to explain the hallucination of the frightening stout woman in black whom Marcel Proust, the author, saw just before he died.

---

[10] *The Past Recaptured*, pp. 387–402.
[11] *Ibid.*, p. 400.
[12] *Ibid.*, p. 399.

And it is because they thus contain all the hours of days gone by that human bodies can do such injury to those who love them, because they contain so many past memories, joys and desires, already effaced for them, but so cruel for one who contemplates and carries back in the domain of Time the cherished body of which he is jealous, jealous even to the point of desiring its destruction. For after death Time withdraws from the body, and the memories — so pale and insignificant — are effaced from her who no longer exists, and soon will be from him whom they still torture, and the memories themselves will perish in the end when the desire of a living body is no longer there to keep them alive.[13]

In Marcel Proust's life, and in his writing, there was always the motherly image who both protected him and caused jealousies and great fear, from the fear of offending his own mother through his aggressive or sexual urges to the mysterious anxieties typified in Jupien's Temple of Dishonor at the end. Marcel's intense need for love was connected with his destructive jealousy, as he tells us. His research into the past has followed the vicissitudes of his own history of love and its ambivalence, almost as a psychoanalytic procedure takes the patient back into the past.

In all of art, there are few examples of the fantasy of one individual intentionally pursuing in detail, with all possible sincerity, the almost clinical revelations of preconscious feelings, with so much genius for observation and expression, and such painstaking erudition.

The psychoanalytic patient's account of his innermost psychic life, during therapeutic treatment, is accomplished with the aid of another highly trained individual, and without aesthetic domination of the form of expression. The technique of interpretation of the transference feelings (the "phantoms"

[13] *Ibid.*, p. 401.

which are uncovered and their origins traced), in psychoanalytic treatment, permit the verbalization of unconscious forces. In Proust's work, aesthetic standards (telling his story in a way which would have met with his parents' approval) perform some of the functions of the transference to the analyst. In psychoanalytic treatment, it is the therapist who directs intellectual as well as emotional insight and helps to explain the interplay of conscious standards, repressed emotional patterns, and unconscious standards derived from the parents.

Masochism such as Proust's is better understood now than it generally was in his day. With no psychoanalytic assistance, no Freudian theory, at least in his earlier years, Proust attempted to work out a way of dealing with his sense of remorse and guilt on the basis of the aesthetic standards his mother once established for him as all-important. In *Jean Santeuil*, he explains his evocation of the unconscious more clearly than in the second version of his novel, and also the connection of his guilt, his writing, and his mother's strict ethical standards. Toward the end of the book, Jean says that when he was writing, he brought out what he did not yet know about himself, things that he invited from imagery, from hidden feelings that were symbolic, instead of writing what reason recommended as intelligent and beautiful.[14] Then Jean goes on to describe how inured he has become to his own vices, how he feels justified, not full of regret as he used to be when young and remorseful, now that his gift of poetry is the focus of his moral existence. Good is what favors his inspiration, and bad is what paralyzes it.

Although in *Jean Santeuil* the author makes this claim of

---

[14] *Jean Santeuil*, Paris, 1952, Vol. III, p. 301. "Une fois devant son papier il écrivait ce qu'il ne connaissait pas encore, ce qui l'invitait sous l'image où s'était caché (et qui n'était en quoi que ce soit un symbole) et non ce qui par raisonnement lui aurait paru intelligent et beau . . . "

adjustment to his inner conscience on aesthetic grounds, nevertheless *Jean Santeuil* the novel is supposed to be published as a posthumous work, given to Marcel by a great writer (implying or forecasting a punishment of death when the writing is completed).

In *Jean Santeuil*, Jean explains how his mother's ethical standards gradually decline, so that she accepts more of what would have shocked her. In *The Past Recaptured*, Marcel deals with the evolution of the writer's internal conscience, but he never really solves the problem of his sense of guilt toward those he feels he has offended by his erotic urges all his life. His final attitude is to make atonement by sacrificing all his being for the sake of his art.

We rarely find anything so close to confession interwoven with such free imagination in the work of one man. In mythology, which is often more of a group product, we are more apt to find it. Many gifted writers are able to express remarkable intuitive insight into human emotions, but Proust attempted an integration which encompassed the main emotions of his own life, in unusually crystalline form. In his early stories, and *Jean Santeuil*,[15] and *Contre Sainte-Beuve* we have the distorted, early shadows cast ahead of *Remembrance of Things Past*, and if we study these we understand the final novel more definitively. Proust's resort to facts of the outer world occurs at a minimum, because the author went back into his semi-forgotten memories, and not to the current scene or other books, for his material. His daily life was devoted to this reliving.

It is his nostalgia which provides the matrix of his work.

---

[15] *Jean Santeuil*, Vol. II, p. 253. Here the author says he has lived all the scenes he has described, and their essence has escaped him until later when he wrote about them.

A Comparison of "Remembrance of Things Past"
with Thomas Hardy's "The Well-Beloved"

In a letter to his friend Robert de Billy,[1] around 1909,
Proust said that Thomas Hardy, in his novel, *The Well-Beloved*,[2] accomplished something "slightly resembling" what
Proust was trying to do in *Remembrance of Things Past*,
"only a thousand times better." He added that Hardy's book
"does not lack the touch of the grotesque which is an essential part of all great works." After the sophisticated tone of
Proust's novel, we may be led to expect something abstruse;
nevertheless, if we turn to Hardy's tale, we find it is dreamlike, but of the utmost simplicity of structure.

The Well-Beloved deals with the return of a renowned
sculptor to the small Wessex community beside the sea, where
he first lived as a boy. There this successful, urbane artist falls
hopelessly in love, on a series of visits, with three generations
of the same girl, Avice. She represents to him all his nostalgia
for the simple group of coast families from which he stemmed.

[1] Mina Curtiss, *Letters of Marcel Proust*, Transl. and ed. with notes by
Mina Curtiss, New York, 1949 (date is approximate, as Proust did not
date letters).
[2] Thomas Hardy, *The Well-Beloved* (reprinted from a story printed in
the *Illustrated London News* in 1892), first published as a novel 1897.

His own mother is dead. Toward these women, "phantoms," all a composite, formed of three generations, with whom he falls in love, he feels a mixture of benevolent idolatry and cruel disillusionment. Of the three Avices, he complains, "I am aching — have ached ever since this jade of an Ideal devised the unconscionable trick of inhabiting one image only." Until the age of sixty-two he remains a youth, in his own estimation of himself. When he at last renounces his love for the image of Avice, after an illness, and finally admits to himself his true age, he loses his power of artistic expression and settles down to a peaceful, platonic marriage, glad to be rid of the torments of his search for the Well-Beloved. In this lyrical story of Hardy's we see the vicissitudes of a man's search for a lost mother-image in three generations, morally reassuring in its impossibility because the three Avices stretch over a time span too great for reality. Avice is three times renewed to him in his virile manhood, always as a youthful creature, never an educated, refined person like himself, but forever blossoming, naïve, sensuous and seductive. It is she who has made advances to him, in the first place. (There is some similarity to the story of Aline, the nun, in *Jean Santeuil*, especially her being replaced by another Aline at the convent.)

In the clarity of Hardy's story, Proust recognized a directness which the vagaries of his own book's roundabout search for a return to past happiness did not permit. Without going into a clinical study of the oedipal source, and employing poetic images instead of adopting the outspoken manner of Freud, both Hardy and Proust make very clear in their novels the fact that a man's deepest love may very well be for a nostalgic phantom [3] which inhabits the bodies of a series of individuals, and provides artistic inspiration.

[3] Proust, *Cities of the Plain*, Vol. II, p. 218.

Hardy compares his hero to Ahasueris, the Wandering Jew, who conquered Time, in that he never died but wandered forever searching for a love he could not gratify. In the myth of Ahasueris, we have projected into the future a search for what occurred, at least in fantasy, in the past. Proust, who also has called his story that of a Wandering Jew, states in the last volume of his novel that any true paradise is necessarily lost in the past. He tells us that art and life are an attempt to relive, to recapture something from a past existence, and he indicates in a more mystical way what Freud sought to trace in specific unconscious conflicts and trauma. Proust penetrated the intangible through poetic precision, but ultimately Proust and Hardy conveyed many of the same impressions: that our emotional paths are laid out for us to follow because of past events which are veiled from consciousness. Freud explored the role of the unconscious in determining human behavior and the development of insight as related, not to aesthetics, but to therapy. Proust and Hardy indicated awareness of oedipal forces, as a result of their aesthetic sensibilities (as the best writers have done at times).

One may easily discern a great similarity between Proust and Hardy in their techniques of whetting the reader's curiosity, especially in regard to jealous love. In *The Well-Beloved*, spying upon lovers, conjecturing about their feelings toward each other, and reacting to the loves of others play an important role — just as in *Remembrance of Things Past*. In Proust's writings, as in his personal life, curiosity was insatiable; its source regarding his mother is described at the beginning of *Swann's Way*, and often referred to. Marie Scheikévitch, who knew him in his mature years, tells us in her book, *Time Past*,[4] that Proust followed strangers at the Casino at Cabourg in order to observe them and listen to what

---

[4] *Time Past: Memories of Proust and Others*, Boston, 1935.

they were saying, and that his pockets bulged with news-papers and notes. Curiosity and jealousy were, for him, the amalgam which connected present and past, writer and reader, lover and loved object. Breath-taking, seductive curiosity, with a sense of approaching something ultimate, definitive, always upon the next page, is a tense atmosphere which his writing creates. In reading of Swann's spying on Odette, and of Marcel and Albertine's relationship, and the degenera-tion of Charlus, we are made to feel exceedingly curious. Marcel's prospective meeting with Mademoiselle de Stermaria, who never materializes, represents perhaps the epitome of falling in love with the disembodied phantom whose chief claim to our interest is the curiosity she arouses — since she never appears at all, except as a fleeting image, but is so highly recommended as a seductive woman. Similarly, Dal-tozzi, in *Jean Santeuil*, pursues strange women on the streets at night, always hoping to find a gratifying love, and receiv-ing, usually, cuffs and blows.

Occasionally, in psychoanalytic work, one may note both the act of falling in love with a stranger and the telescoping of time into a love for several generations of the same girl in the dreams of patients.

One example comes to mind: A man who dreamed of fall-ing in love with an unknown woman was a patient whose conflicts were connected with keen rivalry for his mother's affection with a younger brother. He dreamed of falling in love with an unknown woman as a way of avoiding dealing with rivalry toward his brother and father. If he did not know who the woman was, he did not have to know who might rival him.

Another patient had a dream of a recurrent love that spanned generation after generation, just as in Hardy's *Well-Beloved*. He had been dealing with the problem of homo-sexuality and then retreated from it to his early love for a

little girl cousin who was a faintly disguised version of his
mother. The truth hidden behind the fantasy of loving several generations of the same person is this: The original love
for the mother can be unconsciously transferred to her baby,
that is, the brother or sister — and also, as we see in dreams,
it may be reflected back to the grandmother, or to aunts, and
so forth. Love, transferred from the mother to the baby
brother, in Proust's case, probably contributed very largely to
his homosexual tendency.

We often see in psychoanalysis the operation of a process
in which feelings about emerging conflicts, such as those over
repressed homosexual drives which are currently being mobilized, are diverted back into fantasies related to a brother
or sister, and these in turn disguise the original rivalries and
incestuous drives toward parents. All this is usually involved
in a complicated pattern into which early figures [5] are interwoven, perhaps not clearly but in dimly comprehended, preverbal images. In fiction we do not often see the operation
of this process portrayed so well, because most authors do not
understand or reveal themselves so clearly as Proust or Hardy,
and because one of the aims of literature seems to be to

[5] Cf. a part of Freud's self-analysis, as he describes it to Fliess (Letter
No. 70): " . . . My 'primary originator' (of neurosis) was an ugly, elderly
but clever woman . . . I welcomed my one-year-younger brother (who
died within a few months) with ill wishes and real infantile jealousy, and
. . . his death left the germ of guilt in me. I have long known that my
companion in crime between the ages of one and two was a nephew of
mine who is a year older than I am . . . he visited us in Vienna when I was
fourteen. We seem occasionally to have treated my niece, who was a year
younger, shockingly. My nephew and younger brother determined, not
only the neurotic side of all my friendships, but also their depth. My
anxiety over travel you have seen yourself in full bloom . . . I still have
not got to the scenes which lie at the bottom of all this . . . You see how
the old liking breaks through again. I cannot give you any idea of the
intellectual beauty of the work." *The Origins of Psycho-Analysis* (see
Bibliography for full title), ed. Marie Bonaparte, Anna Freud, Ernst Kris,
transl. Eric Mosbacher and James Strachey, New York, 1954.

complicate and disguise the primitive "transferences" and conflicts out of the past, in order to make fantasies diverting, acceptable, pleasing, and anything except provocative of complete insight. Most fantasies, in ordinary fiction, tend to stimulate only partial insight, with much effort to allay guilt and reassure the reader that painful subjects are unreal and far removed.

Hardy tells in simple terms the story of giving up the original incestuous love, and with it some of the romantic coloration of life, and separating oneself from the wellsprings of artistic talent. In *The Well-Beloved*, he indicates how physical illness and admitting one's age are connected sometimes with renunciation of this great nostalgic source of erotization. Ambivalence toward the "jade of an Ideal" is the subject of Hardy's novel. In the end, a platonic marriage and tranquillity, with loss of talent or genius, becomes the sculptor's solution.

Proust's hero, at the end, does just the opposite of Hardy's. Hardy's hero, through repression, achieves a desiccated semblance of normality, renounces art and becomes happily married, whereas Marcel, at the end, lifts his repressions in order to arrive at artistic fecundity and shuns marriage, deep loves or friendships in the present, and even life itself except for its representation in his writing. Hardy's book, more than Proust's, suggests a counterpoise to the idea that life means progress. In Proust's work, succumbing to the force of regression is accompanied by a conviction that rebirth promises to recapitulate the past on a higher level to restore lost joys.

It is not accidental that in both novels the background and symbolism of the sea predominates, coloring these loves with a regressive element.[6]

[6] Sigmund Freud, *New Introductory Lectures on Psychoanalysis,* New York, 1933, p. 122.
See p. 139, and footnote 11, p. 217.

X

Symbolism

If one takes the analogy of thought to a melody, it is obvious that no amount of histological study, no matter how advanced, could show in a brain more than the pattern left by one note. The sequence of the notes in time makes the melody. Ideas are such sequences.[1]

IF WE HAPPEN to reread a favorite book after a number of years, we are usually surprised to find passages which seem to have sprung into the book since our last reading of it; we cannot recall having read these precise things before. Paragraphs, marked with our own pencil, may be completely forgotten in the course of time. Similarly we may, if we come upon old letters we have written, find the wording unfamiliar, as if composed by a stranger. This demonstrates how the process of repression blots out a portion of our abstract thinking.

We forget some of our most crucial early experiences, and yet we can recall certain unimportant details: the face of a

[1] Stanley Cobb, "On the Nature and Locus of Mind," *Archives of Neurology and Psychiatry* (Feb. 1952), Vol. 67, No. 2, pp. 176–77.

small friend in school whom we did not like particularly, the name of a tradesman we visited on a superficial errand about ten years ago, the exact wallpaper in a rented room where nothing special happened, the plot of a play we thought mediocre, and words of advertising jingles which we have deliberately tried to forget, and could not. Most of us remember a few nursery rhymes and fairy-tale characters from our childhood, but have forgotten others, and we cannot tell why the memories of certain of them have remained with us. We have memories from childhood in which we stand apart like an objective observer and view ourselves as a child, which illustrates how a mixture of fictitious and true ingredients in some of our early recollections represent the *screen* [2] of earlier, forgotten events.

Our thinking and remembering are tied into patterns, constellations, by a symbolic process. Thought occurs in some animals, as well, on a symbolic basis, related either to body processes or internal, physical needs connected with the outer world, and perhaps involving a desire to communicate. The earliest symbolic processes employed in individual human communication were probably connected with mating, religion, and responses to external threats. Group co-operation and therefore group symbols in early mankind seem to have developed from irrigating, farming, and primitive warfare, as well as an inherent drive toward collecting in groups in order to worship and to satisfy social needs and mating instincts. Primitive artistic expressions encompassed all of the basic emotions, symbolically, as if following a basic need to communicate.

Egyptian and Chinese writing represent a transition from symbols closer to primitive pictures than ours, and are akin

[2] Sigmund Freud, *Collected Papers*, London, 1925, Vol. II, p. 368; Vol. IV, p. 359, and II, p. 48.

to some of the hieroglyphic forms in modern advertising. Our writing and printing are based on a simple series of abstract symbols, using straight lines, curves, and dots. As J. Z. Young points out in his book, *Doubt and Certainty in Science,* our ability to communicate through abstract symbols seems to be increasing, depending on educational methods and possibly on inherited skills. People of musical talent and training, who can bewilder us by reading and remembering pages of complicated musical script, may be forerunners of many of our descendants who may be able to read pages of mathematical symbols that would startle us today.[3]

The symbols we first learn as infants are related to basic needs and become partially repressed and amalgamated with each other during bodily and mental growth, and for the most part they are lost to consciousness in their original aspects. If we reflect, we will realize that a vastly complicated set of symbols help to determine our adult thinking, feeling, and action, as well as communication. We cannot think without symbols, yet their unconscious meanings are responsible for much of the confusion of human thought. The symbol of a flag, of a church spire, a tombstone, a Phi Beta Kappa key, a life preserver, lightning, and so on, evoke immediate responses, and when several symbols are condensed, like flags flying together, their messages increase in import by permutations and combinations. The symbols on a printed paper make us smile, weep, alter the course of our lives. We cannot respond even to the simplest symbols with complete unanimity because we are ambivalent. Our innermost lives are filled with universal human symbols and also with more highly personal symbols than we have ever taken into account. The idea of the part of town we prefer to live in, the labels on clothes, or the make of car we would like to drive, the kind

[3] J. Z. Young, *Doubt and Certainty in Science,* Oxford, 1951.

of acknowledgments we hope to gain from others, the dread of certain particular kinds of symbols of failure — we can easily rationalize. But there are hosts of other, less reasonable preferences, which make human nature eternally diverse, fascinating to study, but dangerously incohesive, centrifugal, lacking in ability to communicate.

Symbols are in constant flux, as educational and social mores change, so that many of the symbols of one generation differ, at least superficially, from those of the next. There is bound to be some ambivalence toward the symbols with which one's parents were closely identified, so that each generation feels compelled to retain deep respect for some and reject or transform other favorite ideas and symbols of the preceding generation. The symbol of the national flag tends to increase in importance from generation to generation, particularly when there is a history of parental sacrifice and suffering for patriotic reasons. But styles and fashions, such as taste in architecture and furniture, tend to shift back and forth, owing to the interplay of nostalgia and flight from parental domination. Rebellion manifests itself in systems of thought, philosophies, art, superficial fads, and scientific trends. The child brought up in today's modern home with abstract paintings on the walls may seek for another sort of painting to refresh his own home, someday, going back to the past for a form of rebellion, just as the boy whose father has founded a business and looked forward to the day when his son would share it with him is frequently attracted to another career. There is bound to be a natural, largely unconscious ambivalence attached to the various symbols which surround the older generation's way of life. These symbolisms, connected with old loves and rivalries with parents, brothers and sisters, and with people in childhood, repressed or fallaciously recollected, are responsible for many seemingly inexplicable feelings which dominate our choices in life. Even the most complicated symbols which are connected with success in the adult world are based on our earliest configurations, just as rings on a tree trunk follow the pattern of the first growth. Body symbolism has preceded the ability to talk. Developing conscience and a sense of shame make even the small child repress or distort some very primitive bodily urges connected with his first needs, loves, and anxieties. These earliest patterns are always with us, sublimated socially; as a mass expression of ideas, emotions, and traditions, they distinguish our culture from other cultures distanced by time, place, or tradition.

We cannot understand Oriental music at first, but somehow we feel we ought to understand all paintings more readily than music — and to appreciate almost all perfumes. In our own culture, we are accustomed to accept certain symbols instinctively, and to reject others, responding preconsciously rather than consciously. We place an enormous amount of faith in what we feel deeply. Opposed emotional symbols become focal points for man's inhumanities. Speech has established definite lines of communication, and it is through speech that we are accustomed to trying to control our own disintegrative tendencies, personal and social, and to converse silently with ourselves, to think. There is another kind of thought process to which we refer as "intuitive." Many times we depend on a sense we cannot define, to augment words. We look into our dreams, our fantasies, to know ourselves, and we enjoy works of art because these products of carefully delineated symbolism, liberated from everyday verbalizations, convey meanings to which we can respond directly. Words serve their purpose of communication but many words have, in certain respects, outgrown their usefulness, and create a lag in our understanding, particularly in scientific terms — and perhaps also in some of our literary and artistic approaches.

Symbols, employed in religion, abstract thought, and in the most ordinary and primitive communication, are not enough; we use our hands in gestures, and facial expressions, whenever words seem insufficient. What is the type of thing we generally seek to express, when words seem most clumsy or archaic? [4] The subtleties which words could not catch interested Proust most keenly. Proust said he tried to cultivate a new sense in his observations, and to create a new form of communication in his writing. He felt dissatisfied with what the novel had generally accomplished in the past, as an art form. His two favorite books, *The Arabian Nights* and the *Memoirs of Saint-Simon*, were not novels. Living feelings, sincere awareness of life, were what he wanted to observe and communicate. He groped toward music and painting to help him express more than words. The "stonemason's geometry," he saw in all Hardy's work is symbolic of something more than words. He felt that by being satisfied with the outward forms, without plumbing the depths of true feelings,[5] human thought could quickly descend to the level of barbarism. He did not mean to negate the value of logical thought, but to establish its subservience to emotional insight, emphasizing the need to explore unconscious feelings more

[4] Perhaps it is true, as J. Z. Young has pointed out in *Doubt and Certainty in Science*, that biologists do not pay enough attention to communication as a basic biological need in men. Young points out the tendency of all nature to arrive at more complicated conformations in which organic matter dominates the inanimate, evoking a notion of time without beginning or ending, and a concept of continued change in the direction of higher complications which create problems for one species after another, so that one species tends to succeed another. This is a biological view not dissonant with Proust's. Also see William Morton Wheeler, *Essays on Philosophical Biology*, Cambridge, 1939. Wheeler, an eminent biologist, implies that research based on Freud's theories may lead to great truths which biologists may not otherwise attain. He states on p. 70: "The great fact remains . . . that the knowledge that is being gained of the workings of our subconscious must eventually profoundly affect animal no less than human psychology, since the subconscious *is* the animal mind."

[5] Marcel Proust, *Jean Santeuil*, Paris, 1952, Vol. II, p. 127.

closely. The difficulty of actually achieving further insight
into one's unconscious is the history of his novel. He points
out twice, in *Within a Budding Grove* (once in regard to
Bergotte and once in regard to Elstir), that the artist's pursuit
of certain images within himself leads to true expression and
success as an artist, but at the same time these images tend
to become rigid, to be idolized, to form habitual outlets, and
to set a limit, eventually, to the artist's effectiveness.

When we observe imaginative narrations, dreams and fantasies, we see in them bits of communication subservient to
memory and composed of modified reality. Certain works
of literature more or less successfully throw off the shackles
of words and the repeated habits of thought that are mere
rote. Rebelling against pressure to conform at all moments,
men are impelled to take flight into imagination freely in
dreams or fantasies, in beautifully harmonious forms, or in
obscure and "difficult" art, especially if the latter wins some
sort of public acclaim. The great fascination which musicians, writers, actors, and other emissaries from the world of
emotional expression hold for the majority of people is related to the "transferences" even the most sophisticated,
highly educated individuals may readily feel. Men seem to be
bursting against restraints, to find expression beyond ordinary
words. The symbolism of the unconscious pushes toward
communication. We are speaking here of something partly
related to, but not identical with, the literary school of Symbolism as contrasted with Naturalism or Romanticism, according to which literary critics so often insist upon classi-
fication. When we talk of unconscious symbolism in human
thought, we refer to mechanisms at a level below consciousness, courted by consciousness, but not directed by it. The
Naturalist or Romanticist writer may be symbolical also; but
Proust, referring to writers of "great imagination" or "highly

symbolical writers," appears to be referring, very often, to those who struggled with the relation of unconscious images to the integrating factors in literary creation.

What are the essential differences between dreams, fantasies, and works of art? In the dream, the elaborations of an unconscious wish and its penalties, merging with past memories which the wish evokes and the present-day stimuli which lend their reassuring reality, in even the simplest individuals, are often expressed with crystalline form. But our dreams exist privately, and upon awakening, conscious memory is usually cheated of most of them.

Fantasy is semiconscious, and constructs, even against our will, configurations that spring up grotesquely distorted and disguised. In our fantasies, punishments for censored impulses may be detached from their immediate causes; persons change into other persons or animals, or inanimate objects; reality, dominated by two kinds of morality, conscious and unconscious, and shaped by memories, is infused with desires that may diametrically oppose our conscious, adult picture of what we think and feel. It is this protean, veiled, constantly changing character of fantasy that makes it eternally attractive, and may at times give it the power of expression, far more than reason, logic, or direct verbalization. We fear the products of our fantasy; they are among our greatest fears.

Those who engage in artistic efforts often feel that they achieve inadequate conveyance of a crude fantasy. We allow ourselves to receive impressions more readily than we can shape them in artistic symbols. Thus we receive real, but passive contact with otherwise inaccessible depths of others. We gain from certain works of art a glimpse into the intimate feelings of others, and we feel reinforced by a sense of the compassionate universality of basic human emotions. (Proust wonders, in *Within a Budding Grove*, if there is a large,

universal form of intelligence, in which we participate.) The
rigid forms conventionally employed by art have attempted
to create sanctions, religious, social, and aesthetic. Thus guilt
is relieved, for the expression of otherwise tabooed desires
and anguish. The termination of this artistic sharing would
be a shattering loss, as we reflect when we think of what
modern weapons can do.

Proust often communicates feelings that are not profoundly
buried from consciousness, but simply are not habitually
expressed. Repressed feelings are released by some authors
mainly in wit, or in highly special settings like the "light French
novel," which, if sufficiently entertaining, is not expected to
be moral, or in myths that break the bonds of conventional
realities: religious tales, folk art, and other writings upon
which public approval has bestowed the term "classics." Art
has a tendency to break habits of thought and yet to form
new integrations, and thus to reassure.

Through changes in our media of communication, art
forms may have begun to change at an accelerated rate. It
seems tedious to read enormously long novels, now that time
has been speeded up in every way. We have been slipping
back to visual communications, on a compact, swift basis.
Yet, at present, novels that are quite long are popular. For
some, Proust has been a determining influence; others find
him too tedious to read.

It may be that novels will, in the future, concentrate on a
more exact rendition of preconscious content which writers
like Proust have struggled to find within themselves. Greater
stamina in exploring human relationships may be the direction
of the novel. If this is so, it will not suffice to copy the clinical
findings that psychiatric research has contributed to human
thought, nor to use the method of free-association as a slipshod,
downhill path to the unconscious. Joyce's innovations in the
use of stream-of-consciousness as a style in writing led to

something different from the psychoanalytic use of the free-association method. Partly forsaking vision, which was so typical of Proust, Joyce tried to *hear* the unconscious. But Proust was apparently closer to psychoanalytic exploration of the dynamics of the unconscious and an approximation of the nature of insight (for example, he said he hoped to learn more about himself from his reading of Gautier, indicating that emotional insight might sometimes be gained from reading books). Proust refined the use of language, dissected and made more precise the symbols which language had evolved, by going into his own highly personalized images behind such a phrase as "to be loved" and "to be free." His feeling that aestheticism was more than a means of enjoyment suggests the idea of communication on a level not necessarily higher or lower, but different from that achieved by ordinary speech. Art, as an effort to communicate, takes us into the unconscious but also into new experiences, previously unexpressed.

We will know more about our integrative processes, our personal and group goals and standards, when we learn to look into ourselves more successfully and to communicate clearer insights.

Experiments conducted in the last few years have brought biologists back to the theory that latent instinctive patterns are inherited, so that factors within the human mind, and emotional patterns, for example, may be potentially present and never elicited. Environment has recently been shown to play a great role in determining the expression of physical as well as emotional patterns. Inheritance, in the course of time, possibly reacts with environment reciprocally, to some degree; according to the most recent work of Tinbergen and Lorenz, for example,[6] the alteration of instinctive patterns is conceived of as possible — at least it is a modern biological

[6] See *Group Processes*, Josiah Macy, Jr., Foundation, New York, 1955. Also see p. 292 of this book.

question. Aesthetics is related to this, because where instinctive biological patterns exist, it is possible an aesthetic sense, as Proust divined, may intuitively detect such patterns and, in a primitive manner, attempt to express them. We may also learn from art more about how our integrative processes function. (For the psychiatrist or biologist to study aesthetics is not easy, since a lifetime of laboratory training gives one the feeling of approaching art with a spectroscope, a measuring apparatus — yet it was the Parisian impressionists, among the artists, who, in Proust's time, began to study their own craft scientifically, applying modern physical theories of light.)

When *Remembrance of Things Past* was being written, symbolism, which emphasized the *nuance*, rather than the color, was the new dynamic force in art, particularly in poetry and painting. Those days also saw the publication of Freud's *Interpretation of Dreams*, with its exposition of the symbolism of dreams. Symbolic expression has been further studied not only psychoanalytically and artistically, but in the neurophysiological laboratory. Research into the symbolic process, from a physiological point of view, has lagged behind the writers' and artists' utilization of symbols. It still seems as if the scientist, particularly the psychiatrist, must apologize for invading this territory. But some new, interesting ideas about symbolism have come up in the past few years. Do they amplify or contradict the implications of artists of great imagination, or do our artists and scientists labor in hermetically sealed seclusion?

As Lawrence S. Kubie has pointed out in his studies of the symbolic process,[7] the body image, in part or as a whole, con-

---

[7] "The Distortion of the Symbolic Process in Neurosis and Psychosis," *Journal of the American Psychoanalytic Ass'n.* (Jan, 1953), Vol. I, No. 1, pp. 59–86; "The Central Representation of the Symbolic Process in Psychosomatic Disorders," *Psychosomatic Medicine* (Jan.–Feb. 1953), Vol. XV, No. 1, pp. 1–7.

stitutes one pole of the symbolic process which evolves in the human organism, making possible the organization of psychological tensions. Eating, breathing, elimination, genital functioning, or involvement of the body as a whole, create imagery in the very earliest phases of development. At the same time, there is an opposite pole, which evolves along with the growth of each human organism's internal symbolic process: this is the external imagery, relating inner, subjective perception to the outside world, and finding expression, eventually, in speech, thought, fantasy, poetry, mathematics, and many highly integrated processes. Kubie reminds us that the ability to make abstractions is man's highest mental function (i.e., abstract thought, generalizations). Isolating fragments of experience and synthesizing them, making new concepts out of memories, may occur consciously, preconsciously, or unconsciously, and so shape thought, language, dreams, and even symptoms and psychosomatic illnesses. Kubie uses the analogy of a hammock, pointing out the dual anchorage of every symbol to "I" and "Not I." Gradually increasing ability to distinguish the outer world in infancy leads to development of the capacity to form images of oneself and of the outer world which can represent *each other*. This is illustrated by children's games, very often, when the child runs around and imagines himself an airplane or horse. And vice versa, when he sees a dog he may bark, when he sees an injured person he fears for his own well-being, since he is not quite able to distinguish himself from outside images. Repression (obliteration into unconsciousness) may take place at either pole, in relation to the outer world or the inner feelings. In sleep, we use visual symbols; that is, visions of the outer world which we see in the mind's eye, and body imagery apparently is scanty. If the same course is followed during waking life as in dreams, the external world is used to represent internal feelings without restraint, fantasy and visual images take over completely. This separation from the binding force of reality is characteristically found in psychoses. (To some extent, the fantasy which is given loose rein during artistic construction may be anxiety-provoking, leading away from comfortable defenses. The task of an artist, to draw on fantasy and yet to control his own reactions to fantasy, presents difficulties beyond the mere mastery of a craft.) Proust was aware of the process of integrating personal feelings, evoked through the symbols which constitute language, with the highly ramified patterns of fantasy crystallizing in his entire novel's course. Trying to hold apart from this process objectively, to some degree, he called his literary function "reflective," meaning mirrorlike. He also likened himself to Einstein [8] in his exploration of new relativities and depths. (Freud, too, identified with Einstein.)

The outlines of *Remembrance of Things Past* are embellished, or rather reinforced, by lesser themes within the novel, and sometimes most sharply delineated in the rather bizarre sketches in Proust's earlier, unfinished draft of the novel published as *Jean Santeuil*. This book has been referred to both as a different novel and as the earlier draft of *Remembrance of Things Past*; both statements are correct, just as a recurrent dream can come back with certain alterations. Every echo of both manuscripts corroborates the same basic attitudes and the same aspirations and conflicts. As in the early dreams of patients in psychoanalysis, the earliest most naïve writings of a highly subjective author tend to express basic points of conflict in the least disguised forms. In *Jean Santeuil*, Monsieur Lepic and his wife, tied together by sado-

---

[8] Proust speaks of identifying with Einstein in a letter quoted by Princess Bibesco and mentioned on page 156 of Maurois' biography of Marcel Proust. Freud speaks of his resemblance to Einstein in a letter to Fliess.

masochistic bonds so strong that one could not survive the other, the nymphomaniac nun of Anvers, Daltozzi, the young man in ill health who risked pneumonia chasing women on dark streets at night in the rain, vainly pursuing an ephemeral stranger he believed could truly satisfy him; the young girl in the Confession story; Honoré, the young man who was consumed by jealousy, whose mistress still cared for him devotedly after he lost both legs in an accident — but who still was tormented by jealousy until death ended it — all these earlier images outline the themes we later find in *Remembrance of Things Past*.[9]

Even those of us who are not in the least artistically gifted have specific tendencies toward certain symbolic expressions, and our own special use of language. There are apt to be certain standard symbolic figures which we all engender, perhaps as standard as the symbols on dice. But in the course of our personal development, our own individual symbols become like loaded dice and tend to fall into the same sets of patterns over and over. In Proust's writing, for example, there is constant repetition of certain conflicts, and of such images as his seascapes and symbols connected with the ocean, churches, natural landscapes, flowers, hats, and so forth — also his references to bowls, jars, urns, and other vessels — and to constellations, stars and the sky, and birds. For some, Proust is far more satisfying than for others, but all readers recognize in his fiction something of truth about themselves.

As to specific symbols, sea and birth symbols predominate. Marcel admits he has fallen in love with Albertine because she was part of a frieze of girls outlined against the sea. At the theater, he describes the Princess wearing both a plume and nets with pearls in her hair. He thinks of Albertine as being

[9] See Appendix for summaries of some of Proust's early stories and excerpts from *Jean Santeuil*, freely translated.

as much a part of the sea as a gull, and the Guermantes profile as birdlike — of Robert as half falcon. Robert's eyes are the color of the sea. Vinteuil's "little phrase" is like moonlight on the sea.[10] Many scenes are described as subaqueous, or celestial. Elstir's paintings are frequently connected with rivers or the sea, such as regattas, coastal views, scenes of the vicinity of Rivebelle. The dream of the cathedral partly buried [11] in the sea in *The Guermantes Way* seems to be inspired by Monet's paintings of cathedrals and of water. Albertine, first seduced by a laundress, carries on her affairs with young girls at a bathhouse. The scene of the night raid on Paris is symbolized by fear of a deluge of lava flowing on the streets, like the inundation of Pompeii, which at the same time acted as a preservative. Charlus is beaten with chains from a ship, and needs the stout arms of a sailor; Venice, the city with watery streets, has been Marcel's ideal as the place to visit; Noah was Proust's favorite biblical character, evoking great pity at first, but later envy, because Noah could see more deeply into the world from his seclusion in the ark during the Deluge than he could on the surface of the earth. Proust likened the rudimentary nature of mankind's spiritual existence to the status of the whale, among mammals. All of these marine or celestial images, typically Proustian, are usually connected with unconscious references to pregnancy, birth, or womb. In a sketch called "Penmarch," [12] in the second volume of *Jean Santeuil*, we have a description of a stormy sea which is designated by the author as the nucleus of his search for lost memories. Every man has his Penmarch, he

[10] *Swann's Way*, p. 268.

[11] *The Guermantes Way*, Pt. I, pp. 195–96.

[12] *Jean Santeuil*, Vol. II, p. 207 (freely transl.). Cf. the storm at sea, briefly referred to in *Swann's Way*, p. 496; also see p. 338 of *Cities of the Plain* where the word "Pennemarck" is used in a discussion of curiosity about words. This demonstrates how a small allusion, certain to be skipped by many readers, may be packed with the author's associations.

tells us . . . In this sketch, he describes "the violence of the torrential sea, as at the commencement of the world after a combat of the gods, with all the chain of the Alps installing themselves, peak after peak, colossal but calm, and between them majestic valleys in which one could not have distinguished a man — and the sun shining on the glaciers, the cascades thundering in the breast of the calm peaks and abysses." Here is an allegorical study, focused on birth symbols, epitomizing his literary effort.

Also we have the simple letter of a laundress announcing the death of her son, which Proust likens to great literature, in *Jean Santeuil;* again a reference to water, and to the death of a child.

At the end of the second volume of *Jean Santeuil,* listening to the wind at the parental estate of his close friend, Henri de Réveillon, the poetry of the recapture of lost moments is first described. Jean feels that in the future he will not devour life in anguish at seeing its joys disappear, but taste life with confidence, knowing that one day or another the reality of those minutes would return to him again if he did not seek them — in a sudden recollection, in a gust of wind, in the odor of a fire, in a low sky, sunny but with rain approaching. "We do not know reality while we live it, but recollection allows us to float between present and past in their common essence, finding ourselves. We have not found our true selves in the past, but we recapture our ego, as a delicious honey. . ."[13] (See footnote to page 194.)

With water, air, birth, and death predominant, symbols of not very extraordinary nature, such as rooms, hats, the sea, flowers, and so on, are invested with enormous emotional significance in Proust's work and are, in themselves, the cause of strong reactions in people. For instance Marcel falls in love

[13] *Jean Santeuil,* Paris, 1952. Vol. II, p. 339. See also Note 8, p. 286.

with Albertine because she is connected with the sea. Marcel's farewell to the hawthorn flowers, his fear of strange rooms, his love for the familiar, low-ceilinged room at home, his sea-scapes, are like impressionistic paintings filled with impact through no action, but through the emotional qualities in-herent in symbols. An ordinary train to Paris, from Venice, is a matter of life or death at the end of *The Sweet Cheat Gone;* a hotel room at a beach resort is threatening at one time, another time fraught with searing memories. Symbols are laden with dramatic impact in Proust's writings, just as in dreams, where they may be alluring, anxiety-provoking, reassuring. There is a dichotomy of feeling about most of these symbols. Their coloration may include diametrically opposite aspects. Action is at a minimum, feeling at a maxi-mum, in Proust, and therefore feeling is attached to symbols most candidly.

Proust's heterosexuality was repressed, very largely — and his curiosity about heterosexuality, pregnancy, and birth dominated his use of symbols, or broke through in peripheral, sadistically colored side-issues, seemingly inconsequential to the story, or else these most repressed impulses found expres-sion in some of the more frankly oedipal material of his earlier work, such as the "Confession of a Young Girl," the "par-ricide" article in *Figaro,* and "La Religieuse Hollandaise," the prostitute-nun story in *Jean Santeuil.* (Also, for example, in the frank primal-scene material and oedipal conflict of the "insignificant" character in Jupien's brothel, who spied upon his embracing parents when he was a child.) Instead of being given direct expression, positive oedipal conflict is usually indicated in Proust's writing through sublimated imagery, or such equivocal "phantoms" as Albertine, Charlus, Madame Verdurin, Odette and Swann. Marcel's love for his mother and grandmother is chaste and unsullied. But intra-uterine symbolism, apparently bearing out Freud's [14] conviction that this sort of symbolism implies a wish for union with the mother, on a sexual basis, is omnipresent, suggested by Marcel's hyperconsciousness of rooms, the sea, and the enchanted atmosphere connected with Combray, Venice, and the time when he was with his mother. Proust's deepest symbolism seems to refer habitually to his mother as a sexual object, and to her pregnancy. Probably Marcel's falling in love with Albertine because she is part of a frieze of girls outlined against the sea really corroborates the fascination he had with the idea of his mother's pregnancy, and with the real brother, Robert — but repressed.

Just as his imagery turns the raging sea into the peaks of the Alps, which are colossal but calm, and as the lava upon the streets of Pompeii is also a preservative, we always see ambivalence, a need for reassurance in the midst of fury, in connection with Proust's birth or death symbols. In his references to the sea, we sense a need for maternal approval of his loves, and we see why the sea is always in the background, why Robert and Albertine have blue eyes like the sea, and why there is always a domineering woman, who runs a salon, or someone like Jupien, or even the "Marquise" of the comfort station, in charge of loves and of bodily functions. There is almost always a brother-image, with whom maternal love — or desertion — tends to be shared equally.

Proust, who so fearlessly revealed all sorts of subtleties when tackling such difficult subjects as the problems of the homosexual, had a tendency to guard from his own consciousness but to express through fantasy his great anxiety, curiosity, and fascination regarding what may be interpreted as symbols of birth and pregnancy, intra-uterine symbols. His destruc-

[14] Sigmund Freud, *New Introductory Lectures on Psychoanalysis,* New York, 1933.

tive reactions to his own brother's birth were probably connected with this struggle over water symbolism, and his asthmatic symptoms and anxiety are probably tied in with it also, as we shall later see in more detail. It is amazing how simple a core runs through such a complicated artistic work.

Proust always felt close to death because, for him, it was related to love; it was the logical terminal point for jealous love, which required complete domination of the beloved and allowed no room for jealousy, yet depended upon jealousy to keep it alive. His guilt for oedipal wishes demanded the penalty of death, unconsciously. He needed love so badly, never felt that he received it adequately, and because of incipient rage at the beloved and at himself (himself scarcely distinguished from the beloved, external person) — he needed constant protection; this sent him back in time to an innocent, infantile, symbolic reunion, physically, with the mother who once carried him within her. Imminent fear of death and ill health diverted him from the consequences of physical, heterosexual, adult love, and at the same time evoked protective demonstrations of affection of the sort whereby an invalid dominates others, and in return is dominated. Like the city of Paris about to be inundated, in *Cities of the Plain*, Proust himself was constantly at the point of being choked, suffocated in his struggles with his symptoms.

Before we try to trace more precisely the relationship of the symbols in Proust's books to what he may have felt or repressed within himself, let us compare his intellectual objectives with those of Freud, who was engaged in systematically exploring the operation of the unconscious at roughly the same time. The plot of *Remembrance of Things Past* seems to center about Proust's unconscious attempts to deal in various ways with his oedipal conflict. All his heterosexual urges tend to remain tied up forever with mother-figures. While pure, nonphysical love for his grandmother and mother are expressed throughout the book, sexuality is split off and the novel recounts many types of attempts to deal with it. Bisexuality is expressed through innumerable images. As so often happens, when the original emotions regarding the parents constitute an insoluble problem (in this case, brought to a head by the mother's pregnancy, it appears), loves and hates are transferred from the parents to the sibling, or other early family figures, with a great deal of strength. Thus we see much of Albertine, Robert de Saint-Loup, Bloch, Henri in *Jean Santeuil,* and others — based on Proust's real brother, Robert. And the symbolism of the sea, rooms, vessels, the dungeon within Marcel's self in which Albertine existed, all are connected with the mother's pregnancy and the author's preoccupation with "eternal union" [15] with his mother, in which he escapes competition with his father and his brother by retreating to a time and place which preceded his birth, when he and his mother were really united.

No psychiatrist would base final judgments on a fantasy, even a very long, detailed one, supplemented by only fragmentary data. Yet one is frequently called upon to hazard an intuitive guess when working in the new, difficult, and often very intangible field of psychiatry. Behavior that has the least logic, according to ordinary ways of thinking, often makes sense to the psychiatrist, who has been applying himself to studying man's behavioral expressions and adapting his ear to the symbolic language of one person after another. This is particularly true where communication of unconscious drives is attempted. Proust felt that by evoking patterns of imagery in addition to verbal content, he could communicate something that was beyond the limits of ordinary articulation. He discarded *Jean Santeuil,* the first draft, because comprehensive

[15] See Appendix A, p. 277.

form was absent from these comparatively raw, untempered sketches. The sketches themselves were often extremely revealing, but they were not part of a complete, harmonious form, in which each part would elucidate and be necessary to the other parts. Proust saw in Hardy's *Jude the Obscure, The Well-Beloved,* and *A Pair of Blue Eyes* the same nucleus. He recognized the same basic content in all the work of any one artist. In all Proust's work we see the same strong urge to evoke the past, to speak the language of music such as Wagner's, and of painting — the supraverbal, nonverbal or preverbal language of instinct raised to a high level of artistic sublimation.

To the psychiatrist, the many artistic variations which a limited number of basic human themes may take are of enhanced interest; here, in Proust, is the fascination of an integrated, sublimated presentation, instead of the fragmented sort that is customary. Proust's organization of unconscious, preconscious, and conscious material, by its own tendency to create a new kind of order, is impressive and calls for an attempt at understanding.

Marcel Proust and Sigmund Freud

A T WHAT infinite point do the parallel lines of fiction and psychiatry tend to meet? Proust was something of a clinician despite himself. Freud's aim was purely scientific, but he wrote extremely well. Freud worked out some of his problems in the form of letters, and Proust's literary style has been termed epistolary by some critics. Both men were trying to elucidate themselves, to draw out feelings they did not understand, and to interpret their own feelings in accordance with general laws derived from observation of others. They made use of a literary process, as well as cultivating a technique of introspection, to try to eliminate some of their own blind spots. Freud conducted his own analysis in private, but confided its progress and many of his general observations, even a few intimate details, to his friend Fliess.

Freud notes in his letters how his early patients tended to trace back their neuroses to fictitious traumas.[1] In Proust's

[1] Freud thought that his hysterical patients' stories of sexual seduction by their parents in childhood were true and were very important sources of their neurotic symptoms, but later he discovered that these stories were untrue. Nevertheless the patients reacted to their own fantasies of parental seduction as if they were true. In Proust's story there is a different situation: the mother stays with the boy all night, in his illness, and this was based on fact.

novel, Marcel blamed everything on the night his mother
spent with him when he was ill. This is somewhat similar to
the typical traumatic fictions in Freud's patients. But in
reality Proust's mother did spend a month in his room when
he was ill. The memory of this was probably a screen for
much earlier events that set his neurosis into its patterns.

In Proust's work, events tend to repeat themselves always
in a new way, and these events, repeated with variations, lend
harmony to all his writing, as does repetition, with variation,
in music or in the work of a painter like Matisse; but these
patterns also suggest some real occurrences in the forgotten
past, which we probably will never be able to trace completely. For example, the hand of Norpois which Marcel
wants to kiss, a gesture which later is used as evidence of
Marcel's foolishness — the hand of Servais, the medical student, in *Jean Santeuil*, which seems so cruel and then so self-
lessly compassionate that Jean wants to kiss it — and the
coachman biting Bergotte's hand in Bergotte's nightmare
before he dies — suggest some forgotten impulse regarding a
man's hand.

Apparently Proust was not wholly conscious of the strength
of his need to substitute erotization for aggression; for example
in his ambivalence toward his actual brother. He apparently
did not fully understand the regressive nature (the infantile
erotism, soiling, retreat from the biting stage to earlier stages)
of his earliest impulses toward his mother, and how these impulses colored his later imagery; nor his compulsion to confess,
and to seek reconciliation, as it was related to the fear of losing
the mother's love through infantile erotic and aggressive impulses toward her and the baby brother, and expressed itself
in the constant exhibiting or confessing of "bad habits" and
their partial exoneration, in his writings. Nor did he fully
understand the nature of his submissive urge toward his father,

his rebellion against this, and his compromise need to be punished by the father as a source of reconciliation and reassurance along with gratification. His linking of the idea of pregnancy with death and rebirth, in his own person, was related to much of his imagery, and this must have been unconsciously connected with his mother's pregnancy and his identification with her.

He had a tendency to generalize, to draw psychological laws of cause and effect,[2] which he himself also saw he used as an intellectual escape. He realized that our impressions tend to be wrong in the first place, in regard to other persons, so that he was aware of the limitations of his own efforts at psychology. Paradoxically, he showed us his attempts to understand human nature, and the reasons why he must fail specifically in regard to those most important to him. He felt that every man must face his emotions alone, and that no one can really help him, yet he believed that, to some degree, art might stimulate the process of insight. Toward psychiatry he is reluctant to give a genuine appraisal. Psychoanalysis in Proust's time, even in the 1920's, had not reached anything like its development today. It was being introduced in America. In Europe there were a few psychoanalytic institutes and training centers, and such outstanding names as those, for instance, of Karl Abraham and Ernest Jones had been added to the roster of Freud's pupils. Psychiatry as practiced at present was something about which Proust did know something — but not very much. Yet he had a related approach, in many ways. His avowed purpose was to establish the relationship between voluntary and involuntary memory. In psychoanalytic work, we deal with this problem constantly.

Proust gives us a history of anxiety and inferiority feelings in a sensitive, sickly boy, his need for doing well, for being

2 *The Past Recaptured,* p. 128.

doted upon, for exhibiting himself as a success and then always having this triumph break down (presumably out of competitive guilt). For example, Jean is acclaimed and admired, in *Jean Santeuil*, at the opera, on the arm of the King of Portugal, to the exclusion of his rivals, but then he overhears remarks about his femininity. Usually, his femininity creates an uneasy situation and must be projected: he sees homosexuality all around him; and besides, he is convinced that love does not really matter because time devours all, and only art is real.

Wherever Proust's characters walked, wherever they attended concerts, salons, art exhibits, they were conscious of their curiosity, and of the eyes of others upon them, in return. Erotization constantly absorbed anxieties, and created fresh fears. As did Marcel in the book, the author constantly fell in love with thinly disguised brother-substitutes, who would more normally have been his main rivals; and he fled from heterosexual temptation back to its origin in his mother, and to such symbolisms connected with his mother as were expressed in his literary imagery and his "neurasthenia." He dared not bring to conscious expression his passive urges toward father figures (instead, for example, he feared "fou rire," in real life, when Robert de Montesquiou gave readings of poetry). In *Remembrance of Things Past* he referred to his fear of kissing his father just above the beard, as he would have wished to do, because his father might take offense. He also refers to Charlus's ideal of a masculine lover as like a "beloved hangman."

He probably felt the more inferior because of illness and passivity, and then determined to please his parents and their images, later incorporated in his own personality, by becoming the greatest writer of his time. This involved him in the mastery of his own unconscious, the wellspring of his creativity, as it did Freud, who had to study himself first before he could draw general laws about others.

It is not easy to track down Marcel Proust's possible contacts with the work of Freud. We know that in 1897 Freud wrote [3] to Fliess, "I have found love of the mother and jealousy of the father in my own case, too, and now believe it to be a general phenomenon of early childhood . . . If that is the case, the gripping power of *Oedipus Rex*, in spite of all the rational objections to the inexorable fate that the story presupposes, becomes intelligible . . . Every member of the audience was once a budding Oedipus . . ." Freud was beginning to work out his ideas about the Oedipus complex and to adapt the already existing concepts of free-association and of bisexuality.

Marcel Proust included psychiatric books in his omnivorous reading. He wrote to Madame Straus, around December, 1905, that he had been reading Paul Dubois' *Psychic Treatment of Nervous Disorders*.[4] In the work of this Swiss author, we find Dubois stating, "If one applies one's self, as Freud, of Vienna, has done, to the analysis of dreams and to finding out their original ideas, one perceives that they often betray our most secret aspirations . . . one could in connection with dreams, say: 'Tell me what you dream, and I will tell you what you are, or rather, as one makes one's bed, so must one lie in it.' " Dubois then refers in a footnote to "Die Traumdeutung. Sigmund Freud, Leipzig und Wien, 1900." While translating Ruskin, Proust must have already been reading Dubois. Therefore it is possible that by the time he wrote the "parricide" article for *Figaro*, he was aware of Freud's statement that the conflict of Oedipus exists in all of us.

[3] Sigmund Freud, *The Origins of Psychoanalysis* (for full title see Bibliography), ed. Marie Bonaparte, Anna Freud, Ernst Kris, transl. Eric Mosbacher and James Strachey, New York, 1954.
[4] *Psychic Treatment of Nervous Disorders*, transl. by Smith E. Jelliffe, M.D., and William A. White, M.D., New York and London, 1905, p. 342.

Although Dubois refers to Freud's work on dreams, in the above quotation, we have, in Volume II of Ernest Jones's biography of Freud, on page 114, citation of an attack on Freud's work by Dubois of Berne.

Marcel Proust's habit of thought was to dissect everything, arrive at his own highly personal impressions, and reformulate his observations according to the dictates of his intuition, never copying another's statements. He refers to this when, in the second volume of *Jean Santeuil*, in an essay on Balzac, he describes the great writer's "indifference to the work of others." As an example of this approach, which was to synthesize impressions and observations from innumerable sources, we are told in his letter to Robert de Montesquiou,[5] probably written in April, 1921, that every character in his novel was composed of eight or ten models and that the "little phrase" and music of Vinteuil's great masterpiece had many musical sources, some of which he names. The church of Combray, also, was composed of many churches. He had a prodigious memory, absorbed a great deal from people, and read day and night, but since he was ill and worked in bed, and did not often document his writings with footnotes or denote sources,[6] there seems to be no direct mention of Freud in his notes. The earliest literature on dreams, which Freud read and described in his letters to Fliess, before he wrote his *Interpretation of Dreams*, seems also to be reflected in Proust's statements about dreams, for example in Marcel's description of the sound which wakes him up and becomes part of the dream.

In *Le Banquet*, their youthful publication, Gregh, Dreyfus, Proust, and the others of their group (it will be remembered) expressed their conviction that classicism, romanticism, and

[5] Mina Curtiss, p. 364.
[6] He mentions having read Havelock Ellis and Schopenhauer (as did Freud), also Krafft-Ebing. Cf. Dostoevsky's reading of *Carus*.

typical French tradition must be synthesized, in order to create great French literature. This gives us further insight into the way Proust utilized such a classical play as Sophocles' *Oedipus Rex*, the story of Ajax, and so forth, in the "parricide" article, and later, the myth of Phaedra in *Remembrance of Things Past*. Even if Proust perhaps was acquainted with some of the works of Freud very early in his career, he still showed remarkable ability to include his own concept of the unconscious in the core of his thinking and to utilize it artistically, as if whatever he read or heard from Freud only corroborated what he felt inherently to be true.

A most interesting sidelight on Proust's relationship to psychiatry is the fact that his own father was co-author of a book on neurasthenia, and to that extent was a competitor, or forerunner of Freud's, among the booksellers. In *The Treatment of Neurasthenia* by Achilles Adrien Proust and Gilbert Ballet, London, Henry Kimpton, 1902, translated by Peter C. Smith, one may read in the preface by the authors that, according to common belief, neuroses are becoming more frequent, but that perhaps this seems to be so only because we now have secured names for such illnesses. Charcot, in France, first ensured the recognition of neurosis, Dr. Proust and his co-author tell us, and many others followed Charcot: Beard, Axenfeld, Huchard, Ziemessen (1887), and others, up to F. Müller (1893) of Leipzig. Drs. Proust and Ballet state that, on the whole, more harm than good is done by medicines in the treatment of neuroses, and that good moral (in the French, apparently this word rather connotes "morale") and physical hygiene, a well-conceived diet, and the action of suggestion in the form of advice and encouragement usually do more for the neurasthenic than complex prescriptions. They list as symptoms of neurasthenia: insomnia, dyspepsia, headache, adding up to irritability in general, and "weakness of nerve elements." They consider gastrointestinal and other symptoms more often the effect than the cause of nervous difficulty. Although they consider that an exciting cause may be in intellectual work, they hold intellectual work alone incapable of causing persistent neurasthenia. Depressing emotions impress them as a source of fatigue more powerful than brainwork — and they list competitive strivings, the physical conditions under which mental labor is done, overpressure in schools regarding examinations, for example, as the real cause of nervous difficulty. Emotional strain is considered a main source of neurasthenia: vexation, anxiety, disillusion, remorse, thwarted affection, and other states of sorrow and disquiet are cited as the usual causes of nervous exhaustion. Life in "society" is said to figure among the possible causes of overpressure. On page 27 of the book, syphilis and heart disease are described as accessory rather than primary causes of neurasthenia, because of the worry and depression which they cause. Charcot is quoted on hysteria, and again in regard to functional disorders, especially headache [7] and backache. The horrible dreams [8] of neurasthenics are described. Both German and French authors are quoted and there are references [9] to German medical magazines from 1884, 1885, and 1890. The instability of the ego's synthetic function [10] in neurasthenia is mentioned. In general, a modern reader is apt to be favorably impressed by the open-minded, kindly and thorough-going approach of these authors. Archaic though some of the terminology and concepts appear to us today, the helpful character of the authors is apparent, shining through a slightly bombastic style, and we come away with a more attractive

[7] Achilles Adrien Proust and Gilbert Ballet, *The Treatment of Neurasthenia*, transl. by Peter C. Smith, London, 1902.
[8] *Ibid.*, p. 41.
[9] *Ibid.*, p. 48.
[10] *Ibid.*, p. 55.

picture of Marcel Proust's father (a handsome, popular man
and a pioneer of public health in France) than the slightly
caricatured deductions we may have drawn from reading
about Drs. Cottard, du Boulbon, and Dieulafoy, and the
politician, Norpois. (In *Remembrance of Things Past*, Marcel's father is Permanent Secretary at the Ministry, not a
doctor; but several fictitious doctors in the novel give voice
to attitudes which mimic statements in the Proust-Ballet book
on neurasthenia.) Evidently it was always necessary for
Marcel Proust to temper his love and respect for his father
with defiance, never to show real submission. If he did know
about Freud, one may suspect this ambivalent attitude would
have carried over to Freud also. In *Jean Santeuil*, a psychiatrist appears upon the first pages of the book, in the place of
Norpois, and gives erroneous advice about Jean, who is a
very nervous child.

There are quite a few statements in the Proust-Ballet book
about bringing up children. Habit formation in children is
described, and the power of suggestion is recommended as an
important aid in "moral education." To get the child into the
habit of believing that he is capable of good and incapable of
evil, make him believe he has a strong will, is considered essential. (We recall Marcel Proust's account of Mademoiselle Vinteuil as not inherently evil, but really good; she engages in
defiant and sexually aberrant acts as a lapse. In "The Confession of a Young Girl," a bad habit is the cause of downfall in
an otherwise loving individual. Marcel Proust frequently
writes of habit and moral will in his father's terms, particularly
accusing himself. On the questionnaire, when asked what he
considered his own worst fault, he had answered, "Lack of
will.")

The importance of always attributing good qualities to a
child is stressed by Drs. Proust and Ballet, who say one must

never say aloud in front of a child that he is lazy, and so forth, one must never judge him as wanting to do evil but only as having made a mistake. In regard to punishment, they tell us, "To teach children to be firm, one must be firm in dealing with them." [11] Chastisement should not be roughly given; what one must arouse in the child is moral regret for having deserved it. (Here we see a source of Proust's notorious moral masochism.) Herbert Spencer is quoted by Drs. Proust and Ballet, regarding how Americans overwork, cannot enjoy life, and develop neurasthenia. (They seem to have had a rather unflattering impression of Americans, as did Freud.) Dr. Proust and his co-author recommend that we, in America, try to change our values and learn to relax, reminding us that prophylaxis lies in good education. The moral influence of the physician, the importance of gaining the confidence of the patient and exerting authority over him, and utilizing this authority constructively to get the patient to live at peace with himself are all discussed. When the patient's intellectual capacity is sufficient, one can appeal to the patient's mentality and his will; otherwise the power of suggestion is important, they state. Hypnotism is discussed, and Bernheim, Elden, Forel, and "many others" are mentioned as using hypnotism. Profound disturbances, the authors state, cannot be permanently and completely cured by hypnotism.

Since Dr. Adrien Proust lived until 1903, presumably he kept up with German as well as French periodicals on these subjects. Marcel Proust lived with his parents. It is quite likely that after the publication of his father's book on neurasthenia, he participated in discussions of hypnotism and possibly some of Freud's papers, even though a translation of them was probably not available in French.

In *Swann's Way*, Marcel mentions associating to a dream which he considered was really about Gilberte, although she

[11] *Ibid.*, p. 107.

appeared as a boy in the dream. Interpretation of this dream he called playing the combined role of Joseph and Pharoah,[12] which, interestingly enough, refers to the favorite son. Frequently, in the later volumes, Marcel Proust refers to the processes of repression and the recollection of repressed memories in a manner that indicates he has already digested many of Freud's basic attitudes. As we have said, free-association was a process then in use by others, preceding Freud; and bisexuality was also a term in current use — but Proust's impressive utilization of these concepts seems to have stemmed from profound intuitive insight plus some actual knowledge of Freud's early ideas, as they began to be published. Yet we must always bear in mind that it was typical of Marcel Proust to remake everything, to put his personal stamp on every phrase he wrote, to be impregnated by what he read and observed, but to wait until it crystallized into something new within himself, reconstructed within his own patterns. So if we see some evidence of Freud's basic ideas in Marcel Proust, they are assimilated, also, with Bergson's writings and go back to the Greek classics, especially Plato's theory of essences, and a wealth of reading including the theories of contemporary French painters and symbolist writers or critics such as Gide. Marcel Proust denied having written a Bergsonian novel, and probably would have denied writing a Freudian novel or any sort of novel that had another man's name attached to its description.

After *Swann's Way* was published, in November, 1913, Proust was interviewed by Élie-Joseph Bois for *Le Temps*, and stated:

> My book might be looked upon as an attempt at a series of "Novels of the Unconscious" — its predominating consideration not only does not figure in M. Bergson's philosophy, but is

[12] In *Within a Budding Grove*, p. 289.

even inconsistent with it. From my point of view, voluntary memory, which is above all a memory through intelligence and the eyes, gives us of the past only faces without truth; while, on the contrary, if a scent, a savour, recaptured in quite different circumstances, brings us back the past almost in spite of ourselves, we find that it is a very different past from what we believed we recalled through the pictures of our voluntary memory.[13]

Toward the end of *The Past Recaptured*, Marcel Proust likened memory to a series of jars at different levels and said that we could go back to the contents of those jars through recollection. While Freud was experimenting with hypnotism and later with free-association and the study of dreams, as an intellectual means of going back into the contents of those "jars," Marcel Proust sought a sensory return to them.

In a letter to Camille Vettard, writer and critic, in September or October, 1922, Marcel Proust wrote:

What I should like people to see in my book is that it sprang wholly from the application of a special sense . . . which is very difficult to describe (like trying to describe sight to a blind man) to those who have never exercised it . . . It is perhaps like a telescope, which is pointed at time, because a telescope reveals stars which are invisible to the naked eye, and I have tried . . . to reveal to the conscious mind unconscious phenomena which, wholly forgotten, sometimes lie very far back in the past . . . As to style, I have endeavored to reject everything dictated by pure intellect . . . to express my deep and authentic impressions and to respect the natural progress of my thought.[14]

[13] Marie Scheikévitch, *Time Past: Memories of Proust and Others*, Boston, 1935, p. 205.
[14] Mina Curtiss, *Letters of Marcel Proust*, transl. and with notes by Mina Curtiss, New York, 1949, p. 405.

In following the natural progress of his thoughts, through his feelings, Proust was perhaps closer to Freud's self-analysis and universal application of the fruits of introspection than to an adaptation of any of Freud's theories.

In another letter, written to Marie Scheikévitch [15] (probably November or December, 1915), discussing Albertine and his volume about her death, he wrote:

> What up to then had composed the sweetness of my life, the perpetual rebirth of bygone moments, became its torment, for the memories of love are no exception to the general laws of Memory itself, ruled by habit, which weakens everything. And so what most recalls a person is precisely the thing we have forgotten, because it was without importance . . . I start to experience, little by little, the strength of forgetting, this mighty instrument of adaptation to reality, destroying in us that surviving past that is its constant denial . . . Regret is really a physical ailment, but among physical maladies it is possible to distinguish those which act upon the body only through the channel of memory.[16]

Probably the most complete summing up of Marcel Proust's attitude as a psychological novelist, expressing his reflective awareness of how he utilized psychodynamic observation, is in his letter to the editor of *Les Annales*, written late in 1921 or early 1922, in which he states:

> I was unfortunate enough to start a book with the word "I," and immediately it was assumed that instead of trying to dis-

[15] *Ibid.*, pp. 286–87.
[16] See Sigmund Freud, "Recollection, Repetition and Working Through" (1914), *Coll. Papers*, Vol. II, p. 368. Here Freud shows how memories of the past may be distorted in order to hide a conflict in the present. Also see Freud's "Screen Memories" (1890) "Ueber Deckerinnerungen," *Gesammelte Schriften*, Vienna, 1924–34.

cover universal laws, I was "analysing myself," in the personal and odious sense of the word. I shall therefore, if you are willing, replace the term "analytical novel" by "introspective novel." As for the "adventure novel," certainly there are in life, in external life, great laws too, and if the adventure novel can unravel them, it is as good as the introspective novel . . . To say a last word about the so-called analytical novel, it must in my view, never be a novel of pure intellect. It has to do with drawing a reality out of the unconscious in such a way as to make it enter into the realm of the intellect, while trying to preserve its life, not to garble it, to subject it to the least possible shrinkage — a reality which the light of intellect alone would be enough to destroy, so it seems. To succeed in this work of salvage, all the forces of the mind and even of the body, are not superfluous. It is a little like the cautious, docile, intrepid effort necessary to someone who, while still asleep, would like to explore his sleep with his mind without this intervention leading to his awakening . . . As soon as the innovator is understood, the school for which there is no longer any need is disbanded. Besides, no matter how long the school lasts, the innovator's taste is always much broader. Hugo vaunted Romanticism as his school, but appreciated perfectly Boileau and Regnard. Wagner never regarded Italian music with the severity of the Wagnerians.[17]

In the above, we see Proust's definition of his own "introspective novel" plus the implication that it is something even more, and contains the roots of expansion beyond introspection; for example, we may find sociological truth also, as a result.

Regarding what we now call psychosomatic medicine, there is a rudimentary account in Proust and Ballet's book. We see something of a sketch of its weaker points in Marcel Proust's novel, in the person of the renowned doctor du Boulbon [18] —

[17] Mina Curtiss, *Letters of Marcel Proust.*
[18] *The Guermantes Way*, p. 412.

described as the man Charcot predicted would "reign supreme in neurology and psychiatry" — who actually hastens the grandmother's death. Proust seems to vie with medical men in expounding the psychosomatic approach and at the same time to outdo them in deflating it, or delineating its limitations. He was convinced that there were strong emotional components in his own asthma, and although he confessed that his illness was largely a nervous habit, he felt certain that if he were cured of his asthma, some other symptoms would take its place. He mentions Dr. Sollier's decision to put him in a sanitarium in his letter to Madame Straus in 1905.[19] And in his translation of Ruskin's *Sesame and the Lilies,* published in 1906, he says:

> . . . we have contemporary medicine appearing to be on the point of telling us also . . . that we are "born of the Spirit" and that it continues to control our respiration (see Brugelmann's works on asthma), our digestion (see Dubois of Berne's The Psychoneuroses and his other works), the co-ordination of our movements (see Isolation and Psychotherapy by Drs. Camus and Pagnies, preface by Professor Déjerine). Doctors said not long ago (and the tardy still repeat it) that a pessimist is a man with a bad stomach. Today Dr. Dubois says in print, unmistakably, that a man who has a bad stomach is a pessimist. And it is no longer his stomach that must be cured if his philosophy is to be changed, it is his philosophy that must be changed if his stomach is to be cured.[20]

An example of how Proust made some of the essential thoughts or attitudes of other writers his own can be seen from his essay on Baudelaire.[21] Three things which he pointed

[19] Mina Curtiss, *Letters of Marcel Proust,* pp. 136–37.
[20] John Ruskin, *Sésame et les Lys,* transl. by Marcel Proust, Paris, 1906. Also see repetition of this Introduction in *Pastiches et Mélanges,* Paris, 1919, pp. 250–51. See Mina Curtiss, *ibid.,* p. 427.
[21] "A Propos de Baudelaire" (June 1921), *Chroniques,* Paris, 1927.

out about Baudelaire: the unusual use of Time, the color scarlet, scattered throughout his work, and his references to ancient cities, all became characteristic of Proust's *Remembrance
of Things Past.* Similarly he may have noted essential approaches of Freud, in his later years, and made them his own.
But his self-observations and his conclusions about sociology,
art — all that concerns mankind — are distilled from his own
absorption of whatever he read as reflected in his own introspection.

Regarding a topic about which he had much to say —
homosexuality — how much light did his writing cast upon
his own deeper self-understanding? And to what extent did
his insight into homosexuality extend itself to broader observations, sociologically, artistically, or medically?

XII

Proust's Homosexuality: Probable Contributing Factors and How They Are Unconsciously Expressed in His Work

THE EFFECT of Proust's homosexuality upon his exhaustive knowledge and candor about it as a literary topic is obvious; his confession by implication, and the resulting guilt coloring his writings and affecting his life, as well as his extraordinary ambivalence toward men and women, especially the latter, as rivals, are frequently quite clear; his identification with female characteristics and the feminine viewpoint is noticeable; he himself implied that his writing lacked virility. But more subtle, more difficult to see, is the way the unconscious derivations of his homosexuality tend to repeat themselves through the delicate traceries of all his literary imagery, as well as in the broader outlines of his narrative.

If we attempt to apply the psychoanalytic method of approach, so far as we can, wherever data about Proust are available to speculate as to the type of traumata he suffered in his early experiences, and how they influenced his literary work, of course, instead of free-association, we must resort to his attempt at self-revelation through the patterns of his novel, plus his letters, biographical data, early writings, and constant comments about himself. The lacunae and blind spots are ob-

vious; there is much we cannot know. Still, as the most self-re-
vealing of all authors, he is a natural choice for such an ex-
periment.

If we can raise some interesting questions, without certainty of any final answers, particularly regarding the relation
of the arts, and the general problem of communication in
words, to psychoanalysis, that is about all we can hope to do.

It is probably true that Marcel Proust's actual brother, the
real Robert, was not made a character in the novel directly,
because of his great importance in Proust's emotional life. It
was easier to weave a varied fantasy of ambivalent love for
him, and identification with the bisexual image which he represented to Marcel, by extracting from the real Robert the
varied facets he contributed to Proust's concept of Robert
de Saint-Loup, Albertine, Gilberte, Morel, and others, and
then to eradicate him again, to cast doubt upon his character
and eventually to re-establish it, to eliminate him and to per-
petuate him at the same time, without being burdened by a
designated brother for Marcel in the story. The beloved
brother-figure who later is outgrown, also, in *Jean Santeuil*, is
Henri, whom Jean loved so well, and later Bertrand de Réveillon, and Servais, the attractive young bicyclist, who became a medical student and moved away. Like the "silent
beat" in music, which draws attention to itself by omission,
and to which we referred at the beginning, the absence of
Marcel's brother in the novel, despite the wealth of autobiographical data based on truth, draws attention to the real
Robert's absence, and to the presence instead of other notable
pairs of brothers, such as Charlus and the Duke de Guermantes, of which one was homosexual and the other was
Odette's lover at the end. (At the beginning, Charlus, the
homosexual, had been acknowledged to be her lover.) Proust

habitually interchanged the images of brothers as favorites of the mother-figure, as in "La Religieuse Hollandaise" (in *Jean Santeuil*), and Marcel and the Duchess de Guermantes *versus* the Duchess and Robert de Saint-Loup, and so on.

We have noted that Robert de Saint-Loup undergoes a complete change of character just when Albertine leaves Marcel. It is as if Marcel's frustrated rage at Albertine spills over onto Robert. After Robert fails to bring back Albertine, he is discovered to be a cheat, a conniver among servants, an accused but exonerated spy. Finally he dies valiantly, and his good qualities are remembered. The narrative does not particularly require Robert de Saint-Loup to become a homosexual, except that the author apparently wanted to think of brother-figures like Robert as separated from women. We are told that the original blond, blue-eyed model for Saint-Loup also ended in "bimetallism."

Robert de Saint-Loup lives in Swann's old home, Tansonville, married to Swann's daughter, Gilberte, toward the end, as we know, and Gilberte confesses she really was in love with Marcel, in her youth. This is like the pattern of the Duke de Guermantes, Charlus and Odette, but with variations: the least worthy brother always proves to be the secret favorite of the mother, on an ambiguous basis.

Proust was struggling to express his concept of bisexuality in a literary way at around the same time Freud was working out, in his own mind, the possible universality of bisexuality and its role in neuroses. Freud first became interested in bisexuality [1] through Fliess's writings about periodicity, in which bisexuality was an important topic. How much of

---

[1] Sigmund Freud, *The Origins of Psychoanalysis* (See Bibliography for full title), ed. Marie Bonaparte, Anna Freud, Ernst Kris, transl. Eric Mosbacher and James Strachey, New York, 1954, p. 38. In 1902, Weininger published *Sex and Character* in Vienna, making use of Fliess's theory of constitutional bisexuality.

Proust's interest in demonstrating the bisexual nature of many of his characters was due to his reading of psychiatric or medical literature is not known. However, we can see from his novel that bisexuality was often a key which led back to the nostalgic past, always tempting and never fully satisfying. (The bisexual object represented the sibling loved by Marcel, as his mother loved him, and then, in frustration, he goes back to the original love — as when he goes to Venice with his mother, after losing Albertine — soon he turns back to the brother — as he seeks refuge in Robert, when the Duchess de Guermantes considers him a nuisance.)

The rearrangement of Marcel's introjected and projected loves and hates, tied to the phantoms which were composites, so carefully constructed and always in flux, constitutes the material of Proust's books. These patterns build up the "universe" based on the "lost paradise," which he spent his life re-creating. The immediacy of his feelings rests upon a return to vivid screen memories. The original memories are vague, preverbal, unattainable; only the links to them, the screen memories, are really available. Proust wove together from his feelings a tapestry that has been likened by his critics to an Oriental carpet. He fused remembered or imagined persons with contemporary people.[2] Even more, perhaps, did Proust connect his characters with works of art which he admired, such as the pregnant servant girl, Eulalie, at the beginning of *Swann's Way*, who was so much like a Giotto figure, Swann's impression of Odette as like Botticelli's Venus (rising

[2] For example, it is common knowledge that Charlus was based only in part on Count Robert de Montesquiou who died December 11, 1921, and Morel, in part, on "the Angel," Léon Delafosse, a pianist with a beautiful singing voice, whom Proust introduced to Robert de Montesquiou, and so forth. Charles Haas was one of the models for Swann. Laure Hayman, whom his father and uncle knew, contributed toward Odette. See Mina Curtiss, (*Letters of Marcel Proust*) p. 364 (letter to Montesquiou, Apr. 1921).

from the sea), or Jethro's Daughter, Zephora, in the fresco of the Life of Moses in the Sistine Chapel by Botticelli — Marcel's impression of himself as an Arabian Nights character, Berma as one of the "beautiful primitive virgins on the Erechtheum," Balbec as the scene painted by Whistler, and so on, are typical of his descriptions. A cigarette lighter composed of two English pennies, with a fine patina, as if the profile of Queen Victoria had been done by Pisanello [3] — even this — was based upon a real cigarette lighter, which Proust borrowed for a time, and then returned when the description of it was completed.

It has been conjectured that the original model for Albertine, among many others, was Alfred Agostinelli, Proust's intelligent, attractive chauffeur who took up aviation and was killed in an airplane accident. There was also an Albert, whom he befriended, who was more like "Jupien," an ex-valet turned brothel keeper, for men.

At the same time that Proust's characterizations and design are rich, there is a wraithlike quality about his people, a transience, a mythological element, because they are all parts of his heritage of art and culture. Their histories are told as parts of his own. His literary style is a sentence-by-sentence evocation of his own self, his past. He has traced his innermost self back to precise patterns, and co-ordinated his feelings, like a series of genes in a cell, each nucleus related to the nucleus of all the rest. That is why his sentences are emotionally direct even when they are endlessly long. His proliferated style is not as haphazard as it may seem; his verbalizations follow the true line of his emotions.

His homosexuality, whatever its physiological components, definitely seems related to the pattern of a love he felt toward his beautiful, sensitive, somewhat nervous and domineering

[3] *The Past Recaptured*, p. 31.

mother. This love was unbearable, partly because of jealous rivalries (with the father at the most repressed level, with his brother on a more conscious or preconscious level). The torments of this love resulted in introjection of his mother image, identification with her femininity, her sensitivity, ambition and talent (increasing his own wealth of sensitivity and talent). He actually duplicated her appearance in many respects (like Andrée in the book). Her self-sacrificing love for her husband and sons was a model for his devotion to his writing. His Duchess de Guermantes and Madame Verdurin are largely derived from his mother's and his own virtues and faults as they were projected outward again, from within himself. He emphasized domineering tendencies in Madame Verdurin, seductiveness and social know-how in the Duchess, as well as unpredictable kindnesses and cruelties in all his characters.[4] Madame de Villeparisis and Andrée are "bluestockings," like his mother and grandmother. Mixed with feminine characteristics in all his female characters, there are usually erotic tastes or character traits connected with masculinity. Eroticism is represented, especially, by frankly bisexual images who are under the domination of parental figures.

In the questionnaire Proust answered at twenty-one, it will be recalled that he said he most admired masculine traits in women, such as frankness and comradeship, and in men, feminine charm. We see these preferences portrayed in his main characters. It is as if he wanted to assure himself that women had phalluses and men were really not potent; then he could identify, safely, with either one, and there was no danger of impregnating or being made pregnant, no identification with the completely submissive women or sadistically dom-

---

[4] He described this unpredictability as characteristic of his father more than of his mother.

ineering men. He was immensely curious about everyone, in reality, as if unconsciously trying to verify their true nature, and perhaps to prove his surmise about their sexuality correct or incorrect.

When we read about the evolution of an individual's emotional life, either in novels or in psychological treatises, some of what we read strikes us as obviously quite true, some of the psychodynamic theory we grasp intellectually as logical, and some theories seem far-fetched. Yet certain of the latter theories suddenly take on tangibility and a convincing reality when we observe our own children. The nostalgic attraction which even a child feels for the earliest period of infancy — when the mother-child relationship exacts very little responsibility from the infant, and anticipates every need, providing unstinting warmth, love and gratification — is something we tend to forget in adult life. The urge to return to that period when the mother offers a conflict-free environment is stimulated by frustration which the child encounters during developmental phases. We recognize the full sense of the word "nostalgia" when we read of Marcel's longing to return to a beautiful spot in Venice, with an *Arabian Nights* atmosphere, where he went alone one afternoon while on his trip there with his mother,[5] but could never find a second time. And we recall how, in Venice, his "hopeless" invalidism won for him his mother's fullest affection, since he was beyond being hurt further by it. We can see something of this same enchanted atmosphere in the loving care with which Marcel previously spent his time selecting, ordering, and paying for, every choice garment that might make Albertine more beautiful. In his description of great music and art such as Vinteuil's and Elstir's, we again feel there must be nameless glamour from a lost paradise in these works of art, such as

[5] *The Sweet Cheat Gone.*

the madeleine dipped in the cup of tea evoked. The attraction Proust describes comes from deep within the past, rather than something promised in the future.

An infant's experience of bodily understanding with its mother is soon broken up. Separation from the mother occurs in infancy, particularly when biting results from acquiring teeth; then the breast is withdrawn, and other things in the outside world begin to be grasped with the hand, put into the mouth, tasted, explored, smelled. The bad begins to become more sharply distinguished from the good, at this time — in a rudimentary way. It is also connected with the first experience of nostalgia, an urge to return to the passivity of uninterrupted relationship to the mother, with a sense of omnipotence through having one's wishes anticipated and gratified. We learn from anthropologists how the collective magic of primitive tribes abounds with ceremonies trying to make up for whatever misdeeds might have removed the anxious, frustrated personalities of primitive folk from the lost paradise which was their original home,[6] according to traditions in so many sections of the world. (On Sundays and holidays we tend to search, still, for elements of a lost happiness which we seem to remember, but which it is practically impossible for us to describe with words, because it was forgotten before the learning of speech.)

Those in close contact with a child less than two years old need no reminder of how dependently small children cling to those they love. The torments of jealousy and insecurity they experience when forced to give way to rivals often is like that described by Proust. We are familiar with the way curiosity means not only touching and tasting, but smelling — and how the latter is closely connected with sexual curiosity. As to the period of training to cleanliness, although it is almost impossible even for older children to recall it subjectively

[6] See: Erik H. Erikson, *Childhood and Society*, New York, 1950.

in later years, it is a time when excremental products are the only real possessions, the only part of the child's self possible for him to dispense at will. His excremental products in the first two years may be withheld in rebellion, proffered at the proper time as praiseworthy gifts, or angrily expelled in rage as his most harmful, destructive products. Time first begins to make itself felt, as a force connected with sphincter control, in these early years.

The child in his first two years exists very much like a primitive savage, feeling deeply, expressing himself mainly through basic body processes or their sublimated imagery — repressing his own body processes altogether at times, because of anxiety. Words are an awkward, superficial means of expression, often used to hide or contradict his true feelings. Incredulities, possibly allied with a sense of shame regarding nakedness and his strong inner feelings (such as erotization, hostility), make reality the less certain, the more difficult to express. The child cries under varied circumstances: whenever he needs the attention of another person. His way of showing love and hate, which are fused, and are not always distinguishable from each other, lies in a mixture of expressions and acts which eventually are somewhat repressed. But in his babyish way he must repeat the human history of transition from fetus to independent existence as he experiences cultural, biological, and immediate environmental influences, and thus he sets the patterns for his future. He is beset with the danger of losing the protection of those he depends upon and of incurring mysterious, frightening punishments (perhaps fear of the loss of the body part that feels most pleasure). The result is a dilution of his emotional drives, a shunting back to the body processes where they originated, but the symbolisms of art and poetry may evoke these drives in increased intensity once more.

We often choose to ignore the battles going on in the

child's world, with its toys, angelic facial expressions, and bodily grace. But it takes very little for us, as parents, to confess doubts about how much is really known — for instance, about homosexuality. Especially in regard to the beginnings. Fortunately, nature, if unobstructed, often seems to take over so successfully that with the years comes inner strength, and after latency and adolescence, the child normally grows in the direction that leads toward procreation.

Something happened, in Proust's development, to impede his masculine, procreative function. The usual "fight or flight" mechanism, as a response to external threats, also seems to have been too frightening for him to develop. We note the passivity in his writing, typified in the description of the three steeples [7] and three trees, where movement is the result of his being drawn along in a carriage, seeing stationary objects which appear to change their own positions: movement is the result of time, and of his passivity in time. This has been his reaction to many situations in the course of the story. Where rivalry existed, spying and conjecture and psychological observation took the place of action. Illness frequently took the place of rage at others. Protection was always a prime necessity, whether it was in a salon, Jupien's Temple of Dishonor, or the familiarity of a well-known, often tested room, or through the utter unreality of a hired, faked attacker, or an illness that was really in part malingering, or a dream brought on by drugs at an hour when one summoned sleep, under one's own control. Approval — or else protection — was forthcom-

[7] In adolescence and adult years, he still looked upon these symbols from the viewpoint of a child measuring heights. We note his regret at having renounced something connected with the three trees, and later the dizziness connected with the great height of the steeples, at the end of the novel, where literary success is becoming a reality. The Duke, the masculine, successful man, grown old but still Odette's lover, "wavered as he made his way along the difficult summit of his eighty-three years, as if . . . taller than church spires . . . " See *The Past Recaptured*, pp. 401–2.

ing on the basis of being injured, feminine, punished enough already, quite harmless, puerile — or through the self-sacrificing cultivation of his genius. The urge toward physical flight was apt to be translated into a longing for travel that could rarely be satisfied, or into frequently changing from one love affair to another, and was actually a source of separation-anxiety. In fiction, as in real life, Proust took flight mentally. His endlessly varying fantasies never arrived at precisely the same form a second time. The urge to real flight was probably one source of his ubiquitous separation-fear. In fantasy, he could flee and stay, contradict and partially satisfy all his urges, through complete control, through the magic of imagination.

Psychoanalytic experience has shown the presence in the unconscious of impulses to attack, to destroy or drown out the fetus in the mother's womb. This impulse may be represented in body language and in alteration of function. The body may react with denial; holding back, evidence of anxiety, an urge to cry for help, or other symptoms may replace the ejecting impulse. We see in the analyses of adults and the play of children the expression of these destructive impulses and reactions against them. Symptoms of nausea, vomiting, diarrhea, constipation, and so forth, may develop out of conflict with these disturbing urges. Years after childhood conflicts over a prospective rival carried within the mother have faded into oblivion, the body repeats, like a broken record, its old statements in body language, symptoms, patterns of feeling. From preverbal imagery stem the figures of preverbal, oral aggression (such as the lion in the cage about to be swallowed by the python, in *The Sweet Cheat Gone*). In Proust's case, breathlessness and fear of smothering were apparently tied to early, repressed aggression.

Where one first fails to go through a developmental phase

successfully, one establishes a pattern, and every important subsequent step tends to be undertaken in the same terms, with the same strategy as that which first failed, no matter how inconsistent.

Inability to accept the rivalry of a baby brother or sister is usually based on an oedipal situation that has already made this adjustment too difficult. Then the natural hostility toward a sibling rival may become a permanent focus of conflict. The older toddler may overcompensate, show excessive love for this baby and for the mother, in order to hide fears of destructive attitudes. In adolescence, the pattern of renouncing competition may be more firmly entrenched.[8] From then on, the boy loves younger boys. This insures a protective love; his aggression is erotized; his own position with his mother is kept a protected one. But in real life, this in turn leads to a dangerous situation, because if brotherly love is given physical, erotic expression — and there is aggression in the homosexual seduction of the other boy — the result may be the mother's forsaking him, shocked at his homosexuality — and ostracism from all, socially. This dilemma furnished the nucleus of the problems of love about which Proust wrote. His understanding of how the seduction of younger people to homosexuality is also an aggressive attack on them is demonstrated by his handling of this topic in relation to Albertine and Morel toward those they seduce.

In psychiatric treatment, the resignation of competition in favor of a parental or sibling rival is frequently seen. But it is not the only factor in homosexuality. There is usually a mixture of various types of homosexuality in most of the male homosexual cases under treatment: flight from incest, identification with the mother, castration fear,[9] a history of sexual

[8] Sigmund Freud, "Certain Neurotic Mechanisms in Jealousy, Paranoia, and Homosexuality" (1922), *Collected Papers*, Vol. II, p. 232. London, 1924.
[9] The reader is probably acquainted with the vast psychoanalytic literature on this subject, based on Freud's theory that the little boy expects

seduction or intimidation, masochistic and sadistic elements, anal fixation, fear of the female body, and so forth.[10]

We see in Proust's life and his writings how important was the search for love, the inability to find it on really satisfying and at the same time socially acceptable terms, and then its renunciation, leading to a search for something essentially the same; but in a new kind of love-object, this cycle is repeated an infinite number of times, based on homosexual loves in Proust's real life but fundamentally on remnants of incestuous ties to his mother — usually turned around so that he loved a brother-image as his mother once loved him.

The mother's sanction is represented in the Duchess de Guermantes' tolerating her husband's affairs, Marcel's mother permitting Albertine to live under the same roof with him in the apartment at Paris, and, in *Jean Santeuil*, the Duchess de Réveillon's not knowing (or not concerning herself about it) when Jean was sleeping with their maid, and the Duchess de Réveillon herself whispering tender words to him in the woods.

In schizophrenia, a return to early infantile periods and even fetal passivity may be the decisive drive, because for either physical or emotional reasons, or both, the earliest adjustments of infancy were not accomplished sufficiently well to place life's goals in the future. Instead the main goals of schizophrenics seem to revolve around the past, in a dis-

---

bodily injury as a result of his competitive, destructive urges toward his father in rivalry for his mother's love, the talion principle. Fears of birth and of death may be closely connected with castration fear, as well as the original trauma of losing the mother's breast, as an infant. In Proust's fantasies, death and rebirth seem closely connected; and we get the impression that he hoped, unconsciously, that by reunion with his mother orally, at the breast, in his symbolic imagery, and also in his unconscious, erotically, some lost element of himself would be restored.

[10] Sigmund Freud, *Collected Papers*, Vol. II, pp. 66, 152, 241; Vol. III, pp. 251, 446.

sociated, regressive way. The nostalgia which typifies Proust
is different. It is on a higher level,[11] connected with his conscious research into the past, and combining insight with a
search for emotional sources in the unconscious.

Proust differs from the majority of men in that his outward
evidences of heterosexuality apparently began and ended with
his love for his mother, except, perhaps, for the Marie Bernadaky of the Champs-Elysées whom he gave up, but who was
not absent from his writing, and Madame Pouquet, and others,
whom he loved without success.

If he loved his mother so intensely, why did he almost never
find another woman to love equally, in her image, after this
Marie? Why did he apparently have no heterosexual affairs,
although he wrote about them? And, if it was merely the
arrival of a baby brother, or his rivalry with an imposing,
overwhelming father — or the father's frequent absences
which left him mainly female images with which to identify
— that upset his development and prevented masculine identification, why could he not grow beyond these emotional
impediments as many people do? In other words, why was
life especially difficult for him?

Congenital factors must have played a role. Robert Proust
seems to have been robust, from the start. Marcel's mother
was ill before she bore Marcel and he was a frail child. In
addition to physical resemblance to his mother, and inherited
inner resemblances, which seem to have reinforced the idea
of his being a replica of her, interreacting anxieties undoubtedly caused his harassed mother to lavish excessive love upon
him, hoping to impart her strength to the child whose sufferings she could scarcely bear to witness. This sort of relation-

---

[11] It is a reaction to a later level of development. There is little doubt that
Proust experienced in his first two years a secure and very gratifying relationship with his mother, in contrast to the history of many schizophrenics.

ship is described in Dr. Adrien Proust's book, and one feels in the description a reprimand. Seductiveness that is not at all intentional or conscious may result from overly demonstrative, constantly coddling, caressing attitudes. In Marcel Proust's first two years, his father was away a good deal, and his mother and grandmother showered attention upon him. Their ambitions for him were great, their standards supreme, as we see from their endeavors to cultivate his literary sensitivities at the earliest possible age. They omitted all the love scenes from the books they read to him; their easily offended, puritanical attitude, their tacit disapproval of all heterosexuality, probably reinforced his sense of guilt and shame. Hence, his later preoccupation with sinful sex, the need of his characters to confess, to pay the penalty for sensuality, to seek forgiveness, to create something worthwhile out of personal suffering, as an atonement for sexual pleasure. There is little question about his mother's dominating attitude as we know from the sort of letters they wrote to each other,[12] their quarrels about the boy's enforced submission to her will. Perhaps there is biographical truth in the touching scenes at the beginning of *Jean Santeuil* where Jean is made to substitute classical studies and literary pursuits for friendships and youthful heterosexual love.

Marcel Proust's mother must have become, as are all objects of great love, especially in very young children, an object of intense frustration. Before his brother's birth, there must have been other disturbing feelings. These were intense physical urges, later remembered perhaps as pleasure in kissing his mother, but also because they were bound with frustration,

[12] See Maurois, André: pp. 81–82. In these letters, Madame Proust reproaches her son for living a life of fashion and insists that he work. He writes, in reply, that he has caught a cold, and if it turns to asthma, she will be perfectly sweet to him again, and he comments how miserable it is not to be able to enjoy "both health and affection simultaneously."

as a sense of having been denied the longed-for kiss. (So Proust has designated the visit of Swann, a kindly father-image, and an image of himself as well — to be the first reason Marcel has missed his mother's kiss.)

The actual birth process, as small children secretly piece together their ideas about it, excites fears and sado-masochistic fantasies mainly connected with odors, beatings, digestive processes, illness, and childish anxieties of every sort, based on early fantasies. Many children combine with their vague notions of the relationship between the sexes a beating fantasy such as the scene in *The Past Recaptured*, confusing punishment and satisfaction (and linking it, as did Proust in the narrative, with "primal scene" and masturbation). This attitude toward birth and parental sexuality may be a factor in the repression of heterosexual feelings. The early sexual problem, in addition to the task of becoming adjusted to sibling rivalry, after a new baby comes (and continuing rivalry with the father), complicates castration-fear with fear of birth.

The new baby's demands on both parents and on the entire household, and the older child's feelings of jealousy are connected with confused impressions about the mother's pregnancy. The older boy may retain a fixated interest in the pregnancy that preceded the birth, and in the baby who is already alive but is not yet part of the world,[13] and sadistic erotized fantasies regarding the mother's body. The birth then becomes a traumatic event around which the older boy's conflict may crystallize. The boy may retreat from the emotional storm of the little brother's birth by suspicious withdrawal from all women as sexual objects and focus his

[13] It will be recalled that the young man for whom Albertine leaves Marcel is one Marcel had formerly derided with the name "I-am-in-the-soup." This is typical of how Proust's imagery seems to fit his unconscious patterns.

admiration on boys where no body-part [14] is apparently miss-
ing, or on masculine women who seem to be as strong as men.
There are apt to be great fears of submission. The impregnating, virile father-figure, the competent, strong, successful man,
is terrifying; he must be defied (as Marcel stamps upon Charlus's hat); he must be proven feminine, inferior in some way,
or made into a grandfatherly, elder figure (as in *Jean Santeuil*,
when Jean sits in his stern grandfather's lap, after his parents
rebuff him).

In *Jean Santeuil*, at the beginning, there is a description of
an author's gratitude toward those on whom he models his
characters. The author is likened to a pregnant woman giving
birth. In *The Past Recaptured*, Marcel likens himself to a
suffering, sick mother, sacrificing herself for her son.

We recall once more the real Robert Proust's early memory
of Marcel's infinitely tender, motherly attitude toward him.[15]
André Maurois tells us that their relationship made the term
"brotherly love" a reality.

The psychoanalyst who reads Proust cannot fail to be impressed with the unity and simplicity at the basis of his complicated narrative and descriptions. The conflict over his
mother's relationship with his brother, her pregnancy, and
her relationship to the father, behind this — and the effect of
the trauma of her pregnancy — reminds us of Freud's discovery that such traumata influence an entire life in all its
aspects. This is one of the great discoveries of the era in
which Proust lived. It is also striking to see how the symbolism in all of Proust's writing revolves around a few basic
patterns, particularly intra-uterine symbols connected with
water, air and rooms (prisons or cages), and clothing. As

[14] See psychoanalytic literature on fear of the female genitals as a component in male homosexuality.
[15] Harold March, *The Two Worlds of Marcel Proust*.

Einstein discovered in the most complicated mathematical formulae a basic law of relativity, Proust's work, like Freud's, seems to illustrate a fundamental law of how, in a pre-existing unstable situation, a traumatic event (in Proust's case, his mother's pregnancy) affected a human life and the entire fantasy life and aesthetic expression of a man of genius.

Love is the most persistent force in Proust's writing. The images related to his loves change constantly: therefore it is hard to put his patterns of feeling into any words except his own. It is almost impossible to explain the complicated interplay of "phantoms" in his stories except by reducing them to the basic elements of his own early problems. This is largely a study in symbolism because of the primitive, preverbal nature of his conflicts. We are given an infinite number of variations of the theme of his mother as an erotic object, taboo and frightening, transferred to the brother — merged with himself — then needing to be extricated from himself — and the need for the presence of a protecting father, defied, effeminized, but still loving (like Charlus). He emphasizes, by his images, the enclosed, womblike aspect of return to the mother. The author's withdrawal from heterosexual feelings in real life is a strange counterpart to Marcel's heterosexuality in the novel. We are given the assurance, again and again, that the fictional Marcel is not in rivalry with any man, and that his erotic interest in the women he loves is never designed to impregnate them, but only to find their "perfume and music," to recapture what was rightfully his, "the breath of a lost paradise," which can really be found, after all, only in the arts. What words can convey only crudely, symbols delineate, deny and prestidigitate into endlessly changing, ephemeral expressions, unified in an imposing entity, which Proust himself likens to a cathedral (implying it must be a sanctioned, lofty, admired work).

When Marcel loses Albertine, and envisions a python about to swallow a lion in a cage, we have not only an image of arrested movement, to express the furious biting and swallowing up, the instinctive reaction to loss of his beloved — but also emphasis on the primitive nature of his reaction. His asthma, as well as his homosexuality, seems to be closely allied to this arrested swallowing, suffocating image, which condenses so many of his reactions to an early trauma, and suggests again the attack on the intra-uterine content.

We will turn, next, to an attempt to trace some factors related to the psychological side of his asthma, and the latter's relation to his writing.

In regard to the *cage* containing the lion, and the concept of Albertine as imprisoned by Marcel, his captive — and to Marcel's paralyzed feeling when Albertine is staying with him in his apartment, so that he is unable to go on the streets with her, we have the elements of what psychoanalysts were later to observe about the dynamics of street phobia: the fear of going out on the streets — especially as this fear occurs in men with feminine tendencies. The inhibition of the erotized use of the legs, and of exhibitionism and looking, is related, in street phobias, to prostitute fantasies on the streets. There is an unconscious urge to have an affair with a casually encountered stranger, in lieu of the father, and, with infantile logic, immediately to effect a pregnancy, within oneself, with a concomitant abortion wish and restitution fantasy. All these urges, bound up with castration fear and birth fears, contribute unconsciously to fear of going on to the streets, unless accompanied by a protective parental figure (as Jupien always has to be with Charlus in his later years). Most of these same components may also be related to the psychological constellations conducive to asthma attacks, but with some differences as we shall soon discuss. Even this relation of asthma to street fear is implied in Marcel's confession that his illness, which kept him tied to his room when the affair with Albertine was at its peak, was partly malingering, and was a "paralyzed" feeling, a fear. Not only was Marcel jealous of Albertine in the story, but probably the author identified unconsciously with Albertine's prostitute tendencies, and later these same tendencies were projectd to Charlus, in the last volume.

Usually, in psychoanalytic work, we find that the difference between the conflicts in asthma and in street fear are as follows: In street fear, the erotized emotional components are nearer to the point of actual expression in the form of acting out prostitute tendencies, and the street fear is an emergency measure which prevents it, psychologically,[16] without necessitating physical illness. In those asthma attacks which derive from emotional conflicts, it has been found that the attack is very often associated with an inhibited cry for the mother which is repressed in order to avoid fear of sexual wishes.

To recapitulate the main fantasy, as it was shaped by the forces that also anchored the author firmly to his homosexuality, in his own development: We see Albertine as the main love of Marcel, in the book, after he has worked out a scheme of emotional values. The Duchess and Madame Verdurin and Madame de Villeparisis are images like his mother and grandmother and aunts. The glamorous, "blue-stocking," and sensual, debased, or tenderly loving elements are divided among the ladies of the book, including Marcel's tabooed amorous feelings for the Duchess. Homosexual elements regarding Albertine are projected to Morel and Charlus. Pregnancy-fear is projected to Jupien's niece, and Eulalie, the servant girl

[16] Milton L. Miller, "On Street Fear," *International Journal of Psychoanalysis* (1953) Vol. XXXIV, Pt. III, pp. 232–240.

who dies — both peripheral figures. Jupien's niece is said to
have been in trouble long ago, yet it is almost forgotten —
still "the trouble" comes to light and Morel calls this girl
dreadful names, and does not marry her. She comes to a
tragic end, only after being aided financially and given a title
and dowry by Charlus (a symbolic disguise for impregnation
by an effeminized father-figure, who loves the girl and shows
his love by giving her a fortune). Still, with all the carefully
prepared fantasy, Marcel cannot be imagined happy in his
love affair with Albertine. Aggression against her breaks
out. She must die in the story, because it is the only solution.
Heterosexuality cannot lead to marriage and childbirth —
the punishment occurs first. Then Marcel reverts to the
original fantasy of unsullied love, for his mother, in Venice,
the symbolic womb, with its watery streets — a submerged
Combray, where his mother lavishes unlimited love upon him.
At the same time he fights this regressive urge by trying to
become a great writer, and a promiscuous lover. Robert, the
brother-figure, himself occupied with a degraded sort of
mother-figure in Rachel, the ex-prostitute, is no longer necessary to the story after Albertine is gone. When the mother-
figure, which is one component of Albertine, is lost, the
brother-figure in Robert no longer persists as an object of
Marcel's affection. Robert dies shortly after Albertine does,
and in fact he is really part of the same concept. The unconscious mechanism that has created Albertine later is the motive
for turning Robert into a homosexual: a bisexual brother-
image loved as Marcel's self.

Marcel's two trips to the sanitarium precede the outbreak
of more overt aggression, in the form of a fantasy of seeing
Charlus being beaten, a scene in which the author probably
identified with all the characters involved. The threat of dis-
solution of the narrator's personality is projected to the city

of Paris, and to the many "respectable" homosexual men who
are patrons of Jupien's Temple of Dishonor. After the most
unrestrained expression of aggression in the book, which is
portrayed through spying and conjecturing, without much
activity on Marcel's part, we see the release of high ambition,
in the form of fecundity, literary gifts which Marcel discovers
as if by accident. He finds that he does possess great ability
within himself, at the point where the despicable Madame
Verdurin, who is nevertheless a mother-figure, a dominating
and overly ambitious one, is experiencing her greatest triumphs. Now the ambitious woman is appeased; the main
father-figure, represented by the aging Duke de Guermantes,
is also at the height of his success, in a parodied sort of way,
because he is the lover of Odette, who still looks young (recalling the ageless "jade of an Ideal" in Hardy's *The Well-
Beloved*).

Marcel now attempts to solve the problem of his oedipal
situation by identifying with the pregnant mother, making
restitution in this way for the destroyed images of the brother
(Albertine and Robert, eliminated as the mad Charlus would
have murdered Morel). He reunites with his mother in her
matriarchal, fecund function, receiving the love of the father
by this impregnation. But this, too, is an anxiety-ridden situ-
aton. The narrator, identifying with a pregnant woman, fears
an accident. Like the image of Madame Saint-Euverte's niece,
in the blatantly scarlet, configurated dress — mysterious, re-
clining as if in illness, rocking the cradle of Time, suffering,
it seems, from a pregnancy or miscarriage, a neurosis, or some
unknown difficulty — perhaps merely posing — the author
presents himself enigmatically, motionless, but filled with
drama. At the end, he races with death against Time, to try
to fulfill his mother's ambitions for him. When not writing,
he turns his mind toward death, toward sleep, toward the past.

A recapitulation of the entire book occurs at the end. It closes the circle of an endlessly repeating fantasy, with lights shining now here, now there, like the play of insight which comes and goes.

Regarding the truly feminine side of "Marcel," as it is projected to others, much has been said [17] about the incident of Mademoiselle Vinteuil's friend spitting upon her father's photograph, ritually. In the first place, this activity involves the father, his image looks upon them (like the mother seeing the "primal scene" in "The Confession of a Young Girl"). Second, Mademoiselle Vinteuil commits various symbolic acts all condensed into one, when she spits upon his photograph. Partly, this may be related to infantile sexual feelings on an oral level; and partly it is a reaction with soiling. A submissive attitude toward the father is denied, by defiance.

Mademoiselle Vinteuil's female partner, as co-conspirator, is a mother-image participating in the act, therefore mother and daughter need not fear each other's disapproval and revenge for involvement with the mutually desired, depreciated father. The father can neither seduce nor revenge himself upon them, for he is already dead. And besides, Mademoiselle Vinteuil is really a good daughter, the author makes this clear (like the overly demonstrative daughter in the Confession story, and like the dutiful author who ruins himself to become the great writer his parents wanted him to be). Mademoiselle Vinteuil's defiance and sexual sinfulness are a temporary lapse, for which she makes up later by putting her father's marvelously beautiful musical work in order, with her friend's aid. Here we have the author's feminine identification carefully worked out: at first, defying the father-image; at the

[17] Charles Briand, *Le Secret de Marcel Proust;* Edmund Wilson, *Axel's Castle,* New York, 1931.

same time submitting to participation in a forbidden act with both parents and a sibling image involved. But Marcel is only an onlooker. And finally, the result is beautiful and constructive: the music, the novel. The pattern of Mademoiselle Vinteuil's homosexual episode is repeated later in Albertine, who says Mademoiselle Vinteuil and her friend were "mother and sister" to her. Thus Albertine doubly involves the sibling-and mother-images. Also, Albertine is both a mother and a version of Robert to the "Marcel" of the book. But he fears she might be the incestuous lover of Mademoiselle Vinteuil and her friend, Albertine's own "mother and sister" of long ago. The fine-spun ramifications of all this are very difficult to follow. That is precisely why it required so long a novel (with such long sentences) to sketch out the fantasy, of which this is just one essential series of facets. Every act seems to be counterbalanced by an image of its reverse. The passive and active sides appear, if not in the actual narrative, then in a dream or doubt.

The scorn expressed by spitting on the image of Mademoiselle Vinteuil's father is also related to Marcel's stamping on Charlus's hat. In the latter incident, it is Marcel's rebellion against his own fear of homosexual submission to Charlus that precipitates his defiant act. (We will think about the defiant stamping again, when we discuss a lover's loss of both legs in two early stories. All this is related to the inhibition of the use of Marcel's legs, erotically and aggressively, and the importance of his grandmother's tying his shoelaces, for him — and suspicions of homosexuality aroused at the sight of Marcel's walking with various men such as Monsieur d'Argencourt's raised eyebrows when he sees Marcel taking a walk with Charlus, Charlus's occupations when Marcel walks with Brichot, and so forth.)

We also may note, in passing, that when Marcel sees Mademoiselle Vinteuil's friend spit on her father's image, it is the opposite arrangement of the pattern in real life that first suggested the episode of the beating of Charlus [18] where it was really an eminent, devoted father who had to make insulting remarks about his son, before a prostitute, in order to be potent with her. Thus we see incestuous ties involving parents and a sibling frequently rearranged in the intricately interwoven Proustian personalities. There seems to be a reduplication of family or clannish relationships among all the characters.

The blending of defiance and sexual attraction is especially marked in Proust because, within a masochistic homosexual make-up such as his, the need to submit to the strong male tends to be counterpoised against the simultaneous compulsion to deny this submission. Identifying with a female, in the likeness of Madame Verdurin and Mademoiselle Vinteuil, the author demonstrates fundamentally harmless aggression against such father-figures as Vinteuil, the great musician, and Charlus, whom Madame Verdurin separates from the worthless but beloved Morel. But as a submissive female, yielding completely to Marcel, at the beginning of *The Sweet Cheat Gone*, Albertine loses her life. It is the submissive female who is really endangered. True femininity is a peril, in Proust's scheme of things. The unworthy, foul-mouthed young Morel or Maurice can be loved by the father-figure. The author's femininity always has to be mixed with defiance, and even so, it is largely repressed insofar as it is related to really potent, virile father-figures who might impregnate. In real life, Proust fell in love with young boys; he was emotionally like a domineering woman with a younger one; he was a seducer —like Albertine and Morel, when they seduced younger people. Love affairs of this type caused him the least anxiety;

[18] See page 102 of this book.

the suffering they invoked was largely jealousy, moral anguish, or fear of ostracism and separation. But more subtly, in his unconscious, it seems, he feared the overwhelming nature of complete submission to a virile man, which seems to have meant to him not only castration but identification with the birth-giving female, death, and at the same time some hope of rebirth (by what he considered might be an act of memory).

He tells us of Charlus's yearning for a really virile man whom he conceives of as a "beloved hangman" and therefore fears. One suspects that the author was never truly satisfied, in his homosexuality and bisexuality, by his beloved brother-figures, yet his yearning for really strong men mobilized on the surface his repressed urges toward defiance (exemplified by the "fou rire" attacks, when he listened to Montesquiou read poetry). The mere hint of his passive dependence on Montesquiou aroused him to a duel.

Proust's repressed impulses to express defiance no doubt increased his symptoms, particularly his insomnia and asthma and possibly his tendency toward "street fear," as well as the verbal asperity against which he always had to remain on guard.

Toward the end of his life, as in *The Past Recaptured*, the feeling that by producing a great book he had unconsciously somehow begun to achieve the perilous birth-process and to identify himself, therefore, with a submissive woman seems to have been the real reason he was so convinced that to create a great literary work was to race with death.

Elstir, Proust's artist of great imagination, is described as looking sad at the mention of the fame he was about to achieve — Marcel rationalizes this sadness, as forecasting in the painter's mind, a time when he would be deceased.

This brings us to still another point. (It seems that one may start almost at random with a phrase of Proust's and find suitable material for a dissertation upon his entire personality.) In *Within a Budding Grove*, Part II, page 193, there is a description of some of Elstir's early allegorical work, where there is a scene reminiscent of the storm at Penmarch,[19] depicting what is really a birth fantasy, in which "a little human personage in old-fashioned attire seemed often to be stopped short on the edge of an abyss." Why should this small figure have antique dress, or any clothing at all? He is dated by the fashion of his garment. In the archaic quality of the little figure, just as in the old-fashioned manner in which Proust carried out his own exaggerated forms of social observance (and in Jean's retreat to his grandfather's lap, in *Jean Santeuil*, after a scene of disruption with his parents — also in the author's emotional retreat from the Republican Government), we see the theme of escaping from directly submissive contact with father-figures by a retreat to a generation before his father's, for supreme authority. Just as he splits off the purely loving, asexual qualities of his mother, and projects them back to his grandmother's image, he frequently splits off his submission to the traditional authority of his father, directing it toward a more conservative, archaic, grandfatherly source. But in the voting story, in *Jean Santeuil*, after the unusual experience of having his mother's love all to himself for an entire day, he does the opposite: this time he makes restitution, submits to his absent father's wishes, by voting for the man his father would have chosen, to the detriment of the man he really favors.[20] We always see this reversal, this symmetry, in Proust, and it seems to spring from an instinctive need in the author, rather than from a purely intellectual concept of literary symmetry. It makes his work the more

[19] See Appendix A, p. 280.
[20] *Jean Santeuil*, Vol. III. Also see Appendix A, p. 279 of this book.

satisfying to some readers who respond with a similar reaction, an unconscious feeling of reassurance perhaps — from the sense of balance, the lack of emotional commitment, the symmetry of the narrative. As in Hardy's *Well-Beloved*, it requires a fantasy of at least three generations to work out these balanced feelings.

XIII

Neurotic Components of Proust's Asthma

Supplementing the physiological, allergic basis for his asthma, Proust doubtlessly precipitated frequent severe attacks by the way he lived and worked. He wrote of accepting his asthma largely as a nervous habit, almost a form of malingering, but preferable to the ills that would have replaced it if he relinquished it, and a necessary penalty for the cultivation of his sensibilities and talents. In his Preface to Ruskin's *Sesame and Lilies,* he quotes Brugelmann on the psychological origins of asthma and gives his own idea of the importance of what we now call "psychosomatic" aspects.[1]

Again, in *Cities of the Plain,* Proust says, "By dint of supposing yourself to be ill you become ill, grow thin, are too weak to rise from your bed, suffer from nervous enteritis. By dint of thinking tenderly of men you become a woman ... The obsession, just as in the other instances it affects your health, may in this instance alter your sex." [2]

Around 1901–2 Proust wrote in a letter to Antoine Bibesco [3]

[1] This Preface was reprinted under the title of "Journée de Lectures," in *Pastiches et Mélanges,* Paris, 1919. [2] Vol. II, p. 76.
[3] Mina Curtiss, *Letters of Marcel Proust,* Trans. and ed. with notes by Mina Curtiss, New York, 1949.

that he consulted a doctor who told him his asthma was a
nervous habit and that he should go to an institution to break
the habit as one demorphinizes the morphine fiends. Another
doctor, he wrote to Lucien Daudet, had said to him it would
be possible to make the asthma disappear but that he did not
want to do so because "to the extent to which you are
asthmatic . . . your disease is for you an escape and enables
you to dispense with other maladies."

In *The Past Recaptured,* Proust says:

> And even our physical ailments, at any rate those which
> affect the nervous system rather closely, are they not in a
> way special preferences or phobias developed by our organs
> and our bony structure, which thus discover that they have
> contracted for certain climates an aversion as tenacious and
> inexplicable as the fancy some men shew for women who wear
> eyeglasses or for female circus-riders? The desire that is
> aroused each time at the sight of a woman circus-rider, who
> will ever say with what persistent, unconscious dream it is
> connected, as unconscious and mysterious, for example, as is
> the influence which one who has suffered all his life from asth-
> matic attacks, may suddenly feel in some city, apparently the
> same as all the others, but where for the first time he breathes
> freely?
>
> Now, aberrations are like love affairs in which the morbid
> condition has spread and affected the entire being. Even in the
> maddest of them, the underlying love can still be discerned.[4]

He then goes on to describe Charlus, where he is being
beaten, as s.arching unconsciously for virility proven by tests,
and adds that Charlus remained faithful, in a way, to Morel by
preferring his accomplices to resemble Morel in appearance.
Proust thus appears to tie, by association, his asthma and

[4] P. 159.

homosexual "neurotic defect," [5] but he always felt that both conditions were so mysteriously rooted in the unconscious that they were incurable except at the sacrifice of a tenuous adjustment which permitted him to put the maximum of himself into his literary projects.

In *Jean Santeuil* [6] he describes the sensitivity of superior individuals, their egotism, excessive nervousness and brilliant excess of intellect.

In *The Guermantes Way*, the doctor says, "We enjoy fine music, beautiful pictures, a thousand exquisite things, but we do not know what they cost those who wrought them in sleeplessness, tears, spasmodic laughter, rashes, asthma, epilepsy . . . Neurosis has an absolute genius for malingering. There is no illness which it cannot counterfeit perfectly." [7] (In this reference to epilepsy, the author was very likely thinking of Dostoevsky.)

To a large extent we may piece together an account of Proust's own insights in regard to his homosexuality, including his realization of his abnormal interest in his mother, his renunciation of interest in girls, his strong identification with the women in the family, probably also his secret wish for, and fear of, a truly virile male partner. But we find available very much less self-analysis regarding Proust's asthma, except that it seemed the penalty of artistic achievement. The conflicts that were symbolically represented by his asthmatic symptoms seem to have been most obscure to him, least verbalized, most deeply related to the earliest, inarticulate levels of body expression, including those vague "Proustian" symbols connected with the sea, rooms, or air. Proust recognized that some emotional components of his asthma did exist, and he

[5] Mina Curtiss, *Letters of Marcel Proust*, p. 246, Letters to Louis de Robert, 1913. Re the term "neurotic defect," also this book, note, p. 102.
[6] *Jean Santeuil*, Vol. III, p. 308.
[7] P. 418.

tied them up inconclusively with his homosexuality. He knew, only too clearly, the nostalgic importance of breathing and of odors. Fragrances of Combray recall most vividly for Marcel the reality of childhood days. Marcel's senses are the key to recall. Evil odors are frequently his villains: for instance the poisonous smell of the staircase that separated Marcel from his mother, in *Swann's Way* — or the odor of asparagus by which Françoise tortured Eulalie. Charlus, in fits of haughty derision, refers to excretion and disgusting bodily odors. "To cattleya," Swann's and Odette's phrase for love, refers to a species of orchid, hence a fragrance. Flowers (popular as literary symbols of the day) were prime messengers of love and beauty for the real Marcel Proust, but flowers and the perfume of princesses were especially intolerable to him in later life, because of his illness. In general, he seems to have connected flowers with forbidden, alluring odors, and unconsciously with female sexuality.

In Proust's writings, we have dawning insights alternating with dreamlike lyrical images in which his inverted oedipal (homosexual) feelings are in constant struggle with the positive oedipal (heterosexual) strivings. He regresses particularly from the latter, displaces his heterosexuality, projects it, confuses the sexes, to avoid it. Marcel is always on the verge of desiring or expressing triumph over a father- or brother-image, possessing the beloved woman, in the story; then he exhibits masochism and destruction along with his triumph. At the end, we have another sort of triumph, a literary one. But first we are told of Marcel's ill health, Charlus's madness, and Madame Verdurin's great wealth and high social position (restitution to a mother-figure). It is only as a pregnant woman, or a man fearing an accident, an illness, the loss of all, that Marcel feels convinced of his potency as a writer, at the end. Marcel has won the indulgence of others, their forgiveness and their special consideration through illness. But in addition to what he wrote, the author's asthma and Marcel's in the book spoke a supplementary language.

Proust knew that this bodily language existed, that it was necessary, and that in his case it was in part a neurotically determined symptom (although undoubtedly with a complementary physiological basis). Hence, one must look for the primitive, least verbalized, or else the most unacceptable and ego-alien side of his great personality to understand the dynamic neurotic components in his asthma. Perhaps the neurotic contribution to his asthma is, after all, inexpressible in words or he would have expressed it. But perhaps he really did so, portraying it in symbols or combinations of symbols that we can learn to decipher more clearly.

In Charlus's masochism, in the seduction of the very young boy by Charlus, and Charlus's confession of the intent to murder Morel, we perhaps have an illustration of more than Proust may have been conscious of: the image of his father as a homosexual, dangerously seductive toward him — he wards off such a fantasy, and has revenge on the father at the same time, identifying with the aggressor and masochist, both. Here is a vicious circle of anxiety, mostly repressed, pushing toward expression in fantasy.

Proust's "inverted Oedipus complex" involved him in conflicts with the women of his family, and other women throughout life, for the affections of men. This competitiveness for men, against the women as rivals, is a cogent factor in the homosexual man's existence. It is minimized in *Remembrance of Things Past*. For example, Charlus does not mind Morel's engagement to Jupien's niece, but if we follow this young lady's fate in the story, we find that Morel insults her and leaves her, Charlus generously gives her money and a title, but she becomes ill the day of her marriage to the Cambremer

boy and dies a few weeks later, her widowed husband becomes
a homosexual, and Charlus's lover. (Jupien's niece dies, like
the brother-figure, Robert, not because she is the object of
anyone's aggression — but death overtakes her. Thus fantasy
deals once more in passive terms with repressed aggression.)

In *Within a Budding Grove*, Marcel expresses the wish to
kiss his father on the cheek, above where his beard begins,[8]
when his father is unexpectedly kind, but he does not yield
to this desire for fear of annoying him. And, in *Swann's Way*,
Marcel says he feels his only hope of becoming a great writer
depends on his father's arranging it. Later this fantasy is
carried out, to some degree, because, as is merely hinted,
Norpois, his father's friend, recommends Madame Villeparisis
to go to the Grand Hotel at Balbec. There she will meet
Marcel and his grandmother, and introduce them to Robert
de Saint-Loup, Charlus, and the others who will be links to
all the main characters in the book. Thus Norpois, Marcel's
father's friend, the very man who does not understand Marcel's writing nor sincerely wish to help him, unwittingly
brings about introductions to those who furnish material for
his literary career. In Proust's actual life, his father made it
possible for him to write because of the income he provided
for him. But in the story, Marcel's gift of money to Albertine
enabled her to buy the horse that killed her, and presumably
Charlus's gift of money was connected with the typhoid fever
and death of Morel's ex-fiancée (at least in the author's
unconscious).

Most of Proust's writing gives us the impression that father-
figures, such as doctors and statesmen, lent their prestige and
aid to him at the cost of a kind of physical submission, against
which he rebelled. The gradual disclosure of the fact that
Charlus is a homosexual is one of the fundamental motifs of

[8] P. 75.

the book, a theme about which much of the story revolves. The protection given to Marcel by strong, somewhat masculine women and tender, loving men, with constant reassurance that Marcel himself is sexually intact, potent erotically, heterosexual, although frail in physical health, is essential to the story. At the very times when Marcel is sick in bed, we note that he has love affairs. It is as if the whole novel were written to create a kind of milieu in which this fictitious "Marcel" could feel most loved, most at ease, most in touch with his nostalgic paradise, combining past and present. This paradise was always in flux, resisting flight through time by changing patterns, always intermittent between reality and poetry, and, as Proust phrased it, "not lacking a touch of the grotesque."

Although Proust depended on one vast, interdigitated set of involuntary memories to evoke the intense bliss of love in his writing, in his actual life his allergies and what perhaps also amounted to phobias (not only of the street but of chill, dampness, dust, noise, pollens, and so forth) constantly protected him from another set of involuntary memories, the recapture of all the intolerable stimuli which had become connected with parts of the past that he could not bear to recapture. He stressed the recall of values that might be turned to positive use, by their inclusion in his artistic masterpiece, but he must have struggled to achieve constant repression as well as recall. Erotic drives were always a threat and had to be evoked under special circumstances. Allied to repressed erotic taboos were all the sounds, smells, and stimuli he could not tolerate physiologically, partly perhaps because recollections might rush into consciousness too disagreeably to be coped with.

In asthma, the threat of sexual drives unacceptable to the sufferer is one factor that is able to cause an asthmatic attack. Erotic impulses which may bring about maternal rejection and

disapproval have been found as a rule to upset the balance of
adjustment in the asthmatic child, or asthmatic adult, who
frequently craves special demonstrations of esteem. Violence
of feeling, fears connected with infantile misconceptions about
sex, may cause sexuality to remain repressed and still operate
unconsciously. Identification with the mother's pregnancy,
the strangely interpreted content of her pregnancy as anal
content or urine, and infantile misconceptions of the violent
acts that caused it (perhaps injection and expelling through
flatus or breathing) can create panic in the most primitive
portion of the mind which knows only symbols engendered
in infantile years. Suffocation is more than a fantasied punishment. It is a real threat where physiological allergy and actual
asthmatic disease are present.

To avoid all erotic temptation, except under the conditions
that have become habitually acceptable, combining atonement, reassurance, and the symbolic, incestuous gratifications
most desired, evidently set a pattern in his own personal life.
"Like the famous race horse that was fed exclusively on
roses," [9] he needed to maintain his homosexual life in order to
keep functioning.

Guilt stood between him and everything else. He was never
free of guilt in connection with his erotic life. He always had
an urge to confess, and a fear of the result of his confession,
as evidenced in "The Confession of a Young Girl," the "parricide" article in *Figaro*, the long sections on homosexuality
in his novel, and his frequent dissertations on morality in connection with sexuality. There always seems to be a necessity
for reconciliation with the parents through confession. (Even
C., the author of *Jean Santeuil*, has to reconcile, after a misunderstanding with the boys to whom he gives his manuscript.)

Besides this urge to confess, which is typical of many asth-

[9] *The Past Recaptured*, p. 332.

matics, tears and sobbing are particularly frequent in Proust's narratives. For instance, one early story was based on an image of drinking the tears of the beloved. Another example: André Maurois quotes Proust as writing, "Quite recently I have begun to hear distinctly, if I take the trouble to listen, the sobs which I struggled to repress when my father was present, in which I was free to indulge only when I was alone with Mama. The truth is, they have never ceased . . ." [10]

He seemed to find it necessary to share both his tears and his love with his mother and never break the sense of indissoluble union [11] with her by arousing her disapproval. Sexual temptation was a threat to this union with her. Frustration and rage which might make him flee constituted a threat to it. But tears seemed to return him to her, along with confession and forgiveness. By self-restraint and turning his fantasies into a great artistic achievement, he felt certain of her approval. And yet the self-revelations of writing led him to confess his homosexual loves by which he risked her wrath, on moral grounds, and also as her rival. But her wrath would not be incurred if the boys were portrayed as "girls" or represented himself, in illness (loved by his mother) — and at the same time represented the brother loved by him — as the "phantom" of Albertine — all a fantasy, shifting, unreal.

In his research into the past, Proust selects memories which would not have estranged his mother too completely. Sadistic references to birth are objective, peripheral, and infrequent. Homosexuality is projected to others, and is looked on with repulsion by Marcel.

Proust exacted constant proofs of endearment all his life, as did the fictitious "Marcel." He was unable to take the

[10] André Maurois, *Portrait of a Genius*, New York, 1950, p. 112.
[11] Perhaps most important of all was Proust's tendency to identify with his mother in what he considered the indescribable agony of her fecundity, and then the birth process.

simplest steps in his daily life, without advice from friends. In his stories the main character frequently struggles to become the cynosure of deep affection from all sides, or else someone's lack of love for him becomes the chief problem, in the plot.

In relation to competition with others, a peculiarly stolid inertia typifies his characters. They grow like stalagmites or stalactites by intricacy of crystallization, by formative powers from within, and thus achieve their goals.

Eventually it was an immovable object that killed Albertine. She fell against a tree, hitting her head. It was when Marcel lay ill in bed that she became his mistress.

The motionless person, spying upon Charlus, waiting hopelessly for the beloved, as Swann did, the paralyzed Marcel at Venice undecided whether or not to rejoin his mother, like the canvases of the great symbolist painters, convey frozen drama. Holding back, and controlling what is about to be expressed, is very important to Proust, typified by the retention of his breath when Françoise tells him Albertine is gone. Restraining respiration is his means of preserving his composure, and not betraying his true feelings, to the hostile servant.

Early articles on asthma published in England, France, Germany and Holland, and elsewhere tended to stress the emotional factors. For example, there was the famous case of the paper rose that precipitated an attack of rose fever, the painting of the storm that set off an asthma attack in a patient sensitive to weather, and the mere mention of place names which caused asthma attacks in other patients. With further medical research in allergy, there began a swing to purely physiological theories and a diminished interest in psychological factors. In the most recent decades, with modern research in psychosomatic medicine, allergists have renewed their studies of the interaction between physical and emotional factors in asthma. Some have adhered to their skepticism, while others have swung to the opposite attitude of attributing fairly definite personality profiles to certain types of asthmatics whose attacks often seem to have a neurotic basis.

Proust's belief in the fact that emotions may cause illness seems to have been greater than his faith in any return to health through emotional insight. He gives the impression of having made a bargain, trading health for sensitivity and genius. His writings reflect a feeling that doctors generally tend to prolong illnesses, rather than to cure them, and that doctors contradict their own theories; but we know that this attitude toward doctors must have been colored by his need to see flaws and effeminacy in the men who represented authority to him, because his submissive deference was always accompanied by anxiety. (When he was about to enter a sanitarium, he wrote to Madame Straus, as if he needed the reassurance of a motherly woman against fears aroused by the prospect of submission to medical authorities. He was something of a medical expert himself, probably partly in self-defense, out of distrust for doctors.)

André Maurois,[12] in his exceedingly thorough and sensitive biography of Proust, comments to the reader that asthma represents a repressed cry for the mother. This sort of psychosomatic observation in a literary biography is indicative of a change in the past decade. It has become fairly widely accepted, now, that asthma is connected with a repressed cry for the mother, as Maurois reminds us, and that this cry which is held in check is a source of the breathlessness of the asthma attack. The asthmatic's repressed cry seems to be a cry of rage as well as a call for help. But why should this be so?

[12] *Portrait of a Genius.*

And particularly, why should it be important in the case of Proust, who was not loath to express his need for his mother, by tears, by his writing, and by the way he lived? Since he was most eloquent in his expression of his need for her, why did he still require physiological expression of this cry for her?

Fear of separation from the beloved runs through Proust's writing as the essence of love itself. Without this fear, there is no love — and only death can end it, unless the love itself is transferred to another "phantom."

This same dread of separation is typical of psychoanalytic findings regarding the emotional component in asthma. For example, we find this separation-anxiety described in a monograph entitled "Psychogenic Factors in Bronchial Asthma," published under the sponsorship of the National Research Council in Washington, D.C., in 1941, as the result of a research program conducted by the staff of the Chicago Institute for Psychoanalysis. Any situation that threatened estrangement or separation from the mother or her substitute was the cause of acute anxiety in the patients studied. They were found to be typically ignorant and fearful about mature sexual functioning in their youth; they grew up fearing that sexual temptation would deprive them of much needed maternal protection.

In Proust's case, we have his anxiety stemming from two sources: fear of sexual temptation (and competition), and fear of the original aggressive, pregenital urges against which his homosexual impulses were defenses. He was in a state of perpetual anxiety and frustration, constantly needing love and reassurance from every direction, particularly from mother-figures and from his own mother and grandmother, and then turning away from his incestuous ties to them, to brother-figures, and then to the mothers of his friends, always wishing to be the favorite in the salons, and always suspicious that young men friends were derisive of him (a projection of his uneasiness, because of homosexuality, and also because of his competitive hostility to them in relation to people with prestige).

Besides sexual temptation, another situation that threatened estrangement from mother-figures in the asthmatic patients studied psychoanalytically by the Chicago group was actual physical removal from the mother. This Proust describes very well in the account of his first trip to Balbec with his grandmother, and his telephone call home from Doncières, and then in the passage where he is separated from his mother at Venice, and rushes to the train, unable to bear having her go off without him. Sexual temptation has almost held Marcel in Venice in the person of Madame Putbus's maid whom he has always been pursuing. But he cannot face separation from his mother by sexual temptation — and makes the choice which seems characteristic for many asthmatics — that is, he renounces sex and goes back to his mother. In the scene at Venice, where he is so undecided, we see immobility versus action as typifying his main struggle. His story always shows how he keeps anguish and anxiety under control. Similarly, he demonstrates how, when harmonious love does begin to exist for him, a separating factor must insinuate itself. Several times, it is Madame Verdurin who breaks up a love affair. In *Jean Santeuil*, Jean's own mother plays this role at the beginning, preventing Jean from seeing his beloved Marie, or Henri de Réveillon. But toward the end of *Remembrance of Things Past*, the author indicates that his own unconscious hostilities may have caused his separation from his beloved, as he describes his guilt for the "double murder" of Albertine and his grandmother. His special way of overcoming separation either in space or through death is to make time a uniting factor. This preoccupation with time can be traced back to his early twenties, when he wrote a note to his mother: "Darling Mama: . . . (hoping to breakfast with her) . . . To feel that we fill the same period of time with our sleeping and our waking will be for me a dear delight." [13]

In the asthmatic cases studied by the Chicago group, the birth of a younger child which threatened to come between the older child and the mother was at the root of the neuroses of quite a few of the patients. In each one, the conflict was handled in a different way, typical of his own personality development. Some tried to overcome the threatened loss of the mother-child relationship which meant so much to them by turning the situation around and mothering others. A number of women patients who did this had successful careers and were able to look after, or support, younger women, or to have homosexual friendships on a mother-child basis. Among the men, overt homosexuality was not the chief defense presented, in this group of patients, as it was apparently in Proust. There were some who attempted to become independent, and to escape the mother-conflict by becoming impersonal, losing themselves in artistic endeavors or hard work, a sort of "pseudo-independence." [14] Proust's efforts to lose himself in artistic work brought him back again to his mother-conflict because of the nature of his novel, which was confessional, introspective, and personal, and so articulate, and because his mother's lofty aesthetic standards made him work unsparingly for literary greatness.

Actual attacks of asthma occurred, in the patients studied psychoanalytically in Chicago, at the point when the patient's psychological defenses broke down: when the danger of losing the mother was too acute or when the patient was unprepared

[13] André Maurois, *ibid*, p. 64. See note declaring his love for his mother and describing his asthmatic attacks.
[14] Thomas M. French, *The Integration of Behavior*, Chicago, 1954.

to cope with a sudden risk of losing the love-object. The patient was precipitately overwhelmed and the asthma attack was like a suppressed cry of helplessness. (This unprepared state and sudden loss is epitomized when Françoise announces to Marcel that Albertine is gone, and he holds back his breath so as not to betray his desperation; also when Morel unexpectedly renounces Charlus, at Madame Verdurin's, and Charlus, struck dumb, is led off by the Queen of Naples.)

Nearly all of the asthmatic cases studied in the Institute report were allergically hypersensitive, but the attacks during their analyses were not found to be demonstrably related to allergens; in fact, allergic sensitivity decreased in some cases. Some cases improved much more than others. It was thought that where considerable improvement occurred after a very brief period in analysis, it was because weeping tended to relieve attacks, and gratification of the urge to confess matters that had never been discussed before by the patient, with a forgiving parental figure, was an important therapeutic factor. In place of asthmatic attacks, some patients at first tended to cry, and then later they developed an ability to face conflicts openly that had hitherto been repressed. The degree of improvement seemed dependent upon the severity of the neuroses accompanying the asthma. Increased independence and greater freedom of expression were associated with improvement.

All of this makes the confession and reconciliation themes in Proust's novel, particularly Charlus's posthumous confession of his intention to murder Morel, extremely interesting. Confession and exhibiting of weaknesses and faults, and compassionate forgiveness, are marked characteristics of all Proust's work. The desire for forgiveness or involvement of the beholder seems to be at the root of his confessions. There is also a defiant, provocative element, in all of Proust's writing. He expected to lose all his friends after the publication of *Sodome et Gomorrhe* (Cities of the Plain), but was surprised to find he was forgiven. Proust's letters to Count Robert de Montesquiou, who was a contributory model for Charlus, are interesting to read because they show how constantly Proust was at the point of provoking him, without often doing so. Undoubtedly, Proust's punctiliousness about manners hid or made up for his defiant tendencies. His aggressive tendencies, like his erotic drives, had to be held in check, most of the time.

It is suggested in the Chicago Institute monograph, by Alexander, that children who have a hereditary deficiency in adaptability to independent living after birth and at the same time have been exposed to a conflictful attitude in their mothers may at the height of struggle over independence be exposed to allergens in quantity; the lungs then may defend themselves by spasms of the bronchioles, and set the pattern for later asthma attacks. Another possibility suggested by Alexander is that the threshold for allergic sensitivity is lowered if an emotional factor appears which evokes this same bronchiole reaction. It may also be that a hereditary basic defect in adaptability is responsible for both the severity of the emotional conflict and the allergic sensitivity. Saul, in "The Relations to the Mother as Seen in Cases of Allergy," in *The Nervous Child*, in 1946, suggests that under stress, or when the relationship to the mother is endangered, the dermal and respiratory mechanisms may play a role in resultant skin and respiratory allergies related to dermal and respiratory mechanisms of prenatal life.

In Proust's case, probably physiological factors and family inheritance were added to temperamental, "nervous and highstrung" characteristics of mother and grandmother.[15] His lack

---

[15] In *Remembrance of Things Past*, Proust refers to Swann's "racial eczema and constipation of the prophets."

of identification with his father, his inability to cope with the shock of the brother's birth, and his later reaction to the baby brother with a tendency toward homosexual love may have served to increase his separation fears because his sexual wishes were the more forbidden, being homosexual, and originally incestuous, and infantile-perverse in their precocity. He tried in all his writings to deal with the erotism which broke through compulsively. This erotism was a disturbing component in his make-up, constantly causing anxiety and jealousy. It was very often a thin disguise for accumulating aggression. His masochism was his last resort. Literary creativity afforded him an outlet in fantasy to a certain extent, but there was always a reflex anxiety from the fantasies stimulated by his writing. It was probably to seek refuge from this that he turned for so long from literary creativity to his translation of Ruskin. In Ruskin he found a wealth of artistic support and bases for later imagery.

Writing *Remembrance of Things Past* was Proust's attempt at independence and self-respect, to make up for his invalidism, dependence, guilt, and feelings of perpetual vulnerability and need to suffer. The overwork which ruined his health was at the same time necessary to his ego. He was always deeply ashamed of his homosexuality, and eventually frustrated in his loves for young boys. Like Albertine, they were never completely satisfactory objects, they were loved when fear of separation caused suffering, otherwise they were boring. He tells us the main value of his love affairs was to make him suffer, and thus to stir him to literary activity. He was always thrust back to frustrating nostalgia, with its alluring but insoluble conflicts; and he sought to make art greater than life by a synthesis that was his last stand against breakdown and disintegration.

The unconscious symbolism through which the "asthma

conflict" seems to express itself, in terms of body symbols, has been studied in the dreams [16] of asthmatic patients, and seems to center around intra-uterine conflicts in many patients, and a fear of smothering — as talion punishment for the desire to smother the rival within the mother's body, in the patients where separation-fear focused around rivalry with a younger sibling.

This recalls, again, the continuous appearance of the sea, rooms, and other intra-uterine symbols in Proust's work as an active part of the story, always laden with fear or else with reassurance, according to whether the narrator wishes to convey a feeling of being loved, protected, full of hope of gratification — or of shame, rejection, isolation, and danger, and "unbreathable aroma." When Marcel's relationship to his mother and to Robert and other brother-figures is pleasant, the symbolism of the sea is calm and attractive. It does not threaten. But when aggression is mobilized in Marcel, or where sexuality threatens to offend, the room, the sea or the city streets, are ominous, and, as in the image of lava inundating the streets of Paris when Marcel has spied upon Charlus being beaten — sado-masochism is expressed, and suffocation is threatened, very often through intra-uterine symbols.

[16] *Psychogenic Factors in Bronchial Asthma*, National Research Council, Washington, D.C., 1941.

XIV

Themes of *Remembrance of Things Past* Compared with the Theoretical Deductions of Thomas M. French's *Integration of Behavior*

In *The Captive*, there is an indication that verbal inconsistencies and word slips (associations) are more revealing than conscious speech.[1]

Proust, by trying to follow the natural course of his feelings in his style and narrative, seems to have mapped out a history of the main choices and contradictions into which he was driven by unconscious forces in his own personal development. This unconscious determination established the relationships of the main characters, and so made the story. He himself could not predict the future experiences of some of his characters while he was writing, as we know from his letters.

He defined literary style as a matter of vision. His composite images apparently recount his own developmental history in visual terms, very often like a series of paintings. There is also an undercurrent that is like the music of Vinteuil, growing from a "little phrase" connected with love, and the sea, to a great masterpiece with fuller orchestra.

Albertine really *had* to be represented as feminine, with a

[1] P. 112.

masculine side, and no other way, because it seems that she represents his mother predominantly, his brother secondarily — and always the author himself, until she dies and is finally eradicated from within him. Albertine as a person is kept completely separate from any erotic ties with father-figures. She is also safely removed from brother-figures; she loves only young girls, except for Marcel. And still Marcel is hopelessly jealous, as of a beloved brother's interest in girls or in his mother. Separation fears are always about to arouse rage and suffering, in *Remembrance of Things Past*. We can see, now, why Charlus, a father-figure, although so effeminized, was kept thoroughly preoccupied with his great homosexual affair with Morel during the time of Marcel's love for Albertine, in the book. No matter how diluted a mother-image or brother-image Albertine is, along with all the other aspects of her composite existence, and no mater how effeminate and dis-interested the figure of Charlus, in the book they are united in the time of the appearance and disappearance of their great loves. Abstract patterns in art may say whatever the reader wishes to read into them, and whatever the creator may indicate unconsciously. Yet these patterns are retracted in the very stating. The main characteristic of an abstract pattern is that it is a form of control. Rules are laid down rigidly, whether the art be music, painting, or literature — and within the precinct of aesthetic law, fantasy roams without detection, without our surmises being capable of proof.

It is in the latter part of *The Past Recaptured* that Proust talks about the ability of *time* to unite people, because it is the road to the unconscious and to what Proust terms reality.

How contradictory and yet how paradoxically similar is Proust's attitude toward time and that of Freud,[2] who wrote:

_____

[2] Sigmund Freud, "The Unconscious" (1915), *Collected Papers*, London, 1925, Vol. IV, p. 119.

The processes of the system Ucs [unconscious] are timeless; i.e., they are not ordered temporally, are not altered by the passage of time, in fact bear no relation to time at all. The time-relation . . . is bound up with the work of the system Cs [consciousness].

The processes of the Ucs are just as little related to reality. They are subject to the pleasure-principle; their fate depends only upon the degree of their strength and upon their conformity to regulation by pleasure and pain.

Just as works of art, by creating their own patterns, dominated by the unconscious, stand apart from time to a great degree and permit free flow of feelings within their own rigid standards, dreams also are timeless and accessible to all sorts of otherwise repressed emotions in the dreamer. (Baudelaire and Coleridge seem to have understood this also, as we see in their approaches to time and dreams.)

If we had all the dreams of an individual, instead of his waking life, to consult, would we have a re-edition of that person's existence? Would dreams tend to fall into patterns of any definite sort, also?

Marcel [3] says he holds time incarnate within himself and must bring it out in his book. This is very much like what the understanding of a long series of dreams would bring out, at least in part, if the dreams were studied minutely.

There has thus far been only one such detailed study of a limited series of dreams. This has been described in *The Integration of Behavior*,[4] by Thomas M. French. The man studied, whom we shall call Mr. X, was in many respects the antithesis of Marcel Proust in background, physical build, mentality, personal and cultural endowment and in most of

---

[3] *The Past Recaptured*, p. 400–401.
[4] Thomas M. French, *The Integration of Behavior*, Chicago, Vol. I, 1952, and Vol. II, 1954.

his situations in life. But he had asthma, and nervous factors contributed a great deal to augmenting his allergic reactions. He also had a brother about two years younger, whose birth helped to set off the neurotic pattern connected with his asthma. Some points of similarity between Proust and this patient (Mr. X) are clear, others debatable, but it is interesting to compare the patterns of Mr. X's dreams with the patterns created by Proust's writing.

Naturally, we cannot draw permanent conclusions from the comparison of only two individuals. At most, we may be able to show that such studies might fruitfully be made.

Mr. X was psychoanalyzed by Dr. Helen V. McLean as part of the research program in asthma at the Chicago Institute for Psychoanalysis, starting around 1935. Mr. X was later selected by Dr. French for a minute study of dreams, with the purpose of inquiring into the formation of patterns of unconscious emotional life, because Mr. X's record was meticulously kept, thoroughly discussed by all the research staff, and contained several series of simple dreams with associations, fantasies, and so on, of a kind that were suitable for a published study, for which he gave permission.

Mr. X was a forty-six-year-old man who was treated at the Chicago Institute for Psychoanalysis, referred from the Allergy Clinic of the University of Chicago with a diagnosis of bronchial asthma and fall pollen disease. The allergists sent him for psychoanalytic treatment, apparently because they felt they were unable to offer him further therapeutic aid, after a period of six years of medical treatment. He was a masculine-looking, tall, blond man, always very neatly dressed. His manner was quiet and he talked with reticence. He was unusually inarticulate. He had no consciousness of any relation between his illness and possible emotional conflicts. His employment was in a railroad yard, cleaning out freight cars, for the past fifteen years, where he followed his predilection for working at night. He was married and had two children, but did not enjoy his family life.

His father was a blacksmith, who provided comfortably for his family and was once mayor of the small European town where they lived; he was ambitious for his children to rise a little higher than blacksmith work. The patient's birth was a difficult one. During his boyhood he had frequent bronchial colds. At the age of nine or ten, as in Proust's case, a severe asthma attack occurred.

Mr. X's father and brother also had respiratory difficulties, so there was probably an inherited factor. The father was a domineering man who allowed no one in the household to question his will or to make a noise when he was in the house. The children were often forbidden to talk. The mother was attractive, protective toward the children. The patient, Mr. X, was the first of six. He was always sickly, sensitive, and had a tendency to seek refuge in physical debility. When he was around two or three years old, his brother was born. Until then, he had slept with his mother. After that, he slept with her only when ill. He always cried easily and was called a "cry baby." He witnessed his mother and father having intercourse when he was between five and six, and stood transfixed, unable to breathe, then turned and ran away terrified, yelling that his father was murdering his mother.

Dr. French, who gives further details of Mr. X's biography in the first volume of *The Integration of Behavior*, was convinced that Mr. X's dreams recapitulated the main emotional conflicts of his life. His dreams fell into series, which tended to repeat, in a variety of ways, his unconscious feelings of long ago regarding the immediate members of his family. The psychoanalytic process gradually loosened his defenses, and this caused his dreams to change. In the sequences of his dreams, he tended to express dependent cravings for his mother's love, instigated toward increasingly clear expression by the conscious desire to please his analyst, who seemed like his mother. His wish was to receive special consideration and love from her; but this inevitably led to intense jealousy, and aggressive impulses toward rivals, and therefore to great anxiety.

For example, he had an early dream of trying to win a mother-figure's affection by guarding the safety of a girl, reminiscent of his younger sister. (In his history, there was a next youngest brother whom he hated, but five other siblings with whom he got along well. He customarily dreamed of being kind to his sister; this avoided the problem of homosexuality that would have resulted from displacing the first incestuous love for his mother almost solely to love of the brother.)

Mr. X's dream of being good to the daughter of the beloved mother-figure is like the fantasy of Marcel's trying to get attention from the Duchess de Guermantes through his friendship with her nephew, Robert — and also the author's attachment to the mothers of his friends when he was young, in his actual life. Proust's characters often become interested in young men through the older women, and vice versa. For example, it is Madame de Villeparisis, the cultured, elderly lady, who introduces Marcel to Robert, and it is Robert who brings Marcel closer to the Duchess de Guermantes. Charlus gets Madame de Surgis to present her sons to him. Madame Verdurin supervises the loves of Swann, Albertine, and Marcel, and in *Jean Santeuil*, Jean wins the protection of the Duchess de Réveillon, his friend's mother, and thus becomes established socially and makes further contacts.

Similarly, Mr. X's wish to win the affection of mother-figures, and anxiety over separation from them, dominated his emotional life and his dream patterns. His relation to his brothers and sisters was based on the erotization of aggression toward most of them, always in accordance with the degree of his hope of pleasing protective parental figures. His negative feelings were mainly projected onto the one brother who was next youngest.

To go back to Proust, we see in Marcel that the more hope he has of a mother-figure's approval of him, the more he can allow himself to love a sibling image. Madame Verdurin invites him to her home at the cost of being enthusiastic about all her other guests. At the same time Madame Verdurin always has some object of her derision, like Saniette, and even Elstir, in the old days, when she called him Master Tiche (like the one sibling on whom Mr. X concentrated his hatred and projected guilt and shame).

Madame Verdurin and the Duchess de Guermantes are both very lenient about sexual aberrations. The author's own guilt is thus relieved in his fantasy. In Mr. X's dreams, also, we see how he unconsciously wished for similar leniency from his psychoanalyst.

Madame Verdurin and the Duchess appreciate artistic genius and personal charm and are inclined to be tolerant of eccentricities. There is always a constant flow of forgiving love directed toward Marcel, or promised him, until Albertine leaves, and then this cycle is broken up and has to be re-established in different ways. But love, in Proust's work, always runs a course that develops rapidly into a fear of separation, connected with unconscious fear of outbursts of aggression toward rivals and flight to a series of new love-objects, or else diversion to a projected image of homosexuality, spied upon. All these changing patterns of love's intermittances are dominated by the women who run the salons and the matriarchs of Marcel's family — even Aunt Léonie, whose

sofa, given to the house of prostitution where Rachel func-
tioned as a denizen, made Marcel cold and frightened at its
austerity in the bawdy surroundings.

Proust's constant preoccupation with social exclusion and
inclusion, in the salons, and acceptance and refusal as a lover,
is astonishingly similar to Mr. X's constant pressure to win his
mother's love by adjusting his impulses toward a sibling,
erotizing his aggression, in order to retain his mother's good
will. Mr. X also was always in danger of provoking his
mother's wrath, through his incestuously tinged, sexual impulses toward her or toward his siblings. His dreams show
this similarity of pattern to all of Proust's stories and his novel.

The homosexual girls exhibiting at the hotel, and those
who are excluded from salons because they are Dreyfusards
but later accepted again because they are pro-French and anti-
German during World War I, are just a few examples of
Proust's constant preoccupation with the theme of how far
one can express erotic, hostile, or unpopular feelings and not
be ostracized. Proust also employed Mr. X's expedient of pro-
jecting rejection to others: as when Morel screams vitupera-
tively at Jupien's niece, when he learns that she has once been
illegitimately pregnant. How to remain beloved and admired
by all, in spite of one's unconscious infantile incestuous urges,
which also have to do with the destruction of sibling rivals
and father-figures and with mysterious preverbal, infantile-
perverse impulses regarding the mother's body, is at the core
of *Remembrance of Things Past* and of Mr. X's dreams. The
father as rival is dealt with least; active competition gives
way to muscular contraction, a paralyzed, breathless attitude,
and increased sensory perceptivity.

None of Mr. X's dreams succeed in satisfying all his conflicting needs with one pattern. We find in his dreams a series
of partial solutions, each seeking to reconcile some of his un-

conscious, conflicting needs, but leaving other unconscious needs out of account. We find, similarly, that each phase of Proust's novel deals with a partial solution of the old problems of oedipal and inverted oedipal guilt, and then proceeds to the next attempt at solution, the next theme — but in Proust the patterns are all made one, and supplement each other; they are united in form, demonstrating that harmony can exist, when art, or insight, triumphs over time and what we consider "reality."

Mr. X's dreams, as they occurred to him subjectively, made little sense to him. But as we read Dr. French's careful study, we see how they fall, according to Dr. French's analyses of them, into patterns as crystalline as Proust's, and with similar emotional logic.

Mr. X, in the course of his analysis, gradually began to comprehend how his erotic and aggressive impulses habitually threatened him with loss of his mother's love. He was beset with unconscious aggression toward rivals, and compulsively tried to mitigate his hostility by turning it to erotic approaches. But he felt his mother would not tolerate either his sex life or his aggression. He therefore had a tendency which he himself could not explain, to take flight from the women on whom he was most dependent. This is like Marcel's wish to leave Albertine and go to Venice without her. Marcel, in his reunion with his mother at the Venice railroad station, is again like Mr. X who finds a compromise between his fear and dependence, very often, by fleeing from one beloved individual to another (also like the Albertine-Marcel and Charlus-Morel themes so interwoven that when the author tells us about one pair, he constantly breaks the narrative to tell us about the other two).

Later Mr. X, watching at a safe distance, sees in a dream the beating of an iron bar by his mother. This is an expres-

sion of his own sado-masochism, as in the scene of Marcel spying on Charlus who is being beaten. As Dr. French comments,
"verbs are one-act plays whose dramatis personae can be interchanged at will." [5] In Mr. X's dreams and in Proust's writing, no single representation is satisfactory for long. Yet the
total pattern, mobile, constantly shifting, leaves us with remarkable consistency of core. The characters change, the
verbs remain the same. Many varied actors and inanimate
objects are set forth in a harmonious pattern of activity. Rivals always arouse aggressive impulses which are erotized and
are immediately translated to impulses to flee because of
threatened frustration of dependent urges. Frustrated rage
at the parents then tends to break down, physiologically, into
the inhibited angry, vituperative cry and soiling tendencies
which are paralyzed in the helplessness of the asthmatic attack.

The impulse to beat rivals is frequently turned by both Mr.
X and Marcel Proust back upon themselves. Outward physical gestures are held back more in Proust than in Mr. X. In
both of these men, *walking* occurred as an erotic approach
and then was inhibited.

In Proust's work, we often see a subtle, gratifying attempt
to solve the problem of rivalry by thinking of mother-figures'
competition among themselves, as in the Cambremer and Verdurin salons, where they vie desperately for social adherents.

We marvel at how his intellect and imagination provided
projections and condensations which fitted the needs of his
art. But similar projections and condensations were created
nightly, apparently, in the dreams of the far less gifted Mr. X.
What Mr. X did on a primitive level in sleep, Proust, who had
insomnia, did through his concentrated efforts. Proust labor-
iously fitted together the pieces garnered with painstaking
"research" from his unconscious, making his "universe" for

[5] *The Integration of Behavior,* Vol. II, p. 162.

others to understand. Mr. X, through a great deal of real sincerity in his approach to free-association and the telling of his dreams and feelings, attempted to communicate to his therapist what was in his unconscious and to accept the insight, derived from psychoanalytic interpretations. This patient felt that by communicating his conflicts verbally, he was able to win the analyst's approval and interest. As a research patient, he had an altruistic as well as therapeutic urge and made the utmost effort to be honest, just as Proust was painfully honest and sincere. Both Proust and Mr. X invested their credulity in the urge of the unconscious to find a means of communicating itself, no matter how contradictory, trivial, puerile, or paradoxical their thoughts.

Mr. X found that the time when he actually began to lose interest in his wife and to become severely ill was when she became pregnant. He had married to find a mother. His relationships repeated sibling and mother relationships of old, and avoided conflict with father-figures. Toward the end of his analysis, Mr. X blamed all his troubles on excessive jealousy, as did Marcel, in the novel.

Some of Mr. X's images were somewhat Proustian, as Mr. X's dream of the lady blacksmith beating the iron bar, which recalls Proust's image of the cook in the kitchen as a female "Vulcan"; [6] Mr. X's two later dreams of pulling up grass,[7] and Marcel's quotation, "Grass must grow and children must die," so prominent at the end of *Remembrance of Things Past;* the abundance of water and womb symbolism in Mr. X's dreams, as in Proust's work; the prominence of train symbols in both of these men — are examples. Water symbolism predominates in the imagery of both.

As an example of similarity to Proust's fundamental

---

[6] *Jean Santeuil,* Vol. I, p. 215.
[7] French, *The Integration of Behavior.* Mr. X associated to pulling the grass, robbing his mother of his siblings.

imagery, the following dream typifies Mr. X's use of train
symbolism in his dreams:

> [Mr. X] dreamed he was in open country and witnessed a
> troop train turning over. There were six cars that turned over,
> and he could see the heads of soldiers sticking out of the win-
> dows. He associated to a woman, and the heads were like the
> heads of babies sticking out of the woman. There were doctors
> and nurses. Later, he spoke of the soldiers as symbols of youth
> and manhood.[8]

The interpretation of the dream, made by the analyst, Dr.
McLean, referred to Mr. X's fear of sexual freedom (to which
he had likened the open country). The six cars referred to the
six pregnancies of Mr. X's mother (according to his associations).

After this dream, Mr. X discussed his impotence. He was
potent only with prostitutes, and then not always; he had a
desire for a "higher type of woman" but was afraid. He recalled how in childhood he used to sleep with his mother.

Mr. X's robbing tendencies were turned to their opposite
by his unconscious guilt, and they stimulated a tendency to
get rid of his own money, even in his dreams. Strangely
enough, Proust's compulsion to lose his money was recounted
at a ball, to Princess Bibesco.[9] This brings to mind, also,
Proust's lavish tipping and gift-giving, and his reiteration, in
the novel, of how men are depleted of money, by giving it to
the women they love.[10] (All of this money and gift-giving is
probably related unconsciously — as the psychoanalyst readily
recognizes — to sublimated infantile anal erotism and anal
birth theories. The latter phrases would probably have been
avoided by Proust; yet he intuitively, in a more poetic form,

---

[8] *Ibid.*, Vol. II, pp. 90–91.
[9] Marthe Bibesco, *Au Bal avec Marcel Proust*, Paris, 1928.
[10] *The Sweet Cheat Gone*, p. 277; see reference to being robbed.

conveyed similar concepts: for example, in regard to the comfort station "Marquise.")

The orgy of the patrons of Jupien's Temple of Dishonor, in *The Past Recaptured*, in the underground tunnel during air raids, links Proust's images of trains, and sexuality, in a way that is close to consciousness. Trains bring new arrivals and also take people away: they are a combined symbol of birth and death. Trains suited superficial aspects of Proust's story, but — more to the point — they were a spontaneous symbolic expression of his emotions. Charlus first meets Morel at a railroad station. Marcel's envy of Albertine regarding Robert is on a train, as is Bloch's affair with Odette. And the separation and reunion of Marcel and his mother are at trains. Trains are related to time, death, birth, and sexuality.

As in Mr. X, also in Proust's work, water symbolism is connected with hope of pleasing and winning mother-figures.[11] For example, when Marcel sees the Princess de Guermantes at the theater and she smiles to him, she wears ornaments as from the sea in her hair. Sea symbolism is connected with Marcel's drinking and his pleasure, in Robert's company, at the wonderful restaurant at Rivebelle, and with his meeting Albertine. Also sea symbolism is connected with Proust's first exposition of the feeling of nostalgia, related to the storm at Penmarch, in *Jean Santeuil*, where he says that every man has his Penmarch.

But when Marcel (or Jean) finds a woman to love, he always has to share her. Robert tends to share women with Marcel after he, Robert, is no longer interested. Like Marcel, Robert takes flight from person to person.

---

[11] Sigmund Freud, *New Introductory Lectures on Psychoanalysis*, New York, 1933, p. 122. In talking of separation fear and love for the mother, or her substitute, Freud states, "I might mention, incidentally, that the common phantasy of returning into the womb is a substitute for this desire for coitus."

When Robert is alone with Albertine, on just one occasion, Marcel is jealous.

As French points out in Mr. X, whenever there is great separation fear the ego's integrative span is less, and there is less sharing. We find this same principle in the novel.

In both Mr. X's and Proust's unconscious life, fear of offending mother-figures, because of sexual or aggressive urges, leads to an impulse to take flight from the provocative situation, and this in turn creates intense fear of separation from the mother. This is the basis of a constantly repeated pattern.

Conversation, to keep the interest of parental figures, tends to degenerate, in both, under stress, to vituperation (for which Charlus, in the novel, is so famous — also Morel).

The disintegration of the hope of pleasing mother-figures, and of the flight mechanism which would cause separation from these mother-figures, the need to confess, to weep, to expiate, to be forgiven, shown clearly in the early chapters of *Jean Santeuil*, are typical of Mr. X and of Proust. As invalids, somewhat paralyzed in their muscular activities through illness, they took flight into changing imagery, and they were spellbound, particularly by trains and longings for travel which they felt unequipped to carry to consummation.

There is not the slightest hint of Marcel's being homosexually interested in Charlus. Nevertheless he did have an impulse to kiss the hand of Norpois, similar to Jean's impulse to kiss the hand of the young doctor, Servais, in *Jean Santeuil*. Both Norpois and Servais were looked upon as cruel, but at the same time, they were unexpectedly kind. Similarly, we see Mr. X's hesitant struggles to deal with his homosexual impulses toward his stern father.

Most deeply repressed, in Mr. X, was his fearful, but cogent wish to win the love of his virile, powerful father. (This reminds us of Charlus's secret, unfulfilled longings for a truly masculine lover. Charlus always had to be satisfied with far too weak a man.)

Both Proust and Mr. X seemed convinced that love is really a form of suffering. In the unconscious imagery of both, people who love are made to endure agonies.[12]

Proust gives us hints, in the course of the novel, that his love for his father, like the unspoken love of his mother for her own father, is the strong "silent beat" in the musical pattern of his writing. In both Proust, and Mr. X, on the surface of the patterns, the mother seems to take over the complete scene, as avenger and love-object. The father is too frightening. In *Jean Santeuil*, written while Proust's father was alive, there are several references to "sleeping," unexpressed filial love for him. (See Appendix A.)

The actual dreams of Mr. X altered as he was able to penetrate more deeply into his own unconscious, and he attempted to adapt himself more to reality.[13] His integrative capacity was greatest in times of hope, whether expressed in fantasy, dream, or action. Proust's characters show a similar response to hope. When there was less hope of receiving motherly love, aggression, particularly toward brother-images, was inclined to break through.

Proust and Mr. X demonstrated the similarities to which we have drawn attention, probably because (1) they had in common certain basic personality traits connected with their tendency toward asthma on a neurotic basis, and (2) because universal, unconscious symbols seem to be expressed in the dreams of the one, the art of the other.

[12] *The Past Recaptured*, p. 395. Here Marcel's final solution, to become lost in his work, is likened by him to the love of a dying mother who must still fulfill the task of caring for her son.
[13] Mina Curtiss, *Letters of Marcel Proust*, p. 286. Proust refers to "adaptation to reality" in a letter Nov. or Dec. 1915 to Marie Scheikévitch.

Apparently symbolic pattern-formations tend to follow a certain amount of orderliness; some are typical of a group (such as a subclass of asthmatics), some universal. The similarities between Mr. X and Proust, stressed here, should not give the impression that they were expressed identically, or that the two men were at all alike in personality, in their daily lives.

The most marked contrasts between them, in addition to the obvious antithesis between Proust's genius and Mr. X's inarticulate nature and their social and educational disparities, were based upon Proust's overt homosexuality, derived probably from his unconscious feelings toward brother-images — while Mr. X's unconscious erotized and aggressive feelings were focused very largely on sister-images. Mr. X was vastly more inhibited mentally, but less ill physically. Mr. X's need to please his therapist was on quite a different level from Proust's extreme need for popularity in French society. And Mr. X paid off his conscience by being kind to his wife and children, whereas Proust tried to fulfill parental demands upon him by the labors of his writing, and also identified mainly with his mother in this arduous creative process.

Still there is a simple core in each, of dependent love, jealousy, paralysis in dealing with active urges or competitive aggression, and intense fear of impulses toward flight.

If Dr. French's assumptions are correct, then Mr. X's patterns give us some insight into how the unconscious tends to express itself, even in the genius of Proust. By-passing the idea of stream-of-consciousness writing, as a chaotic, free-flowing release, Proust was ahead of his time, because he sought to communicate unconscious feelings in a highly structuralized form. The stream-of-consciousness is composed of conscious bits. Associations as used by Proust succeeded in luring repressed emotions into verbalization, in the form of

lucid patterns, decipherable so far as one can interpret unconscious symbolism. The psychoanalyst, accustomed to ob-
serving unconscious patterns of behavior or verbalization in
others, in therapeutic treatment, is struck by Proust's ability
to portray similar unconscious mechanisms. Proust's ability
must have derived mainly from intuitive sources.

What we do not remember consciously, we are compelled
to express symbolically, or to act out. What Proust did not
recall consciously, he wove into patterns, following an aesthetic urge.

At the end of *The Past Recaptured*, we have Marcel's rise,
as the guest of Madame Verdurin, to the highest salon of
Paris, but he professes indifference to his social success. Nevertheless it is at her door, where all the successful artists of Paris
and the world are drawn, that Marcel feels reassured that he
can unite himself with the best of his past memories. He
feels blissful,[14] because of his power of recollection, just
when his legs temporarily fail him, and he is embarrassed about
being seen purposely repeating his stumbling motion in order
to woo memories. Memories seem to come to him passively,
but he indicates that his whole manner of living and thinking
has painstakingly prepared the way for them.[15] He has driven
himself into the keenest cultivation of sensitivities and insight.
(This assiduous tracking down of the unconscious stimulates
the recovery of lost memories, also, in psychoanalysis.)

The learning process [16] is connected with memory and with

[14] See *Jean Santeuil*, Vol. II, p. 227; here the odor of the waiter's napkin
reminds him of his mother putting him to bed in clean white nightshirt,
clean white sheets.

[15] Thomas M. French, *The Integration of Behavior*, Vol. I, p. 94. Here
French shows how past memories are disturbing and distort the present perceptions and reactions.

[16] Stanley Cobb states in a symposium on The Brain and the Mind, in
1952, "I propose that of all the anatomical and physiological properties of the
brain touched on in this review, the area most appropriately considered as

symbolism. Symbolism seems to determine the form memory takes. This process has never been presented more lucidly than in psychoanalytic case histories, and in the very rare artistic attempts at complete self-revelation, such as we find in Proust's work.

Let us turn to the example of another great literary artist. In an essay on Dostoevsky Freud has come to a conclusion about Dostoevsky's seizures. These spells of unconsciousness were brought on by the fear of death and consisted of a lethargic somnolent condition, which Freud felt must have been connected with a death-wish against the father, identification with the father in death, and at the same time an effeminate, passive love for the father.

> . . . The child understands that he must suffer castration if he wants to be loved by the father as a woman. Thus, both impulses, hatred for the father and being in love with the father, become repressed. There is a certain psychological difference in the fact that the hatred of the father is abandoned in consequence of the fear of an external danger (castration), while the amorous feeling toward the father is treated as an inward impulse danger, although fundamentally it goes back to the above-mentioned external danger.
>
> What makes hatred for the father untenable is fear of the father: castration is terrible, both as a punishment and as the price of love. Of the two factors which repress the hatred of the father, the first, the direct dread of punishment and castration, may be called the normal one, the pathogeneous

mind is the integration itself, the relationship of one functioning part . . . to another." "On the Nature and Locus of Mind," *Archives of Neurology and Psychiatry* (Feb. 1952), Vol. 67, No. 2, pp. 176–77.

See also J. Z. Young, *Doubt and Certainty in Science*. In Young's experiments it is demonstrated that an ability to develop memory, on a symbolic basis, is apparently inherent in protoplasm. His experiments on the octopus, which developed apart from vertebrates, show a primitive form of "learning process."

reinforcement seems to come only with the second factor, the fear of the feminine attitude. Thus a strong bisexual predisposition becomes one of the conditions or confirmations of the neuroses. Such a predisposition must certainly be assumed in Dostoevsky . . .[17]

Freud goes on to demonstrate how the violent nature of Dostoevsky's father established the violence of his own attitudes as a novelist, and the extreme submission, in part toward his own super-ego, inherent in his seizures, which restrained him from action. (In Dostoevsky and in Proust, fantasy frequently substituted for violent or conflictful actions.)

We may contrast Dostoevsky's orientation toward his father with that of Marcel Proust, whose mother and grandmother took over the dominating roles, much of the time, in his early development. In Proust, as in Mr. X, it seems that the asthma was closely connected with a fear of feminine, submissive drives toward a too awe-inspiring father figure, but there always had to be a mother-figure nearby, for whom to call out, and identification with a maternal super-ego within, as a refuge — or a female "Vulcan" to exact punishment, inspiring at the same time, a fear of strangulation.[18]

[17] Sigmund Freud, "Dostoevsky and Parricide" (transl. D. F. Tait) from *Stavrogin's Confession*, by F. M. Dostoevsky, transl. Virginia Woolf and S. S. Koteliansky, New York, Lear Publishers, 1947, p. 98. By permission of Crown Publishers, Inc.

Also see Sigmund Freud: "Dostoevsky and Parricide" (transl. D. F. Tait), *Collected Papers*, Vol. V, London, Hogarth, 1950.

[18] Marcel Proust: *The Past Recaptured*, page 236. The author refers to a reliving of past suffering in a general form which enables us "to escape its strangling grip, makes the whole world share in our suffering with us and is not without even a certain joy. When life walls us in, our intelligence cuts an opening."

X V

How Memory Functions During Psychoanalysis

In daily life we are made aware of the compartmentaliza-
tion of our memories. When we try to think through a problem, we are accustomed to the alternations between logical
reasoning and a more passive free-floating attempt to woo
memories and impressions, in order to permit intuitive thought
to function as a process supplementary to logical deduction.
Memories sometimes come to us when we try to evoke them,
but if we are blocked they may later arrive unsummoned, having worked their way through a series of mental patterns.
Sometimes false memories seem very real.

Why is memory so wayward, and how does psychoanalytic
technique overcome the reluctance of memory? Patterns are
evoked via free-association and dreams, and form their own
special sort of communication, through which memories flow,
along with "transference" feelings and a certain amount of
"acting out" in daily life (the "acting out" is due to the force
of repressed memory that wells up and expresses itself in
action).

Each psychoanalysis is like the creation of an elaborate
means of private communication, a new language which the
analyst must learn, with each new patient.

By contrast, what we find so remarkable in writers of the caliber of Proust, or Dostoevsky, whom Proust so much respected, is the expression of universal human nature in the precise vision of a unique, never-to-be-duplicated individual's scheme of things.

Memory plays an important role, both in literary communication and in forming the substance of free-associations and dreams, in psychoanalysis.

In psychoanalytic work, the relationship between past conflicts and current ones is always of prime importance.

Freud originally developed the concept of fixation to traumatic memories.[1] In psychoanalysis, we often see that traumatic memories are repressed, but the affect connected with them appears in current life. Memories may be a disguise for the past traumatic fixation, a flight from it, or an expression of anxiety regarding the trauma — in other words, memories serve very many purposes.

When we are dealing with analytic patients, it is sometimes possible for the patients to induce the therapists to work on a genetic reconstruction of the past in order to avoid the analysis of current emotional problems which the patient finds it difficult to discuss. The current emotional problems which the patient is trying to solve, or to avoid solving, arouse affects related to repressed memories, to which he reverts, and the defenses against forgotten impulses or urges. To digress from Proust, somewhat, a brief and simple example is the following:

A young man was drafted into the army while in analysis. Consciously, he was willing to do his duty, but he was also extremely reluctant to give up his more comfortable existence. In one of the last hours before leaving, he recalled a memory of kindergarten days when he felt that he could not please the teacher. Here, the difficulty in current life was handled

[1] Sigmund Freud, *Beyond the Pleasure Principle*, London, 1922.

by regression to a situation in which he did not feel responsible
for his behavior because he was too young. When this was
pointed out to him, he admitted he had held back a wish that
the analyst should do something to prevent his being drafted,
and he confessed great annoyance at the analyst for permitting him to be drafted. He had been disgruntled, and had
turned it around — to his inability to please the kindergarten
teacher, in a memory.

Even in this simple example, one sees how distortion and
denial, reflected to the past, operate as defenses against conflicts in the painful present.

Important memories that come up during a psychoanalytic
interview are frequently not parallel, but complementary to,
the main present conflict.

As Freud stated in his paper on Repetition and Recollection,[2] some of the most cogent memories are often not recollected at all. They may take the form of screen memories and
the repressed affect is displaced onto the screen memories or
may be found repeatedly expressed in neurotic symptoms or
character defenses without these memories returning.

In psychoanalysis, when an important piece of therapeutic
work has been accomplished, and the affect associated with a
repressed memory has been worked through, the patient may
react to correct interpretations by a recovery of memories
which confirm the interpretation, and these memories may
hardly need much further elucidation from the analyst.

At other times, patients may attempt to use important
memories during interviews mainly as a defense, in order to
get away from dealing with emotional conflicts in a current
situation. During the analysis of their transference problems,
patients may resort to a retreat to past problems, again using
their evocation of memory as a defense.

[2] Sigmund Freud, *Collected Papers*, Vol. II (written 1914).

Actually, closer inspection of the use of memory will in each case demonstrate that not only is the memory connected with an attempt to solve an analogous problem, but it also demonstrates the emotion with which the patient cannot cope; the memory indicates the general way in which he tries to deal with this affect. (One might speak of the relationship between past memories and their utilization in connection with the handling of current conflicts as related integrative patterns.)

Sometimes memories serve the purpose of "resistance," very strikingly, in analysis. For example, one woman patient went back to a very pleasant memory from the age of three or four, of lying in bed and feeling happy. This memory was evoked by envy, aroused by her mother's visit to her sister in another city, in the current scene. During this time, the patient had been particularly annoyed with her small son, anxious to make him a "perfect specimen," ignoring the boy's needs for instinctual expression, because she was actually competing with her sister in raising children, in order to please her own mother. The sister had three children and the patient only one.

Instead of dealing with all her current conflicts in regard to her son and household, it was easier to go back to a past, passive memory, a nostalgic one, of being three years old and well loved by the mother, for taking a nap and doing nothing. As the analysis developed, this patient struggled against revealing transference feelings which were related to rivalry with her sister. Her envy began to come out in the form of intense curiosity and jealousy in regard to other women whom she considered rivals in the present. Strong, repressed childhood interest in her father was also involved, producing anxiety because it threatened her dependent relationship to her mother and was carried over to women in the current scene.

This patient had come to analysis secretly determined never to have any transference feelings. It was not until months later that she actually admitted great curiosity and envy, connected with the analyst. This demonstrates how one of the simplest types of retreat to early memory serves to hold back from consciousness a great deal of current, and past emotional conflict. The innocence of the memory contrasts with the violence and forbidden nature of the repressed feelings imbedded in it. This is how highly charged patterns of emotion may be expressed in visual images, in memories. Therefore when Proust defined literary style as a matter of "vision," he seems to have been aware of the great emotional charge implied when the term is applied to patterns of memory brought to the mind by visual imagery.

There is close connection between the memories evoked during psychoanalytic treatment and current dreams, as they show different facets of a problem, in various integrative stages. In analysis, after the central conflict has been ascertained, there remains the patient's task of dealing consciously with real, current problems. In Proust's novel, his central problems were the prime core, and from his own conflicts proliferated the variations of his narrative.

As French demonstrates, in the struggle for integration the relief of some of the pressure from one goal-directed impulse, as evidenced in memories, evokes another pressure from another related drive. If one aspect of a patient's problem comes to the fore, it sets off related problems, and we see this in the interplay of past memories and present conflicts and transference, during psychoanalytic treatment. We see something similar in the working out of Proust's complicated psychodynamic relationships in his novel.

The goal of the psychoanalytic process is the patient's insight and an alteration in his essential patterns of reaction. We

are therefore dealing in psychoanalysis with something related, in part, to literary art, such as Proust attempted it. The
communication of essential emotional patterns, with their more
or less universal implications, in psychoanalysis, as in Proust's
art, delineates one individual's path of progress, or of flux and
change. As Proust has apparently woven some versions of his
memories and of his current reality into a crystalline pattern,
there is conviction in what he writes. Unlike an analysis, in
Proust's work the end seems to lead back to the beginning.
Proust gives us static form in the midst of constant flux, and
we have an aesthetic goal, as contrasted with the drastic
changes we hope for in psychoanalytic treatment. Proust
seems to have had a genius for understanding the way the
mnemonic process actually works. He used memories, also
dreams, to serve his aesthetic purposes, primarily. Secondarily
he utilized true clinical observations as part of his fantasy,
creating a challenging puzzle for psychiatrists to decipher.

Proust makes it clear that memory unfolds in patterns. If
we strike the right sensory keys to recall, these emotional
patterns may emerge from the unconscious into poetic images,
and may become the substance of art. "Marcel's" memories,
voluntary and involuntary, constitute the novel.

The author tells us:

> ... What we call reality is a certain relationship between ...
> sensations and the memories which surround us at the same
> time (a relationship that is destroyed by a bare cinemato-
> graphic presentation, which gets further away from the truth
> the more closely it claims to adhere to it) the only true rela-
> tionship, which the writer must recapture so that he may
> forever link together in his phrase its two distinct elements.
> One may list in an interminable description the objects that
> figured in the place described, but truth will begin only when
> the writer takes two different objects, establishes their rela-

tionship — analogous in the world of art to the sole relationship in the world of science, the law of cause and effect — and
encloses them in the necessary rings of a beautiful style.[3]

By telling us Marcel's memories and his dreams, as well as
a few of the dreams of other important characters in the book,
Proust gives us intimate knowledge that allows the reader to
identify more completely with these people — since we know,
usually, only our own memories and dreams. It is interesting
to note that Proust concentrates on telling us Marcel's screen
memories, those of the writer, who deals with his unconscious. He also tells us a few of Swann's memories, for Swann,
too, is literary, although inhibited. The memories of other
characters are rarely mentioned. But when Proust uses
dreams to further his story, which he does fairly often, and
exceedingly deftly, he tells us the dreams of Marcel, Robert
de Saint-Loup, Swann, Bergotte, Aunt Léonie, and others.
We shall examine next the way Proust utilized dreams in
order to give the reader insight into some specific side of the
character under scrutiny, something the character in the
story did not know too well about himself. All Proust's fictitious characters seem to dream and have memories and frequently do not pay much attention to them, but Marcel, who
is the most introspective, most endowed with literary genius,
analyzes his dreams and avidly pursues his screen memories [4]

[3] *The Past Recaptured*, pp. 217–218.
[4] *The Sweet Cheat Gone*, p. 313, re memory and psychosomatic illness.
In *The Past Recaptured*, toward the end, there is a series of screen memories, first of the baptistry of St. Mark's (brought on by stepping on the
uneven flagstones), later of the trees at Balbec, the spires of Martinville,
the madeleine in the tea which evoked his memories of Combray, Vinteuil's
great music — all of which banish doubt of Marcel's literary gifts. The
sound of the waiter's spoon against the plate leads to a feeling of great heat;
the odor of smoke; cool fragrance of a forest setting (see *Jean Santeuil*, re
the trees at Réveillon); the hammer of a workman repairing a train wheel.
The waiter brings in orange juice and petits fours, and Marcel, wiping his
mouth, has a vision of a bluish breast and the thought of the beach, high

until they reveal some hints of the original emotions and patterns first associated with them. This analytic process, in a race against time, is to be used as the substance of Marcel's literary achievement.

---

tide, a napkin — like the towel at Balbec the first day. He thinks of deep blue powerful light, of Venice, water in a pipe — boats — Balbec more intense and real than the original. This might be compared with Freud's statement on the way childhood innocence is resorted to as an excuse for substituting innocuous memories from the past for the present situation fraught with conflict. See Sigmund Freud "Screen Memories" (1899), *Collected Papers*, London, 1950, Vol. V, p. 54.

X V I

The Use of Dreams in Proust's Novel[1]

PROUST apparently thought of the characters in his writing as different aspects of himself.[2] Their histories show the relation of these aspects of himself to each other. Their dreams portray his struggles to convey his impressions of how these characters felt, in their own unconscious; that is, what they felt more deeply than they knew. Therefore the dreams of his characters are of special interest. It is an enticing problem to try to figure out how he constructed these dreams.

[1] Sigmund Freud, *The Basic Writings of Sigmund Freud*, transl. and ed. with introd. by A. A. Brill, Mod. Libr. Ed., New York, 1938, p. 954. "Another path led from the investigation of dreams to the analysis of poetic creations and finally, to the analysis of authors and artists themselves. Very soon, it was discovered that the dreams invented by writers stand in the same relation to analysis as do genuine dreams. [Cf. Freud, "Der Wahn und die Traüme," in W. Jensen's *Gradiva*.] The conception of the unconscious psychic activity enabled us to get the first glimpse into the nature of the poetic creativeness. The valuation of the emotional feelings, which we were forced to recognize while studying the neuroses, enabled us to recognize the sources of artistic productions and brought up the problem as to how the artist reacts to those stimuli and with what means he disguises his reactions." See Otto Rank, *Der Künstler*, analyses of poets by Sadger, Reik and others.

[2] *Jean Santeuil*, Paris, 1952, Vol. II, p. 253. "Toutes les scènes que je vous raconte je les ai vécues" (All the scenes I recount to you, I have lived).

The child, Marcel, continued to dream recurrently of his uncle pulling his curls [3] even after the curls were cut; he also dreamed recurrently of a woman whom he longed to embrace, and with whom he wished to be unified. Both of these images are described at the beginning of *Swann's Way*. Marcel's fear of the great-uncle has persisted, in this form, but the author may or may not have intended to suggest, at the start, that Marcel's main character-defense was femininity. The uncle pulled his girlish curls in the recurrent nightmare; and later, when they were cut off, the uncle could not pull them, but the dream continued to recur. As in life, Marcel was frail and feminine, and so presumably did not need to fear the father's ire on a masculine-rivalry basis, even though he also dreamed of union (and identification) with the mother-image. This pair of dreams at the beginning gives us a special insight: pairing punishment with the idea of embracing a beloved, unknown, presumably an incestuous, object. Here, too, the defense is merged with gratification and punishment, in the dream, for Marcel becomes one with her; that is, feminine.

A long dream of Swann's, toward the end of *Swann's Way*, contains individual elements typical of Proust's basic images: the sexual symbols, renunciation of the beloved woman, conflict over separation from her.

Swann's Dream

. . . He was walking with Mme. Verdurin, Dr. Cottard, a young man in a fez whom he failed to identify, the painter, Odette, Napoleon III and my grandfather, along a path which followed the line of the coast, and overhung the sea, now at a great height, now by a few feet only, so that they were continually going up and down; those of the party who had

---

[3] *Swann's Way*, p. 3.

reached the downward slope were no longer visible to those
who were still climbing; what little daylight yet remained was
failing, and it seemed as though a black night was immediately
to fall on them. Now and then the waves dashed against the
cliff, and Swann could feel on his cheek a shower of freezing
spray. Odette told him to wipe this off, but he could not, and
felt confused and helpless in her company, as well as because
he was in his nightshirt. He hoped that, in the darkness, this
might pass unnoticed; Mme. Verdurin, however, fixed her
astonished gaze upon him for an endless moment, in which
he saw her face change its shape, her nose grow longer, while
beneath it there sprouted a heavy moustache. He turned away
to examine Odette; her cheeks were pale, with little fiery spots,
her features drawn and ringed with shadows; but she looked
back at him with eyes welling with affection, ready to detach
themselves like tears and to fall upon his face, and he felt that
he loved her so much that he would have liked to carry her
off with him at once. Suddenly Odette turned her wrist,
glanced at a tiny watch, and said: "I must go." She took leave
of everyone, in the same formal manner, without taking Swann
aside, without telling him where they were to meet that
evening, or next day. He dared not ask, he would have liked
to follow her, he was obliged, without turning back in her
direction, to answer with a smile some question by Mme.
Verdurin; but his heart was frantically beating, he felt that
he now hated Odette, he would gladly have crushed those
eyes which, a moment ago, he had loved so dearly, would have
torn the blood into those lifeless cheeks. He continued to climb
with Mme. Verdurin, that is to say that each step took him
farther from Odette, who was going downhill, and in the
other direction. A second passed and it was many hours since
she had left him. The painter remarked to Swann that Napoleon III had eclipsed himself immediately after Odette.
"They had obviously arranged it between them," he added;
"they must have agreed to meet at the foot of the cliff, but
they wouldn't say good-bye together; it might have looked

odd. She is his mistress." The strange young man burst into tears. Swann endeavoured to console him. "After all, she is quite right," he said to the young man, drying his eyes for him and taking off the fez to make him feel more at ease. "I've advised her to do that, myself, a dozen times. Why be so distressed? He was obviously the man to understand her." So Swann reasoned with himself, for the young man whom he had failed, at first, to identify, was himself also; like certain novelists, he had distributed his own personality between two characters, him who was the "first person" in the dream, and another whom he saw before him, capped with a fez.

As for Napoleon III, it was to Forcheville that some vague association of ideas, then a certain modification of the Baron's usual physiognomy, and lastly the broad ribbon of the Legion of Honour across his breast, had made Swann give that name; but actually, and in everything that the person who appeared in his dream represented and recalled to him, it was indeed Forcheville. For, from an incomplete and changing set of images, Swann in his sleep drew false deductions, enjoying, at the same time, such creative power that he was able to reproduce himself by a simple act of division, like certain lower organisms; with the warmth that he felt in his own palm he modelled the hollow of a strange hand which he thought that he was clasping, and out of feelings and impressions of which he was not yet conscious, he brought about sudden vicissitudes which, by a chain of logical sequences, would produce, at definite points in his dream, the person required to receive his love or to startle him awake. In an instant night grew black about him; an alarm rang, the inhabitants ran past him, escaping from their blazing houses; he could hear the thunder of the surging waves, and also of his own heart, which, with equal violence, was anxiously beating in his breast. Suddenly the speed of these palpitations redoubled, he felt a pain, a nausea that were inexplicable; a peasant, dreadfully burned, flung at him as he passed: "Come and ask Charlus where Odette spent the night with her friend. He used to go about with her, and

she tells him everything. It was they that started the fire."
It was his valet, come to awaken him and saying: —
   "Sir, it is eight o'clock, and the barber is here. I have told
him to call again in an hour." [4]

In *Jean Santeuil*, there is a version of this dream, with different participants in the action. Jean, who has the dream,
awakens with a pain in his chest and nausea, but upon his
awakening, resumes his ordinary life. In the second version,
in *Swann's Way*, the connection with the barber is added,
recalling to us Marcel's fearful preoccupation with his curls,
as a little boy, in his nightmares.

This long dream of Swann's seems to echo the steps by
which the author himself tried to renounce conscious fixation
on his mother and attempted to appease both parents by identifying with his mother and loving the brother, Robert. Napoleon III, who is in Swann's dream, is the illegitimate father
of Robert de Saint-Loup's commanding officer, Captain de
Borodino, as we remember if we can recall such a small detail
as the name and history of Robert de Saint-Loup's commanding officer at Doncières.[5] As in psychoanalytic treatment,
small details which are difficult to remember, or require all
sorts of special knowledge, furnish clues to understanding the
emotional impact of the symbolic images.

Proust sometimes tied up his Jewish side with the Oriental
atmosphere created in the novel (cf. the fez) and makes this
clear in *Within a Budding Grove*,[6] in connection with homosexuality, and Nissim Bernard as a sort of Jewish Charlus.
(Charlus, in the next volume, fascinated by the Jews, wants

---

   [4] *Swann's Way*, p. 490.
   [5] It is Captain de Borodino who gives Robert permission to go on leave
(to be with Rachel), just when Marcel wants Robert to be on hand to
introduce him to the Duchess de Guermantes, therefore Borodino and
Robert separate Marcel from a mother-figure, at Balbec.
   [6] Vol. II, p. 100.

to hire Bloch to beat his parents [7] so that Charlus can watch, and Marcel interprets this as both hate and love.)

In shaping the material of the dreams he inserted so meticulously into the novel, Proust seems to have used his knowledge about dreams partly to lead the reader slightly astray, for the benefit of emphasizing certain angles of the story. Still, the author's unconscious leaves its mark at the core of all these dreams.

Proust deliberately uses dreams, frequently to forecast the future course of the story, or to counterbalance parts of the narrative. For example, after Swann's dream about Odette, there comes a time when Odette is no longer such an attractive woman, to Swann. It is after this dream that Madame Verdurin begins to take over more of the story. The beloved woman, hated for her betrayal, shunned [8] because of incestuous drives, and also renounced out of submission to the father, suffers in Swann's dream a punishment aimed at her eyes, reminding us of "The Confession of a Young Girl," in that the eyes that ought not to see sexuality are damaged (and reminiscent of the punishment of Oedipus).

But in Swann's dream, Swann has noted a symbolic erection on Madame Verdurin, in the elongation of her nose and

[7] *The Guermantes Way*, p. 396 (also see *The Past Recaptured*, p. 151, re beating of an old woman).

[8] The cold spray on Swann's cheek, reminiscent of the cool pelagic spray of Penmarch, in *Jean Santeuil*, is perhaps related to the freezing of conscious heterosexual interest, in the mother and all women. Cf. the "frozen gutter" dream of Mr. X, Vol. II, p. 233, of French's *Integration of Behavior*. Mr. X dreamed of a frozen gutter when he had been suffering from asthma, indigestion, constipation, and chills. His analysis had been interrupted for a time, and before resuming treatment he had been conscious of sexual attraction to a married woman. The house with the frozen gutter in the dream reminded him of the analyst's house. The dream apparently referred to Mr. X's freezing up of his heterosexual interest. He turned toward a man who spoke to him in derogatory terms of a frozen gutter, in his dream. The frozen gutter, French suggests, is related to the water symbolism, now inhibited and "frozen."

sprouting of the heavy mustache. Here is the repression's source: One must not exhibit one's nakedness to these mother-images nor must one look at the dreaded female genital (which seems to imply castration). Instead, there is affection between men.

This dream recalls the provocative behavior or the voluntary renunciation of love, in advance, based on a deep dread of being rejected, typical of many asthmatics. But after renouncing Odette, Swann begins to be afraid of fire.[9]

The nightmarish quality of the end of Swann's dream is related to the fear of strong men and recapitulation to them, and fleeing, causing the pounding heart, pain, nausea, aimless running about, crying out — (all like an incipient asthma attack, because the consoling, protecting mother figure is gone, at the end).

We see in Marcel's earliest dream, and then Swann's dream, both connected with the barber, a turning away from hetero-

---

[9] Cf. Mr. X's dreams of passive homosexual stimulation symbolized by fire, after giving up the women.

Also see Thomas M. French, *The Integration of Behavior*, Chicago, 1952–54, Vol. II, p. 281, re the symbolism of fire and ashes. Fire gives rise to waste products, and is related to life, therefore suggests symbolism of anal sexuality. (French relates the fire dreams of Mr. X to physiological absorption of sexual excitement by tonic contraction of the lower bowel; it is suggested by French that in Mr. X's dreams fire corresponds to a desire for homosexual stimulation, that is, a feminine sexual wish.)

It is of great interest that Sir James G. Frazer, in *Myths of the Origin of Fire* (Macmillan, London, 1930), p. 220, in summing up, emphasizes the prevalence of the notion that fire was elicited from a woman's body, among primitive human beings all over the world. He considers this partly based on the actual analogy of the working of the fire drill, but also on intercourse between the sexes. This analogy is still recognized and carried out in the ritual of Brahman fire priests who kindle the sacred fire with their wives. On the night before the fire is made, the plunger or upper part of the fire drill is put in charge of the priest and the lower part is put into the charge of his wife, and the husband and wife sleep with these parts at night, the process of fire-making symbolizing coition. He considers this same analogy responsible for the fact that in primitive myths women are often considered in possession of fire before men are.

sexual urges to homosexual urges and then fear of the strong father. The attempt to solve this, in Swann's dream, is by identifying with the mother, and concentrating on loving the brother (the young man in the fez, whose hair is covered, protected). The author may have had some knowledge of dream mechanisms, suggesting knowledge of Freud's Interpretation of Dreams, and he uses this knowledge, probably in alliance with his intuition. The result is partly to reveal, partly to conceal — often merely to suggest the unconscious dynamic forces at work. It is as if Proust interpolated bits of music, or painting, where he interpolates bits of dreams, like poems or impressionistic revelations, probably constructed in part from real dreams of his own, but worked over and deliberately revised. Whatever bits of his own dreams he may have used were apparently well thought-out composites, and became intuitive illustrations, used to elucidate, disguise or allay some of the main problems, as well as to hint at their unconscious nature. We may see that at their core, the dreams in Proust's novel recapitulate again and again his own handling of his greatest conflict: to try to renounce sexuality in order to avoid offending his mother, to drive his erupting homosexual love for young boys into sublimation. Frustrated in his attempt to win his father's love, he envied his father's relationship to his brother and his mother. He always had to fight off an urge to be masochistically attacked by the strong father, burned like the peasant in Swann's dream. He projected femininity to the father — as the novel does with Charlus. Charlus is the virile-looking, attractive man originally suspected of being Odette's lover, who is proved to be feminine, beaten bloody, senile, in the end a potential murderer — finally deceased. The simplicity and consistency at the root of the complicated dreams in *Remembrance of Things Past,* as well as the entire life work of the author, is striking.

It is interesting to note that Swann, in his dream, feels in-
adequately dressed because he is in his nightshirt. At the
beginning of *Swann's Way*, we recall, it was Marcel's father
whom Marcel saw in a nightshirt, waiting for his mother to
come to bed, the night of Marcel's hysterical illness. The main
point of Swann's dream is the renunciation of sexual temptation, by giving up Odette. She is given over to a father-image
combining Charlus, Napoleon III, and Marcel's grandfather
(for whom Marcel's mother felt so much love that she rarely
spoke of it). The severe, harsh, masculine mother-image is
retained instead: Madame Verdurin. The dream ends with
homosexual love. Affection and protection are offered by
Swann to a young man in a fez, which Proust says was
Swann's self.

In regard to the young man in the fez, it should be pointed
out that in *Swann's Way*, Swann's death-wishes against
Odette had previously been made clear . . . "Sometimes he
hoped that she would die, painlessly, in some accident" . . .[10]
then Swann thinks of Mohamet II, portrayed by Bellini (presumably the wearer of a fez). Mohamet II, on finding he had
fallen madly in love with one of his wives, stabbed her to
death in order to "recover his spiritual freedom." (We may
also note the continued reference to hair and the head in
many of Proust's images of love.)

This dream of Swann's deliberately giving up Odette, followed by an image of the weeping young man consoled by
another side of himself, occurred in a simpler form in *Jean
Santeuil*.[11] It is interesting to see how this dream has been
changed in the second version. In both versions, the dreamer
has counseled the woman to go to the other man, as Marcel's
father told his wife to spend the night with Marcel, at the
beginning of the book.

[10] *Swann's Way*.
[11] Vol. III, p. 229.

Innumerable more superficial interpretations might be made in addition, but we have stressed here what appear to be the main dynamics of Swann's dream: renunciation of the incestuously loved woman, in favor of homosexuality.

Marcel has a vague dream of being punished with a bastinado and other strange forms of Oriental torture, in *Within a Budding Grove.*[12] Upon awakening, Marcel says this dream was caused by drinking too much port wine; the night before, he had been "an empty vessel." It is here that he likens dreams to projections on a slide by a magic lantern.[13] Before going to sleep, Marcel had dined at Rivebelle with Robert de Saint-Loup, his newly discovered, much idealized friend. In every girl at Rivebelle he had seen a potential or a past mistress of Robert's, and had heard it whispered, "Some girls do have all the luck" . . . "you would jump into the fire for a man like that." Although not consciously aware of his competitiveness with women for Robert, he felt in the bastinado dream that he had committed a crime and did not know what it was. This was probably a punishment dream for his competitive aggression toward women, also for his guilt over emerging feelings of sexual temptation. He is adolescent. He is just beginning to notice the frieze of girls at the beach, and will later fall in love with Albertine, in fact he is beginning to do so. Charlus has just been introduced into the story, a handsome man, with a black mustache, very attractive to women.

Dreams, like rubrics, interpret important turning points in Proust's novel, but may pass relatively unnoticed, as "just a dream," on first reading, when one wants to get on with the narrative. Actually, the author usually rationalizes the content of the dream or uses the dream to explain something about the general psychology of dreams and their interpreta-

---

[12] Pt. II, p. 166.
[13] Bertram D. Lewin, "Reconsideration of the Dream Screen," *Psychoanalytic Quarterly*, XXII, 2 (1953), p. 197.

tion, drawing attention away from personal aspects that might
be too deeply interpreted, such as blaming the bastinado
dream entirely upon the wine, rather than upon Marcel's
masochistic reaction to mobilized aggression toward feminine
rivals.

One of his most interesting comments is made about day-
dreams: "Dreams are not to be converted into reality, that we
know; we would not form any perhaps, were it not for desire,
and it is useful to us to form them in order to see them fail
and to be instructed by their failure." [14]

Whether he writes of dreams or recounts his narrative, the
author never permits himself to take refuge in pure intellect,
or in conventional, factual description. He evokes feelings
that are almost too intense to bear. These conflictful feelings
are then assuaged by the beauty of the pattern in which they
are presented. His dreams are distillations; still they are typical dreams, as composite as actual dreams. They serve various
levels of purposes, as do all the images in the long novel.
Each dream has its nexus with larger realities. (Marcel is
beaten in the bastinado dream and later sees Charlus beaten.
Charlus wishes to hire Bloch to beat his parents, but actually
hires a torturer for himself. Thus the dreams, wishes, and
activities of the book ricochet, reversing the roles of various
individuals.)

The renunciation of love for Gilberte is begun with a
dream, in *Within a Budding Grove*. Here Marcel comments
upon the "loved, the regretted creature, at one moment so
intensely hateful that one has no longer the slightest desire
to see her, since before finding enjoyment in her company one
would have first to make her suffer." [15]

Robert de Saint-Loup's dream of his mistress having an
orgasm with another man, a rich and vicious subaltern, in

[14] *The Captive*, p. 244.
[15] Pt. I, p. 289.

the house where Saint-Loup is the guest of the Sergeant-Major, is a dream of jealousy, and fear of impotence; it is a dream of homosexual conflict, envy of the other's potency, and repressed identification with the female. Later we shall see it forecasts correctly; Robert de Saint-Loup becomes a homosexual. But when Robert awakens from this dream, he says, quite breathlessly, "It was an idiotic dream." [16]

Marcel's dream of a cathedral, in *The Guermantes Way*,[17] an Oriental edifice in the sea, and his own nakedness, and his longing to attain the impossible, seems to refer to his writing. He connects it with the great allegorical figure of Sleep. His association is to the figures of which Swann had given him photographs — figures by Giotto, especially the one which portrays Envy, with a serpent in her mouth.[18]

Shortly after this dream, the narrative shows us how Robert de Saint-Loup, who has access to the highest aristocratic society, by reason of his noble birth, and is therefore enviable, is not helpful to Marcel. Marcel, lost in hopeless admiration of the Duchess de Guermantes, will not be introduced to her by Robert so graciously as he had anticipated. At this time Marcel's hopeless ambition to become a great writer is unattainable; he feels unequipped; envy interferes with activity.

Although Robert has had a dream of being separated from his mistress, Rachel, Robert is actually the one who, at this time, refuses to unite Marcel and the Duchess de Guermantes. Marcel asks Robert to get him invited to the Duchess's home to see her Elstir paintings, specifically one of "a real thaw." Robert goes off with Rachel, instead, having been granted permission by Captain de Borodino to go on leave.

The author tells us in *The Guermantes Way*, "What one

[16] *The Guermantes Way*, Pt. I, p. 163.
[17] Pt. I, p. 195.
[18] Cf. the image of the python about to swallow the lion in a cage, when Albertine leaves Marcel.

has meant to do during the day, as it turns out, sleep inter-
vening, one accomplishes only in one's dreams, that is to say
after it has been distorted by sleep into following another line
than one would have chosen when awake." [19] He goes on to
discuss the contradictions to the laws of thought which one
finds in sleep, and the preparation of the "hell-broth of imaginary maladies or of the recurrence of nervous disorders."
Here he discusses the effects of various sedative drugs, drawing floral analogies.

Later, in *Cities of the Plain,* he describes a refreshing dream,
which he found stimulating because it was quite the reverse
of any actual possibilities:

"M. de Charlus was a hundred and ten years old, and had
just boxed the ears of his own mother, Mme. Verdurin, because she had paid five thousand millions for a bunch of vio-
lets; I was therefore assured that I had slept profoundly, had
dreamed the reverse of what had been in my thoughts over-
night . . ." [20]

The nonsensical quality of this dream translates itself into
a telegraphic message only if one is thoroughly acquainted
with the novel, and scrutinizes what follows the dream. After
telling it, Marcel says his mother would have been astonished
if he told her Charlus had invited a footman to dinner in a
private room at the Grant Hotel at Balbec. This refers to
a confession of Charlus's homosexuality, not Marcel's, to
Madame Verdurin, who countenances it; it is only a slap at
Madame Verdurin, and not an offense to Marcel's own
mother; it is a father-image and not Marcel who is homosexual; and it is Madame Verdurin who has done wrong, spent
too much for flowers (which are related to sexual imagery
in Proust's writing). Next, Marcel mentions ordering an ex-

[19] Pp. 109–10 (See note at end of chapter).
[20] *Cities of the Plain,* Pt. II, pp. 181–82.

pensive hat for Albertine, thus letting slip the fact that he, like Madame Verdurin in the dream, is extravagant. The hitting, of course, is a theme often connected with Charlus.

In *Cities of the Plain*, Marcel has some very sad dreams about his dead grandmother, in which there is doubt about whether or not she is really dead, but if she is alive, she is apparently ill and suffering. He says:

> . . . for as the dead exist only in us, it is ourselves that we strike without ceasing when we persist in recalling the blows that we have dealt them" . . . "I felt that I did not really recall her save by grief and should have liked to feel driven yet deeper into me these nails which fastened the memory of her to my consciousness . . ."

> World of sleep in which our inner consciousness, placed in bondage to the disturbances of our organs, quickens the rhythm of heart or breath because a similar dose of terror, sorrow, remorse acts with a strength magnified an hundred fold if it is thus injected into our veins; as soon as, to traverse the arteries of the subterranean city, we have embarked upon the dark current of our own blood as upon an inward Lethe meandering sixfold, huge solemn forms appear to us, approach and glide away, leaving us in tears. I sought in vain for my grandmother's form when I had stepped ashore beneath the sombre portals; I knew, indeed that she did still exist, but with a diminished vitality, as pale as that of memory . . . my father, who was to take me to where she was, did not appear. Suddenly my breath failed me . . . "Great God!" I said to myself, "how wretched she must be in that little room . . . I must run to see her . . . the wind is keeping me back . . ." [21] [He awakens feeling crushed, as beneath a huge bell of bluish glass.]

A few pages later, in another dream of his grandmother, he says, "I could hear her breathe . . . But in vain might I take

[21] Pt. I, pp. 222–24. (These dreams also reflect the author's mourning for his mother.)

her in my arms, I failed utterly to kindle a spark of affection in her eyes, a flush of colour in her cheeks . . ." and as in the other dream about his grandmother, he consults his father, but he says, "What can you expect, when people are dead they are dead." [22]

Marcel goes on to say that a few days later he saw the photograph Robert de Saint-Loup had taken of his grand-mother. Actually, that photograph had been a source of vexation and misery. Marcel had thought his grandmother coquettish toward Robert because she had put on make-up, but later Marcel learned she had touched up her face to hide extreme illness, and to Marcel's mother that picture had been a photograph of her mother's disease, of the "brutally buffeted face of my grandmother." (Again, we have the image of a slapped face.)

Later, Marcel says he learned from his dreams that his grief for his grandmother was diminishing because she was in better health in his dreams, an invalid but on the road to recovery; she was the reflection of his own thoughts.[23] At this point in the novel, Albertine was about to become the focus of the story, and was beginning to inspire a desire for happiness in Marcel, although his great passion for her had not really commenced.

In regard to Bergotte's nightmare, in *The Captive*, we are first told of Bergotte's rather base love affairs which stimulated his writing, as "transmuting gold into caresses and caresses into gold" (as so often, in Proust — the symbolism of money occurs in regard to love).

Then in his recurrent nightmare, we are told:

It was as though proceeding from somewhere outside himself that he would see a hand armed with a damp cloth which,

22 *Cities of the Plain*, Pt. I, p. 249.
23 Pt. I, p. 255.

passed over his face by an evil woman, kept scrubbing him awake, an intolerable itching in his thighs, the rage — because Bergotte had murmured in his sleep that he was driving badly — of a raving lunatic of a cabman who flung himself upon the writer, biting and gnawing his fingers. Finally, as soon as in his sleep it had grown sufficiently dark, nature arranged a sort of undress rehearsal of the apoplectic stroke that was to carry him off: Bergotte arrived in a carriage beneath the porch of Swann's new house, and tried to alight. A stunning giddiness glued him to his seat, the porter came forward to help him out of the carriage, he remained seated, unable to rise, to straighten his legs. He tried to pull himself up with the help of the stone pillar that was by his side, but did not find sufficient support in it to enable him to stand.[24]

This dream is followed, in the novel, by a discussion of doctors, who contradicted themselves and each other and did not help Bergotte. Bergotte finally died, after having tried self-administered narcotics for a time, and having entrusted himself to "one of these friends, or enemies." An attack of uremia confined him to bed but he got up to see Vermeer's "Street in Delft" — particularly the exact yellow, the famous Vermeer lemon-yellow, of a wall. He felt his writing should have been as expressive as that. Then he became ill, at first thinking it was merely from eating potatoes, but he collapsed and died.

Bergotte's nightmare about the scrubbing hand is reminiscent of the scene of Marcel's grandmother's death. This time the man is touched by an evil woman's hand (in contrast to Marcel's dream of Charlus slapping Madame Verdurin's face); this is reversed in the next part of the dream by the biting of a hand by the mad coachman.

It will be recalled that in Dr. Percepied's carriage, Marcel had achieved his first successful creative writing, and again,

[24] Pp. 244–46.

in a carriage when he saw the three trees at Balbec, he had a great literary inspiration — once more he was inspired when he alighted from the carriage to go to Madame Verdurin's reception, at the end of the novel. (Immobility, inaction of the legs, is related to being drawn in the carriages; Marcel competes in a very passive way, through imagination and artistry.) Passively, we have Bergotte competing with a painter, stealing the headlines from Vermeer by dying at the art gallery. And Bergotte's dream shows the revenge of a mad coachman.

At this point in the novel, Marcel, who used to envy and admire Bergotte immensely, feels that Bergotte has deteriorated, and no longer writes well (for the very images which inspired Bergotte at first are now habitual, idolatrous, and lack depth of feeling).

For Proust, competition is carried on in illness, sleep, suffering — and with great sensitivity and concentration.

After Albertine leaves Marcel, he measures his changing attitude toward her loss in the course of several dreams. He says: "At other times Albertine appeared in my dream, and proposed to leave me once again, without my being moved by her determination." [25] (Knowledge that she was dead had filtered into his unconscious mind.) His feeling that she was dead was combined, in his dreams, with the sensation that she was still alive, and he conversed with her; while he was speaking his grandmother came and went at the other end of the room. In one dream, part of his grandmother's chin had crumbled away like a corroded marble,

> but I found nothing unusual in that. I told Albertine that I had various questions to ask her with regard to the bathing establishment at Balbec and to a certain laundress in Touraine,

[25] *The Sweet Cheat Gone*, p. 170.

but I postponed them to another occasion since we had plenty of time and there was no longer any urgency. She assured me that she was not doing anything wrong and that she had merely, the day before, kissed Mlle. Vinteuil on the lips. "What, is she here?" "Yes, in fact it is time for me to leave you, for I have to go and see her presently." And since, now that Albertine was dead, I no longer kept her a prisoner in my house as in the last months of her life, her visit to Mlle. Vinteuil disturbed me. I sought to prevent Albertine from seeing her. Albertine told me that she had done no more than kiss her, but she was evidently beginning to lie again as in the days when she used to deny everything . . .[26]

Long after the dream ended Marcel remained tormented by that kiss Albertine gave Mademoiselle Vinteuil, in his dream.

At the beginning of *The Past Recaptured*, Marcel's last pangs of desire for Albertine occur when he calls her name, in his sleep, at Tansonville, where he is visiting Gilberte. Toward the end of *The Past Recaptured*, he says:

The interest I had always taken in dreams, was it not due to the fact that, making up in intensity what they lack in duration, they help us to understand better the subjective element in love, for example? And this simply because with prodigious swiftness they accomplish what would be vulgarly called "getting a woman inside our skin," even to the point of making us love passionately for a few minutes an ugly woman, whom in real life we could have come to love only after years of familiarity and cohabitation and with the aid of some miraculous doctor to give us intravenous injections of love — and quite as possibly of suffering also.[27]

The author describes his fascination with the games dreams play with time. He says that he really lost his grandmother

26 *Ibid.*, p. 170.
27 *The Past Recaptured*, p. 243.

many months after he lost her; in dreams, persons change appearance according to one's ideas of them; one person appears as several; he has seen a lover attribute to his beloved qualities that were only in himself, and so forth. He draws from this the idea that in waking life even political hatred, like France's for Germany, can be colored by emotions and distorted, and that the intelligence of man can build up theories on an emotional basis. He says dreams have been a strong factor in convincing him of the "purely mental character of reality," [28] and therefore he did not intend to scorn their assistance in writing his book. He tells us that when he was selfishly wrapped up in a love affair, a dream brought his grandmother close to him, and that he loved Albertine again when she brought him a version of the affair with the laundress. Dreams awaken desires in him which result in creative work. Marcel then criticizes medicine and politics for their faith in objectivity; he believes in subjective knowledge and says everything came to him from Swann (the aesthete). Jealousy procured his great love for Albertine, and now he is no longer jealous and does not love her any more.

We have been able to sketch only a condensed version of what Proust has to say about dreams, which, like time, are a favorite topic for him, closely connected with the unconscious, in which he finds the source of emotional reality, as does Freud. One might be tempted to make speculative interpretations, from the manifest content, for all of Proust's fictional dreams, but we do not know for certain how much is pure invention or even hearsay from the dreams of other individuals. Still, we do notice uniform tendencies underlying all the dreams in the novel,[29] as well as in the narrative. The

---

28 *Ibid.*, p. 246. See also Sigmund Freud: *The Interpretation of Dreams*, New York, 1955, p. 613: "The unconscious is the true psychic reality."

29 An interesting contrast to the dreams in Proust's novel is afforded by one of the author's dreams, which he recounts in a letter to his mother, written September 8, 1901, and reproduced in Dr. Philip Kolb's *Marcel*

father-figures, typified by Charlus, have sadistic trends, and especially in the dreams, a tendency to beat or hurt women. The female figures are masochistic, suffering, but their defense is a masculine one, like Madame Verdurin sprouting a long nose, like a phallus, and thick mustache, before Swann's gaze. This throws a little more light on why all the characters in the novel, except for Marcel and Swann and just a few others, had to be bisexual. By making all his characters bisexual, the guilt was shared and distributed, the sadism and masochism were allotted more evenly. Marcel is heterosexual in the book, but along with the fantasy of his heterosexuality is the conviction that love is suffering. Marcel, in his heterosexuality, takes over the suffering role — he suffers, as he believes women do, submissively, in sex — but then he assures us he is always masculine in the story, and it is the women who love him most: Albertine, his grandmother — who die, and for whose deaths he feels responsible. In the novel, Marcel is hetero-

---

Proust, Correspondance avec Sa Mère 1887–1905, Plon, Paris, 1953. (Letter LXXXVIII). Before telling the dream, he describes his journey back to Paris from a vacation trip and says he did not sleep well and lost most of the "enbompoint" (an error in spelling) obtained on his trip. He had so desired to show his mother his gained weight that *he dreamed in the night he held it like a ball.* Then he goes on to say that what is more important and delights him is the fact that his mother's plumpness must have been reduced by her long walks. He calls his brother a moral, intellectual and physical pearl. Then he gives his mother a detailed account of his expenditures. He terminates the letter by asking her to request information from his brother as to whether asthma can be caused by worms, and if so, how shall he get rid of them? He sends his mother an article on Compiègne, expressing views with which he agrees.

The dream seems to corroborate our thesis about his unconscious, ambivalent identification with his mother's pregnancy, connected here with the urge toward restitution, praise of the brother, and a request that the brother co-operate in eliminating small, vicious creatures in the body that cause asthma. At this time Proust had already published one book, and was working and gestating, collecting notes for *Jean Santeuil*, and evolving his critical and appreciative thoughts about Ruskin. His dream shows how close to his unconscious his gift of expression really was, how simply he formed an image of his central conflict in sleep, and how he was trying to free himself from this conflict both by regression and by creation.

sexual, like Robert (in real life), patterned more after a
brother than a father — and still he has the women under his
skin, he is identified with the suffering female, sick, unhappy.
The sanitarium does not help. He is suffering, as if impregnated, at the end.

XVII

Some Preliminary Conclusions: Unconscious Insight Conveyed by Symbolic Patterns

I~N~ *The Past Recaptured,* Proust writes about the poet's "life resembling his work, so that he will have scarcely any more need to write, such a faithful forecast of what is to come will he be able to find in what he has already written." [1]

He thus discloses that his work and his life are a unit. But by stressing the universal qualities of his work and pointing out that the reader may see himself reflected in his novel, Proust, to some extent, avoids too personal interpretation of his own unconscious drives. Ostensibly, any individual can see in Proust's novel anything he wishes to see. Yet there remain certain pronounced, emphasized facets: Jealous love, separation fear, constant awareness of bisexuality, the stress on placating everyone and keeping everyone in the novel in protected circumstances, compliance with social amenities, and a somewhat defiant, skeptical attitude toward those in immediate authority, tempered by submission to antique tradition — with the avoidance of open hostility (by distancing and immobilizing aggression, by masochism and by crying out for submissive reunion instead of flight), or an outburst of uncontrolled flight. Flight is made only from one daydreamed love-

[1] P. 235.

object to another, with very little physical action. Love, jealousy, and aesthetic interest play a great role in the thought processes that are revealed.

One purpose of this essay has been to question the myth, implied in Hardy's *The Well-Beloved*, and in many great masterpieces, that a neurosis must be left to run its course, and not be altered, if an artist is to produce great creative work. This fear of insight is an ungrounded one, because with true insight the artist should be further liberated. Otherwise repression inhibits some aspects of artistic expression, despite the expressive nature of certain types of neurotic drives. It is time to examine the adamant partition between literary art and psychoanalysis, since both deal avowedly with unconscious conflicts.

It seems that Proust's novel, like Mr. X's dreams, illustrates the great power of the unconscious and the relatively homogeneous core at the root of an individual's neurosis, as well as the interplay of individual and universal symbolism in every human personality. In Mr. X's dreams, and in his life history, we find a hierarchy of motives and a highly organized series of patterns, centered around excessive love for the mother, jealousy, repressed hostility, avoidance of physical action or flight, and a tendency to turn, for love, from one fantasied individual to another. In most respects, as we know, Mr. X's exterior personality was extremely dissimilar to Proust's, almost diametrically opposite.

French, in his projected five-volume work, plans to give us his analysis of the integrative processes in rational behavior, neuroses and dreams, and to dissect these processes into component factors common to all three. He calls the "cognitive structure" of dreams the pattern of their interrelated meanings. In exploring the cognitive structure of one individual's dreams, and the hierarchy of these patterns, French finds what he terms resonance between integrative fields. This resonance between patterns is perhaps the clue to the structure, crystal-line in nature, which Proust's novel has achieved, through following imagery based on "the natural processes" of the author's emotions.

French demonstrates how integrative patterns continually undergo reorganization. This is very much like the constant flux and change [2] in Proust's imagery, his tendency to tell every episode differently, repetitiously, but with a constant shifting of some part of it. French points out how in Mr. X's dreams there is always a series of partial solutions, because too intense need for the mother's love is a source of problems that cannot be solved, even in sleep,[3] and the impulses to aggression and flight are always about to break through; French also draws attention to Mr. X's tendency to stand and look, not move, when confronted with a strong conflict.[4]

Mr. X's tendency to erotize his hostility toward his sister by incestuous attraction to her parallels Proust's avoidance of rivalry with brother-images by homosexual love for them.

If French's interpretations and deductions about Mr. X are correct, then some of the more inexplicable parts of Proust's novel are also somewhat illuminated by our understanding of Mr. X's unconscious emotional mechanisms. For example, in the history of Jupien's niece: her illegitimate pregnancy, the gift of money to her by Charlus, her typhoid fever just when she marries the impoverished, aristocratic Cambremer boy, and her subsequent death and her husband's homosexual affair with Charlus,[5] are at the periphery of the story. Jupien's niece, like Eulalie, the servant girl who dies of illegitimate pregnancy,

[2] Encouraged by Bergson's philosophy but undoubtedly inherent in Proust's approach.

[3] Thomas M. French, *The Integration of Behavior*, Chicago, 1952, Vol. I, p. 122.

[4] *Ibid.*, p. 167–68.

[5] On page 185, Volume II, French says: "When a cognitive pattern is shifted from the center to the periphery of the dream's field of interest, its more or less complex structure tends to be condensed into a simpler one."

gives us a rather clear-cut picture of the author's unconscious emotional attitude toward pregnancy. When Morel, having fallen in love with Jupien's niece despite his homosexuality, discovers that she has been "in trouble" long ago, he suddenly loses his temper and hurls filthy invectives at her. But later Morel is seen sitting on a curbstone crying bitterly, filled with remorse for his attack upon the girl (we are reminded that French considers the asthma attack of Mr. X as resulting from incipient verbal attack and repressed crying). In Jupien's niece we have only one example of the theme of pregnancy accompanied by emphasis on verbal or aromatic attack, and by a sense of terrible punishment. Another is the ill-fated Eulalie tormented by allergy to asparagus, and the cruelty of Françoise. Other examples of the loss of a child may be found on page 393 of *The Past Recaptured*, where Madame Sazerat has lost her son, and Marcel is ill for days after the effort of writing her a condolence note — and in the laundress's letter telling of the death of her son at the beginning of *Jean Santeuil* — where her sincere simple writing is likened to great literature.

Another example of Proust's "uncanny" intuitive portrayal of clinical truth, is, as we have noted, the strange role the "Marquise" of the comfort station plays in the book. Just preceding Marcel's first orgasm which occurs during his wrestling with Gilberte, this woman and her domain are first described. The second time the comfort station is mentioned is when Marcel's grandmother has a stroke there. Also there is something said about a man, a regular patron, who misses his three o'clock visit only on the day his wife is buried,[6] but continues to return regularly again thereafter. Then in the

[6] The comfort station activities and the "Marquise" of this place, in the park, although they seem to have no important part in the novel, bring us closest to the anal birth and gift theories which Freud discusses in "Character and Anal Erotism" (1908), and which French discusses in Mr. X's dreams where childbirth and defecation are identified with each

last volume, in the Temple of Dishonor, Jupien's male brothel, Marcel overhears patriotic young men employed there (as beaters of Charlus) discussing the war and their soldier friends, and one of them says "Big Jule," who is at the front, has not been heard from for weeks; it is the woman who runs the comfort station, his godmother, who has been sending him gifts regularly, up to now.

What we see in both the tragic story of Jupien's niece, and again in the "Marquise" of the comfort station, is the infantile oral and anal theory of impregnation as a process related to the gastro-intestinal tract, and birth as a dangerous anal product, a gift, but at the same time related to death. The abortive tendency (robbing the mother of the infant or fetus) connected with all this is expressed in cryptic references, reflecting talion punishment for robbing the mother of her son, by a statement of Marcel's being robbed by Robert but forgiving him. This sense of being robbed probably stemmed originally from an unconscious feeling that the author's brother had robbed him of maternal affection, combined with the author's wish he might have robbed his mother, in real life, of her second son — the fantasy of a death-wish toward the brother which the novel carried out in Robert's death in the war.

Proust's great courage in facing his conflicts through his own literary work was like a last-ditch stand against disintegration, in the battle with his own unconscious. When he felt discouraged, he said he used to think of soldiers in the Boer War, and how they kept going through the mud, suffering pain — deserted.

---

other. Probably the fantasy of the "Marquise" of the comfort station represents the result of regression from the genital oedipal conflict. The author goes back to the anal phase of development and finds a similar conflict there. The humor, the sidelights on Marcel's mother's and grandmother's attitude toward snobbery, are of course more superficial aspects of the role of the "Marquise" of the comfort station.

There is always some emphasis at one point or another in the recurring patterns of human nature that makes all the difference in a personality. But as Proust states clearly in his novel, basically there are strong similarities in all human beings. These similarities tend to be reflected in great works of art, and individual though the stamp upon them must be, the artist expresses specifically what all our dreams tend to express in more fragmentary form, through symbolism rather than words. This symbolism is both highly personal and, at a deeper level, universal. Apparently there are basic tendencies toward emotional patterns for which we do not readily find words, only our own series of images. This unconscious realm is the meeting place of aesthetics and psychological or biological inquiry, and symbolism is its means of delineation.

Let us turn from Proust to Freud, and his remarks on unconscious imagery in a story by a writer whom he knew personally, Stefan Zweig. Freud discusses this story, emphasizing how it portrayed some of the main dynamics of gambling

> . . . when it is subjected to an analytical interpretation . . . [the story] . . . represents something universally human or rather masculine . . . it is characteristic of the nature of artistic creation that the author, who is a personal friend, was able to assure me that the interpretation given by me was completely alien both to his mind and his intention, although many details were woven into the narrative which seemed expressly designed to indicate the secret clue.
> . . . This brilliantly told, perfectly motivated story indeed exists in its own right, and is certain of deeply affecting all readers. But psychoanalysis shows us that its invention is based on the extinction of a wish phantasy belonging to the period of puberty, which many people consciously remember. The phantasy embodies a wish that the mother should herself initiate

the boy into sexual life in order to save him from the dreaded
evils of onanism . . . The vice of onanism is replaced by the
passion for gambling; the emphasis laid on the passionate activity of the hands betrays this derivation . . .[7]

Although probably the most basic patterns tend to be
similar in all human beings, as Freud noted, in artists like
Zweig they are close to consciousness. We might also cite
Dostoevsky's writing of *Poor Folk* at the age of twenty, and
Belinsky's exclamation: "It is not possible that you, with your
twenty years, can have understood this." [8]

Undoubtedly, the expression of patterns of integration tends
to vary according to early inheritance, development and traumata. We see that Proust, himself, was aware of his own
unusually sensitive nature and how it was related to his genius.
He says in *Within a Budding Grove:*

And for a neurotic nature such as mine, one that is to say
in which the intermediaries, the nerves, perform their function
badly — fail to arrest on its way to the consciousness, allow
indeed to penetrate there, distinct, exhausting, innumerable,
agonising, the plaint of those most humble elements of the
personality which are about to disappear — the anxiety and
alarm which I felt as I lay [in the room at Balbec the first
night in the strange hotel] . . . were but the protest of an
affection . . . for a ceiling that was familiar and low.[9]

[7] Sigmund Freud, "Dostoevsky and Parricide" (transl. D. F. Tait), from
Stavrogin's Confession, by F. M. Dostoevsky, transl. Virginia Woolf and
S. S. Koteliansky, New York, Lear Publishers, 1947, pp. 109-12. Used by
permission of Crown Publishers, Inc.
See also Sigmund Freud, "Dostoevsky and Parricide" (transl. D. F. Tait),
Collected Papers, London, Hogarth, 1950. Zweig's story is "Vierundzwan-
zig Stunden aus dem Leben einer Frau" (Twenty-four Hours in a Woman's
Life).
[8] Ernest J. Simmons, *Dostoevsky, The Making of a Novelist.* London,
1950, p. 25.
[9] Pt. I, p. 350.

Proust apparently felt that the not very thoroughly repressed patterns into which his emotions naturally gravitated,
and the literary images they tended to create, were kept from
overwhelming his mind and his emotional life by habits of
thought and feeling. "As a rule it is with our being reduced to
a minimum that we live, most of our faculties lie dormant
because they can rely upon Habit, which knows what there
is to be done and has no need of their services." [10]

Proust's term, Habit, referring to a sort of mental and emotional regularity, brings us back to the question of inhibition
of intellectual activity, common to everyone. We all hold
many of our thoughts and emotions in check because of our
anxieties; the physiological reactions and images that must be
held back along with any specific thought might otherwise set
off a danger signal within our minds, or physiological symptoms. Our conscious thoughts tend to revolve into patterns
that are preponderantly nonverbal. Habits of thought tend to
become routine, and typify the integrative process in each
individual. The study of the integrative process brings us into
neuropsychiatric inquiry. Instead of an "age of anxiety," perhaps we shall be thinking about entering an "age of insight,"
as we learn more about emotional and mental functioning.

French's books elaborate his hypothesis about unconscious
insight. An attempt will be made, in these books by French,
to establish whether or not cognitive structures of dreams,
neuroses, and rational behavior are related. If French's thesis,
thus far, is correct, and if we have correctly interpreted the
main unconscious significance of the novel Proust has written,
we may ask whether or not the similarities that appear to exist
in the cognitive patterns in Proust and in the patient described
by French illustrate also the processes of symbolic expression
of unconscious insight, such as Freud described. We may also

[10] *Ibid.*, Pt. I, p. 327.

ask whether the unconscious insight in the dreams of an average person can be compared, at all, with the unconscious insight of a great novelist. Imagination, being a human function, is in some aspects common to us all.

Proust apparently could summon from his own feelings and memories what he called "living" emotional truths, as contrasted with purely intellectual logic. He could not have read all of Freud's work and applied it quite so extensively in his imaginative writing if he were merely basing his ideas on Freud's. He probably wrote so much clinical truth into his work by following the natural patterns of his thoughts — which was what he described as his intent. This is very likely his meaning when he refers to Bergotte as living only for the expression of certain images, and when he refers to writers of "great imagination" as contrasted with those of "intellect." (Like Dostoevsky, he seems to bear out the main contention of Tolstoy's "What is Art?" [11] that truth of feeling is the prime source of great literature.)

It is interesting to see how thoroughly our thinking about Proust, Freud, and authors in related fields of modern psychology and brain physiology involves us in semantic problems. We are dealing with the symbolic language of the unconscious, particularly with the preverbal roots of symbolism, and with the entire subject of communication. Where there are scientific schools of thought, poetic license disrupts barriers. It is refreshing to discover in Proust the material we habitually deal with, in studying human nature, "enclosed in the necessary ring of a beautiful style." Yet the scientist is always on guard, in these literary situations, because the imaginative writer tends to do with an entire novel what Proust seems to have done, for instance, with the invented dreams he includes as part of his novel: that is, to weave his

[11] *Dostoevsky: The Making of a Novelist,* Simmons, p. 11.

own truths into patterns that fundamentally suit his own defenses. There are distortions which go through the core of the artist's observations. Proust has shown us ourselves as reflected in his own "universe," and we thus see our reflected selves with his coloration, or his refraction.

Proust's need for integration was great. His anxiety and the actual danger of fragmentation of his impulses was imminent. Luckily, he was sufficiently gifted to follow the only lines along which both his parents gave their approval: literary creation. He was unable to lead an active life. He had the genius, and one might say, also, the neurosis, for just this one kind of aesthetic sublimation, oriented toward the past rather than the present or future. The content of his emotional life was largely centered around the need to deal with unconscious aggression against those whom he loved very dependently, and his defense against aggression was erotization, which in turn was full of conflict because of the homosexual or incestuous objects to which he was tied. The fantasy of impregnating, in which he tended to imagine himself in the female role, was too terrifying to bring to consciousness, and instead he reverted to masochism (illness, beating fantasies, renunciation of pleasures, conceiving of love as suffering). Whenever his defenses broke down, frustration and actual physical exhaustion collaborated with an established illness to ruin his constitution.

He writes at the end of his novel of external flux and change. This feeling that all revolves and nothing remains the same is really, also, a way of avoiding fixed patterns, and conscious insight into them (rationalized by Bergson's and Plato's philosophy).

Freud's research ultimately led the founder of psychoanalysis to an interest in uncovering specific traumatic memories because they revealed conflicts which, in individual cases, were responsible for each unique personality's development.

Whereas Freud tried to arrive at particular rules related to the functioning of human nature, and to apply these rules individually, with a therapeutic aim, Proust's interests were inclined to be centrifugal, mystical, avowedly introspective, and yet melting away, deliberately, into generalities in flight from himself. By casting his own constantly moving patterns upon a screen for us to see, Proust felt he could elucidate something about every other individual. His novel is so long and so endlessly complicated that it is not easy to scrutinize his basic patterns of cause and effect, and to see the simple nucleus of his ramified themes. But the "inverted oedipal" root of Proust's lifelong literary work is constant, in collusion with positive oedipal drives never outgrown.

As J. Z. Young has pointed out,[12] science advances by putting together concepts that have never been collated before, drawing out of what we know, new comparisons. It might be fruitful to compare the emotional truths drawn from several detailed psychoanalytic records, with such truly imaginative work as Proust's, if possible — in which truth and completeness of expression are dominant goals. It is certainly not easy to find further documents for comparison. Few authors create characters with such emotional truth and such concentration on actual personal experience, to the exclusion of journalistic reporting and of factitious "slices of life" from external sources — such as Proust calls cinematographic. And not all the psychoanalytic case histories which have been recorded thus far can offer sufficiently detailed analyses of dreams to see whether or not they occur in series, for example. What has started as a bit of speculation, an effort at such a comparison, has become a step in that direction, in our present essay. So as not to belabor the comparison of these cognitive patterns in dreams and Proust's writing, for the lay reader, we

[12] *Doubt and Certainty in Science*, Oxford, 1951.

have included our further, more detailed study of them in the Appendix.

The fascination of continual change on the surface of a fantasy, with a sameness of inner theme, is like the attraction of a riddle. Only those who wish to recognize the deepest core need attack the problem of dreams and imagination. The tendency of all men to have a different dream every night is like Proust's tendency to tell us a different version of his conflict in every character and in every situation, with a continual sense of liberation and of flight, and at the same time a constancy of expression of what was deepest in him. The only time he repeats himself is when he is really telling an identical bit in an early rendition like *Jean Santeuil* and then again in some part of *Remembrance of Things Past*, as where he describes the agility of Bertrand de Réveillon, which then becomes the description of Robert de Saint-Loup's leaping over the benches and tables to bring Marcel his wrap. What he wrote in *Jean Santeuil* was revised, usually, as part of the emotional constellation of *Remembrance of Things Past*, every sentence serving to elucidate many connected patterns. Many beautifully or amusingly written portions of *Jean Santeuil* could not serve this purpose, and were left unused, in Proust's notebooks.

Some parts of *Jean Santeuil* have been summarized and added to Appendix A, which follows this chapter, because they cast further light upon the patterns of *Remembrance of Things Past*.

In closing this section, we might point out that Proust offers the same apology that is usually used in primitive magic, to excuse any flaws in the omnipotence of his analysis of human nature, claiming that if his mirror does not reflect the reader adequately it is because it is not used correctly. And probably he is telling the truth about this. He takes account of the scotomization that occurs in everyone. Proust's weakest aspects were in his delineation of parts of life he did not really experience, particularly real parenthood and the genuine heterosexual urges connected with it. The founding of a family, the recapture of nostalgic joys by living one's childhood anew with one's growing children, is not part of his story. His creative urge is tinged with tragedy wherever it is mentioned. The pure joy of successful physical activity is usually absent from his imagery. A virile, masculine attitude toward work, and innate joy of mastery of a physical task, the release of excess energy in physical ways, the exuberance of health, are scarcely a part of what he is equipped by experience to tell. The feminine counterpart of normal virility, the truly feminine woman, is usually absent from his pages, except for his mother and grandmother who are so idealized as to seem somewhat incomplete as individuals. There is an absence of practicality, of the role of machinery in life (which of course can be rationalized by Bergson's influence), but also of muscular competence and of real independence, in the general atmosphere of *Remembrance of Things Past*. (This is not a criticism, only an observation.) Proust lends himself to a comparison with dreams rather than with the behavior of ordinary life, and yet he has parallels in a great many clinical papers, on an extensive range of psychoanalytic topics.

Both Proust and Freud have been accused of a pessimistic attitude toward life. This is probably due in part to the fact that each of these men became aware of the dominant, emotionally "rudimentary" nature of the unconscious, the difficulty of dealing with it, and the thin superficiality of the reasonable logic which we prefer to think governs our actions.

Regarding those who write about the unconscious, the more that is said, the more questions seem to arise. The purpose of this book has been to suggest hypotheses for further inquiry, rather than to arrive at any rigid conclusions. Proust is of interest to all who deal with either psychological or semantic problems. His subtle approach complements our insistence upon a scientific exactitude. He is so perceptive of both conscious and unconscious imagery that the effectiveness of language as communication may be measured by his writing. Here, in this problem of communication, and in this natural tendency of repressed emotions to seek expression in inter-digitated, integrated patterns, and in fundamental simplicity of basic symbols — aesthetic and clinical objectives meet.

Since we are still at the beginning of exploring the depths of latent instinctive patterns in human beings and their ability to change, a study of symbolism is timely. For if human nature is to develop more effectively co-operative, less disintegrative social attitudes, with less "inhumanity of man to man," we must do so with gradual insight into the functioning of our innermost emotions and their expression.

Appendices

APPENDIX A

Some Illustrations of Unconscious Insight
in Proust's Earlier Work (Excerpts freely translated)

A<small>PART FROM</small> their literary value, the early imaginative writings of Proust which are summarized in the following section have been selected as most apt illustrations (self-evident to the psychoanalyst, although perhaps not to the lay reader) of psychological insights typical of Proust. These particularly expressive sketches have appeared in pure culture in the peripheral, less famous, or abandoned parts of what Proust wrote; for example: a story entitled "The End of Jealousy," in *Les Plaisirs et les Jours*.[1] This brief tale describes a young man, Honoré, who is in love with his mistress, and she with him. He tells her he loves her so much that even if he should stop loving her, parts of his body would still reach out for parts of hers, such as his mouth to her neck. He prays God not to let him stop loving her as he has ceased to love past mistresses. He is jealous of men with whom she may be in love. An accident, while riding a horse, leads to the amputation of both his legs. His mistress takes care of him and cherishes him, so that now he has proof she really loves him. But still he doubts her. At last he dies, and that is the

[1] *Les Plaisirs et les Jours*, Paris, *Gallimard*, 1921, originally publ. 1896.

only possible end of his jealousy. This story (like the story of Baldassare Silvande), written by Proust in his youth, shows plainly his unconscious attitude toward masculinity and muscular expression. His craving is to be loved passively, at the price of suffering. Presumably Honoré, in the story, consistent with his name, has endearing characteristics which warrant his being cherished even when maimed, as if mothered by his mistress, but still nothing in the world can assuage his jealousy.

In contrast to the story of Honoré, or Silvande, who also loses the use of his legs, we have another sketch of a frail young man, Daltozzi, in *Jean Santeuil,* who is active and uses his legs to vent his masculine drives in a pathological manner, running after strange women on the streets at night in the rain. Accidentally spied upon by Henri (Jean's best friend) on a stormy night — Daltozzi is seen trying to rape unknown women on the street, and receiving cuffs and blows from men. He has a bad cough, and exposing himself to the rain and mud is suicidal. But still Daltozzi likes to go out searching for young virgins, as if he could gain strength from their vigorous bodies. A photograph of Daltozzi's mother is at Daltozzi's office. One day when Henri shows Daltozzi to Jean, running about like that, in the mud, Jean vows never to expose his mother to such contemplation (here we have oedipal repression in connection with running about, soiling mud and rain, and endangered health). Echoes of this Daltozzi sketch appear in *Remembrance of Things Past* in several places, where Marcel has sexual urges toward unknown women on the street, and in another part where Marcel pursues a woman on the street only to find it is Madame Verdurin — also where the denizens of Jupien's male brothel delight in casual encounters with unknown partners in the darkened underground during air raids.

In relation to Albertine, we recall Marcel's paralyzed feeling, and inability to walk out on the streets with her, because of fear he might become involved in a situation of jealousy. Through the Daltozzi image, we see more clearly how walking and sexual fantasies are tied up with incestuous drives and therefore self-imposed restrictions.

Proust, like Mr. X, suffered inhibition of muscular drives in their erotic and aggressive components, as expressions of masculinity. We see that Proust was conditioned by all his early training to be sensitive first, active second. Proust developed the ability to delineate clearly his own unconscious insights and perceptions through literary forms and subtle imagery (whereas Ruskin, whom he admired, depended more on the inspiration of the art forms of others).

Proust's extraordinary subtlety was noted by the musician, Capet; the latter said he had never played for such a listener, who could reflect back to him the moving pleasure of a Beethoven quartet. "Il était enivrant d'avoir joué pour un tel auditeur qui savait si bien vous renverser ensuite, pour ainsi dire, dans le coeur, tout le plaisir émouvant né de ce quatuor." [2]

How Proust utilized his own perceptiveness opportunistically is reflected in the story of Violante, in *Les Plaisirs et les Jours*. Violante is a beautiful young girl who falls in love with a mediocre boy, and then with another one who is a fatuous socialite. Violante abandons charity, love of nature, and intelligence in pursuit of social climbing, which is easy to accomplish because social life is "stupid," easy to understand. She marries a wealthy man, but she has formed stultifying habits and cannot return to her old self. Conquest by habit, loss of the best part of herself, is the theme of this story.

In a section called "Les Regrets, Rêveries, Couleur du Temps," there is a sketch of a man who falls in love with a

[2] See Preface by Georges de Lauris to Proust's *A un Ami*, Paris, 1948.

mediocre woman because he dreams that she is in love with him, and he with her, and that she drinks his tears. This idea was based on a line quoted from Anatole France. The point of the story is to prove that dreams show the emotions more truly than waking life.

We have another interesting reference to tears in a eulogistic verse to Chopin, in the same book: "Sourire du regret et larmes de l'espoir" (Smile of regret and tears of hope), typical of Proust's ambivalence.

The image of drinking tears is repeated, perhaps, in a different way, by the later image of drinking the tea and remembering the lost paradise of Combray, in *Remembrance of Things Past.*

It is of interest that in May, 1892, a political article by Proust, "L'Irréligion d'État," deplored the fact that "la negation d'une religion ait le même cortège de fanatisme, d'intolérance et de persécution que la religion ell-même. (In 1905 Briand carried through the Separation Law which removed official recognition by the state of all religious bodies. Later, in "En Mémoire des Églises Assassinées," Proust defended the ousted clergy heatedly, against the actions of the government with which his father was connected.)

In regard to politics, he analyzes, in *Jean Santeuil*, the baser motives of a conniving politician, Couzon, the leader of the extreme left, in a strangely turned-about story, in which Jean tries to intervene with Couzon, to defend his own father. He points out that opportunism is the weakest element in Couzon's philosophy.

It is only in the last few years that we know very much about *Jean Santeuil*. In 1952 there appeared in three volumes a French version of the original draft of *Remembrance of Things Past* under the title of *Jean Santeuil*, published by

Gallimard in Paris, and in Ottawa, with a preface by André Maurois. We are told in the preface that Bernard de Fallois, who was writing a thesis on Proust, requested the aid of André Maurois. Maurois then interceded for him with Madame Gérard Mante-Proust, Marcel Proust's niece, to allow him to read over many notebooks and manuscripts which she had stored. Bernard de Fallois, with the utmost patience, pieced together these original notes which were preparatory to Proust's famous masterpiece, and which he had directed to have burned. (In 1955 a translation of *Jean Santeuil* by Gerard Hopkins was published in England and in 1956 in the United States. *Contre Saint-Beuve* appeared in France in 1954.)

Jean Santeuil is presented to the reader as an autobiographical, posthumously published manuscript by the most outstanding French novelist of his day. The narrator and a young friend have met this writer at a resort by the sea, much as Marcel and Robert meet Elstir in the restaurant, in the later version. C., the novelist, has a misunderstanding with the boys. Then he reconciles with them just before he dies, and since the boys are in possession of the only copy of the manuscript, the narrator arranges to publish it. We see in Jean the Marcel of *Remembrance of Things Past*.

Reading this version, one is astonished at the prose style, which Proust himself describes as written at a gallop. In 1896 there were already definite references to his writing this version of his novel, in a dedication to Pierre Lavallée and in a letter to his mother in September, 1896, in which he said he had added 110 pages on his novel to his notebook. He stopped working on it when he translated Ruskin. In addition to the fascination of seeing the transposition and development of his themes and the maturation of his style and imagination, we are also given, in the old version, what is apparently a more exact portrait of his parents — perhaps even caricatured, for emphasis. There is a long description of the goodnight kiss of his mother, just as in *Swann's Way*.

Inappropriate neuropsychiatric advice appears on the very first pages. A professor of medicine is visiting Monsieur and Madame Santeuil, and little Jean disgraces himself and his parents by his weeping for his mother at bedtime. The doctor pronounces Jean "un nerveux" and discusses hydrotherapy; we immediately have a hint of the inefficacy of the medical approach to neurosis.

It soon becomes clear that all the sorrows of Jean's later life were secondary to the sorrows of his early childhood which were a part of his deepest self. He describes his father's majesty and the number of important things his father, who later became Minister of Foreign Affairs, was doing in connection with the government. His father's criterion of literary worth rested solely on the basis of what his colleagues in the government thought of a writer. Yet the father does give assent to Jean's becoming a writer, provided he is a very successful one. The mother is described as vastly superior to the father in intelligence and in poetic and musical gifts, but always completely deferent to the father. Professor Surlande, their medical friend, despises literature as a profession, ridicules writers, and says he hopes that little Jean will be brought up to do something worth while, like following a legal or diplomatic career. Monsieur Sandré, the mother's father, who lives in the household, is caustic and severe, but at the same time we see how he is loved, pitied, and respected by all the family.

In the midst of this family description, we are given a fantastic picture of Monsieur and Madame Lepic, who were imagined to have dined every Sunday with Jean's parents. The monstrous Monsieur Lepic, and the distorted creature he has made of his erstwhile charming and beautiful wife, show us the youthful Proust's intuitive insight into interfamilial sado-masochism. This is a great exaggeration of the feelings of the feminine-masochistic individual, like himself, who reacts to the rigid masculine rules of his family (on a morality basis) — and the head of the family's insistence on long walks, for health, after every meal — with illness. Love is at the root of this sado-masochistic picture, because the Lepics really love each other, and they also adore little Jean. The torture of the Lepics by each other is meted out with the rationalization of morality, health measures, and family affection. Monsieur Lepic dies, and his wife, the masochist, cannot survive without him.

We are next given a glimpse of the little girl, Marie, on the Champs-Elysées, of a higher social class than Jean, patterned on Marie Bernadaky, who was related to Princess Radziwill. (Marie, of the book, appears as Gilberte in *Remembrance of Things Past,* but Gilberte seems to be more merged with a brother-image. Also, in the second version, Marcel hints that he treated Gilberte somewhat as his father treated him, with coolness.)

In *Jean Santeuil,* Jean was so upset by his love for Marie that his mother and father decided that for his own good they must forbid his seeing her again. His mother told him he would, in the future, take lessons from a tutor every afternoon, in the classics, instead of going to the Champs-Elysées. He cried hysterically and called his mother bitter names, but he obeyed. Whenever he was angry at his parents he could not eat. But on that night he ate, and his usually stern grandfather looked at him with the most tender concern while he did so. After supper, little Jean curled up in his grandfather's lap and murmured affectionate words to the usually aloof, cool old man. Long after that, he had opportunities to call on Marie Kosicheff at a valley resort, and did not feel any interest in her.

Thus we see a sad and beautiful portrayal of heterosexual

repression. Many writers would have published much of this moving childhood biography unaltered. To Proust it was the raw material he worked over years later. In his later years when he asked that these notebooks be destroyed, he was following out what he had written about the advice of a teacher, that a young poet should burn his first verses because they cannot be good enough, they are an "early work." In the Preface to *Jean Santeuil*, André Maurois makes an eloquent and convincing apology for our invasion of the author's privacy. The proven greatness of *Remembrance of Things Past*, according to Maurois, warrants a study of all that has led up to it.

Henri and Bertrand de Réveillon, aristocratic youths, forerunners of Robert de Saint-Loup, are eulogized on page after page, stressing their fine intellectual and artistic qualities.

An early turning point in the book occurs when Jean's mother, misconstruing one of Jean's social engagements with Henri de Réveillon, erroneously suspecting it to be an orgy with girls, arbitrarily forbids his seeing Henri again. Jean is devastated by this. He trembles, and feels sentenced, like a criminal. His father, hearing the heated discussion going on, enters the room whereupon his mother walks out, filled with pity for Jean's father, whom she considered too sensitive for such a scene. Then she comes back and says she had dispatched a letter to Henri, saying Jean will not see him on this night nor on any other occasion, for a long time to come. Jean thrusts his hands into his pockets, screams at his parents: "You are two imbeciles," and slowly marches out, banging the door so hard he breaks the glass part of it. He goes up to his room planning vengeance. He thinks of running away to his friend Henri. Weeping, he tries to read. He thinks of quitting his studies completely. Then he develops a migraine headache, which makes him more disgruntled with himself than with his parents. Seeking an inanimate object for his wrath, he breaks his prized Venetian glass, which his mother bought him for one hundred francs. Then, feeling chilled, he pulls out a garment from his closet at random, and instead of one of his own jackets, his hands fall on an old black velvet cape of his mother's, lined with cerise satin and trimmed with ermine, a relic of the happier days when Jean's grandfather was still alive and when Jean was a small boy. This little cape is particularly reminiscent of one night when his mother kissed him very tenderly before going out. Jean puts on the cape and thinks of his mother when she was slender, gay, and pretty. He realizes that she has aged and that part of her present nervousness and impatience are his own fault. Eventually his parents must die. His father works hard to provide money for Jean, even to see that it will be provided for him posthumously. There is so little time in which to express gratitude. Jean overcomes his resentment toward them, and submissively comes down to dinner, still wearing the cape which is his mother's. He apologizes to his mother and asks her to kiss him, but she averts her face. He wants so much to cry that he titters foolishly. He kisses his father and begs his father's forgiveness. But his father, seeing him in his mother's cerise-lined cape, yells at him: "It's hot in here and that thing is your mother's. Take it off right away." At this his mother smiles. Jean knows she understands him, and has insight into everything he has done. He runs to her, kisses and hugs her, and weeps. He whispers to her a confession that he has broken the Venetian glass. She is not angry. Instead, she whispers, "It is like at the temple, the symbol of indestructible union."

Even in his adolescence, Jean is depicted as returning to his past, his earlier childhood, for a solution to his present problem. The stress on "understanding," in love, is a theme we see repeated in his work, also of course the tears, the confession, the verbal attack, and remorse. (So typical of tendencies in many asthmatics.)

In the third volume of *Jean Santeuil*, there is an episode about a duel, which shows how entirely preoccupied Jean is with attaining the most prominent men of Paris as his witnesses; all fear of injury is projected to a fear of not obtaining sufficiently impressive witnesses, on a social level, and then on the fear of having to go to the duel on horseback, for he is afraid of horses.

Also in the third volume is the well-known incident of Madame Cresmeyer's dinner party, a gem of parodied social climbing and a complete short story in itself. In a similar tone, we have Jean's revenge on Madame Marmet, whom Jean describes as a diplomat in the war of social climbing, while her husband is in charge of combat. The Marmets behave insultingly toward Jean, because they do not consider him worthy of being seen in their box at an important "first night" at the opera, *Frédégonde*. The mother of Jean's friend Henri, who is the Duchess de Réveillon, a great social leader, takes Jean under her own wing, and persuades Madame Marmet's guests to cancel their acceptance of the latter's invitation at the last minute. The Réveillons end up with Jean as their guest, parading around the lobby on the arm of the King of Portugal. Jean still wants to pay his respects to Madame Marmet, but the Duchess de Réveillon prevents him, and says she will never allow any of her guests to go to the Marmets' house, and that Jean's mother would approve of her restraining him if she knew, and she would soon tell her. But then Monsieur de Lomperolles, the Duchess's cousin, comes over to complain about Jean, and the flower in his buttonhole, and says, with his typical complaint, that Jean is a real female. Thus we see the Proustian pattern of triumph over competitors as a passive, feminine, charming individual.

In this volume, Henri Loisel, the pianist, is perhaps a fore-runner of Morel. Bergotte is the name given to a painter who later is to appear as Elstir in the final novel. The love affair of Jean and a young woman called Françoise foreshadows the affair of Odette and Swann. In this earlier version, Jean wrings a confession from Françoise about her homosexual indulgences with Charlotte. There is a statement by Françoise, apparently derived from the author's own experience, that after her sexual sin she never again knew a happy moment and never thought of anything else.

"Depuis je n'ai jamais eu une minute de bonheur. Le senti-ment de ma faute, du mensonge dans lequel je vis, réussissant à abuser ceux qui m'aiment, ne me quitte pas un instant. Il est entre moi et tout ce que je vois." [3]

One typical sketch shows us Jean at twenty-two; his father, now Minister of Foreign Affairs, goes off on a trip and Jean spends a day with his mother who devotes herself to him, in-stead of to his father. This day is ideal for Jean. At the end, Jean goes out to vote. Instead of voting for the man who is his own choice, he feels he must vote as his absent father would have voted.

This aspect of his submissiveness to his father is reinforced by still another sketch which follows, of his father at a café, alone, on the trip. A dog is asleep, where his father is. There is a passage about waking a sleeping child, and the smile of innocence on the child's face, opening its eyes as the father enters. The child does not remember the incident the next day (III, p. 293). "Car les petits enfants et le chien qui tout à l'heure a regardé M. Santeuil avant de se rendormir, font avec leurs petit corps des choses graves comme de dormir, comme de mourir . . ." (For little children, and the dog who has just looked at Monsieur Santeuil before going back to sleep, do

---

[3] *Jean Santeuil*, Paris, 1952, Vol. III, p. 216.

with their little bodies serious things, like sleeping, like dying).

On page 301 of Volume II, Jean describes the evocation of hidden images: "Une fois devant son papier il écrivait ce qu'il ne connaissait pas encore, ce qui l'invitait sous l'image ou s'était caché." He refers to these hidden images as symbols. Here, he tells us that *good* was what favored his inspiration and *bad* was what paralyzed it.

Toward the end of *Jean Santeuil*, he describes his aging parents, and the rented boat in which they ride. His mother has ostensibly become more like Jean in her moral code, but not really, because she still secretly criticizes a girl from the past who had a lover. The book ends with a description of Jean's father asleep, watched over by the mother and Jean, who is thinking of his father's death, which must eventually approach. In *Remembrance of Things Past*, we have the sleep sequence at the beginning, related to Marcel, and the discourse on aging projected to others; Marcel's parents are already dead.

Since *Jean Santeuil* and *Remembrance of Things Past* are lengthy works, we have tried to give only a hint of the relationship of the two novels, the first a forerunner of the second, and both dealing with all the exhaustive ways of reworking the same themes. Perhaps the most striking image in *Jean Santeuil* is the storm at Penmarch, a microcosm of *Remembrance of Things Past*. Since *Jean Santeuil* is composed of loosely connected episodes, we have not told them in the same order, and have saved Penmarch for the last, to dwell on at greater length.

Much of the second volume of *Jean Santeuil* is devoted to Jean's pleasant stay with his friend Henri, whom he is now permitted to see again, at Henri's parental estate, Réveillon. Henri is described in the same glowing terms which were later used for Robert de Saint-Loup. Henri's father, the Marquis de Réveillon, is a great aristocrat who is very fond of Jean. Henri's charming mother whispers words of tenderness to Jean in the woods at Réveillon, and the attractive young maid there sleeps with Jean. Jean goes with Henri to vacation at an inn at Begmeil, which is the earlier model of Balbec. Henri and Jean enjoy reading together by the calm bay.

Jean has expressed a desire to go to see a storm at Penmarch, on the rocky coast, if one of its famous tempests arises. Pierre, a fisherman, has promised to take him. At three o'clock one morning, Pierre sends word that a terrific storm has arisen and Pierre is going there to see if they need him to help man a lifeboat. The storm has been brewing for three days. Jean sees through the windows the snapping boughs of broken trees. He has an urge to do something unusual, in such fantastic weather. Preparing to go with Pierre, he starts to take his umbrella, but is told it would be smashed right away; instead Pierre brings a rope to tie Jean for safety, if necessary. Jean is overjoyed at the extraordinary precautions, and the abandonment of ordinary ones. They cannot light lanterns, so they wait until dawn. It is an eight-hour trip by horse and wagon to Penmarch, and very hazardous in bad weather. The peril of being washed away to sea is great, as Ethel, the landlady at the inn, describes it. The maid at the inn gives Jean hot milk before he goes. He is told by women in the kitchen that people are frequently drowned in these storms, and it is the worst one they have had in ten years. They ask him why he must go, when everyone else will be safe in their houses, actually locked in with a key, because the wind blows the doors open; and they warn him to say his goodbyes well. They try to tempt him to remain in bed, and promise him a good breakfast served in bed, but Pierre and the sailor are now waiting for Jean, and he goes partly because he does not want to be rude to Pierre.

The horse gallops through a howling wind, Jean expects to be killed any minute. The sailor who accompanies them holds Jean tightly and puts his own beret on Jean. In the sailor's hat, Jean feels brave. "From then on, like warriors who, eating the entrails of a gallant fighter, wearing his helmet, feel in themselves his bravery, Jean had no more fear." [4] (Dès lors comme ces guerriers qui, mangeant les entrailles d'un brave, portant son casque, sentaient en eux sa bravoure, Jean n'eut plus peur.)

The wind becomes overpowering. They have to leave their carriage at Point L'Abbé and take a little railroad train to Penmarch. An attractive young man is forced to stay on the train's platform in the rain, because he has a bicycle with him. He seems distinguished "by birth and nature," (again an idealized brother-image). Jean insists on taking Pierre and the sailor in a first-class car with him. There are also two women in the compartment, evidently fleeing from the storm to the shelter of an inland village. One is a disdainful young beauty, a "cocotte," it seems, probably an actress who lives with a rich man and is striving to show how little she values anyone's opinion, and by this attitude she demonstrates how very much she does care. Her "subaltern" companion increases the despicable impression: a rouged, clown-faced woman, in an absurd hat. Jean studies the latter's criminal features, leprous red cheeks, forced laughter at every word of the younger woman, and excessive familiarity toward strangers. He thinks of her as the servant of a procurer, the seller of a child, or accomplice of an assassin, combining extreme vulgarity with a disgusting sort of elegance, and giving by comparison an air of innocence to the other woman. But perhaps she is only a companion from the stage, showing her bestial roles still upon

---

[4] *Jean Santeuil*, Vol. II, p. 199. Cf. this wearing of the strong man's hat with stamping on Charlus's hat to express defiance of him, and submission projected to Morel, in the later novel.

her face. The exaggeration and falsity on the faces of actors, the mobility of their eyes and oversuppleness of their bodies — possibly derives from their occupation, Jean reflects. He watches the two women perpetually opening their bags and closing them, speaking of the things they forgot to pack, complaining about the dirt and bad odor of the railroad carriage, and pulling their gloves on and off.

Jean looks out sometimes at the delicate profile of the bicyclist and thinks of the injustice being done: this fine boy of good family and distinguished character, soaked and freezing out there in the wind and rain, while those two creatures are wrapped in their furs in the warm car, complaining besides. Once or twice Jean goes out on the platform to show the bicyclist his sympathy by partaking of his fate so that this boy should not think that, like the two women, Jean despises him. When Jean comes back into the car, he hears one of the women pronounce the name of the Minister of Denmark as if she knew him well.

The train arrives at its destination. The bicyclist departs with the two women. Jean is assured that the young man is the lover of the younger woman, and must play a part in scenes of humiliation, pretention, vulgarity, and charlatanism in hotels and trains with her, he must deal with the men with whom she is stupidly vexed, and with her professional jealousies, and so on.[5]

The maid-in-waiting, as the older woman seems to be, the cocotte, and the young bicyclist [6] with the delicate profile go off, vanishing into a corner of Jean's memory where he thinks he will perhaps never see them again.

When Jean and the two men arrive at Penmarch, Pierre and the sailor discover they have come in vain. The lifeboat will

[5] Here we see a preliminary version of Robert de Saint-Loup's humiliating affair with Rachel, whom he calls Zézette.

[6] Albertine comes to Elstir's studio on a bicycle, and is frequently depicted on one, in the second novel.

not be dispatched because it is impractical to set out on such a rough sea. For the last two days all those who have previously attempted to go out in lifeboats had to come back; two people have perished. Pierre and the sailor say they will remain at Penmarch because they have brought along a young gentleman who wants to watch the tempest. The sun shines on the plates in the dining room where they sit and talk. There is a very expressive painting of the sun, sea, and scenery there, by Harrisson (in the later novel, Whistler's painting of Balbec has greatly added to its charm for Marcel). The luncheon odors are delectable. The wind hurling itself against the doors, the rattling of windows and trembling of chimneys, are almost a lulling, monotonous sound, since one does not have to contend with them. It is hard to realize that this is an accursed village, some day to be inundated by the hostile sea, which meanwhile takes more of its children every winter. The place feels, rather, like a sort of happy retreat, where the charm of art smiles complacently and the sun comes for shelter from the wind.

The sun fades, the room turns black, the windows stream. Jean, Pierre, and the sailor eat rapidly. Then it is sunny once more, and the three, holding close together for greater wind-resistance, go up the street to the rocky coast from which they will look at the sea. The wind is incredibly violent. Water hits their faces from the sea, while it is still far off. It rains but the rain blows away and does not hit them. The men climb with Jean to such a windy place that they have to crawl; they are thrown by the wind, so that they have to hug the ground, not daring to raise their heads. The sailor helps the other two to crawl back to a more protected place. Jean feels that the storm's violence is at its peak.[7] He sees, "as at

---

[7] The sexual and birth symbolism here need no comment. Vinteuil's masterpiece, and Elstir's early allegorical painting, and Swann's dream of

the commencement of the world, after a giant combat of the gods, all the chain of the Alps installing themselves, peak after peak, colossal but calm, and between them majestic valleys in which one could not distinguish a man. The sun shines on the glaciers and cascades which thunder in the breast of the calm peaks and abysses."

At the end of this volume, listening to the wind at Henri's home at Réveillon, the model of the Guermantes estate, Jean recalls Penmarch, and the poetry he still experiences in the recapture of memories of the storm there. This is the theme of "research into the past" in its inception.

It was typical of Proust to indicate, later, how completely Jean misjudged the characters and relationships of the three travellers he chanced to see on the train to Penmarch. The older woman is the wife of the Minister of Serbia, the young girl is of a distinguished family, and the bicyclist is a pre-medical student who does not know the two ladies, but merely responds to their request for directions, for their journey. It is this young man, Servais, who recognizes Jean when they meet again, and recalls to him the train trip. This is the young doctor whose hand Jean later has an impulse to kiss. Servais finally leaves Paris, to practice medicine in a smaller town, and is not heard from again.

Although the theme of recapturing the past and its synthesis with the present, and Proust's whole philosophy about reality and the ego, appear in crude form in Penmarch, Proust did not utilize the imagery of this beautiful sketch in precisely the same way in *Remembrance of Things Past*. Instead, he introduced some of the same images more subtly, by gentler means, completely woven into the new narrative.

---

renouncing Odette, all seem to be related to this imagery; likewise, perhaps the three figures outlined, and the rope (Charlus's beloved hangman), and the inundated city (Pompeii, with "Sodoma Gomorra," on the wall, in *Cities of the Plain*).

The allegorical fantasy of Penmarch contained the basic elements of Proust's imagination in an untempered form — compared with the later novel. Sublimation, as evidenced in the Harrisson painting in the dining room at Penmarch, indicates Proust's way of dealing with the anxiety-provoking imagery typical of birth symbolism through the artistic process. The successful writing of his books probably prevented psychosis. The creative aspect of his whole existence provided restoration,[8] reunion with all he loved most and felt he must have lost, particularly his "eternal union" with his mother.

When we dream, we do not remember most of our dreams because of conflict and repression. But in creative, sublimatory activity, such rare and fortunate artists as Proust are able to utilize the same regressive components which shape dreams, and to combine them, in subjection to the highest integrative functions.

In *Contre Sainte-Beuve*, we have the notes of Proust's attempts to arrive at his concepts of art and criticism. It is of interest that he describes the inner core of his own ego as his

---

[8] "Et en effect il ne dévorait plus la vie avec une sorte d'angoisse de la voir disparaître sous la jouissance, mais il la goûtait avec confiance, sachant qu'un jour or l'autre la réalité qui'il y avait en ces minutes, il la retrouverait à condition de ne pas la chercher, dans le brusque rappel d'un coup de vent, d'une odeur de feu, d'un ciel bas, ensoleillé mais proche de pluie, au-dessus des toits. Réalité qui est celle que nous ne sentons pas pendant que nous vivons les moments, car nous les rapportons à un but égoïste, mais qui, dans ces brusques retours de la mémoire désintéressée, nous fait flotter entre le présent et le passé dans leur essence commune, qui dans le présent nous a rappelé le passé, essence qui nous trouble en ce qu'elle est nous-même, ce nous-même que nous ne sentons pas au moment, mais que nous retrouvons comme un miel delicieux resté après les choses quand elles sont loin de nous, qui nous enchante en ce qu'elle est les choses et les différencie si bien à distance, et nous fait d'un Penmarch une chose si personnelle, et que quand nous voudrions la revoir rien ne nous remplacerait, réalitié que nous répandons tandis que nous écrivons des pages qui sont la synthèse des divers moments de la vie." From *Jean Santeuil*, Vol. II, p. 339. See also pp. 136–137 of this book.

"God," and as a little figure of a friar,[9] such as stood in an optician's shop indicating weather changes by removing his hat or opening an umbrella.

In these early notes, he refers to the Guermantes family as having something serpentine,[10] rather than birdlike about them. It is Marcel who is startled at the sight of the Duchess de Guermantes, like a bird who sees a snake. In the later version, the Guermantes are birdlike, Robert de Saint-Loup is "half falcon."

Perhaps most corroborative of our assumptions about Marcel Proust's relation to his mother and brother are the passages where he and his mother quote from Reynaldo Hahn's opera, *Esther*. In regard to Marcel's brother, Robert, being shut out of Marcel's room, the mother quotes a line about death [11] as the penalty of any audacious person who comes to Marcel without being summoned. Later, his *mother* thinks, correctly, that she hears Marcel calling her, and asks if she should come in. He replies, again quoting from *Esther*,[12] "What do you fear, am I not your *brother?*"

He then tells her he has decided to write an article against the method of Sainte-Beuve. This leads to an exposition of the core of his philosophy and the artistic concepts of his later masterpiece. He asserts that art is not cumulative, like science. Each artist has to start like Homer. Sainte-Beuve wanted to know each artist's place in society, and his personality, but Proust feels that a great book is the product of an ego unknown to the artist's friends, obfuscated by daily relationships. We see, here, how Norpois and Madame de Villeparisis are rooted in Sainte-Beuve. Modern soul-searchings in regard to materialism versus the sensitive search for emotional truth are encapsulated here, in these jottings of 1905 to 1908.

[9] P. 77.   [10] P. 92.   [11] P. 127.   [12] P. 129.

APPENDIX B

Some Further Theoretical Comments
Regarding Proust's Symbolism

FRENCH'S STUDIES, particularly of water symbolism in the dreams of Mr. X, are based on Freud's *Interpretation of Dreams*,[1] and many other psychoanalytic works, also on certain aspects of Gestalt psychology, Kurt Lewin's field theory, the work of G. F. Mead at the University of Chicago, and many others.

Motor inhibition and substitution of talking for action, in Mr. X's dreams,[2] is of great interest, because it is similar to what we see in Proust also. Very often trivial social actions are highly charged in Mr. X's dreams. Instead of active participation, there is spying, looking, and moving things are watched: aggressive behavior is looked at, replacing motor discharge by receptive absorption. The shift from motor discharge to mental comprehension, based on visual projection, verbalization, and integrative functions, are described. We see parallels with Proust when we read French's delineation of the change of aggressive patterns to patterns of sensory discharge [3] and the attempt to share these feelings, to express and

[1] Sigmund Freud, *The Interpretation of Dreams*, New York, 1955.
[2] T. M. French, *The Integration of Behavior*, Vol. II, p. 315.
[3] *Ibid.*, Vol. II, p. 326.

externalize them, in order to prevent being overwhelmed. Cognitive elaboration and tonic motor absorption are in harmony with the asthmatic make-up, in just the precise respects where Mr. X and Proust are similar. We do not wish to overstress these similarities. The fantasy life, like the fingerprints of any two individuals, would naturally tend toward similarities and accompanying contrasts. The main point is that the similarities and differences in the imagery of these two men apparently make logical sense when the unconscious is interpreted.

French has attempted to carry certain aspects of symbolism a little farther than such a study has ever been carried, in his work on the minute study of one patient's dreams, and there will no doubt soon be more written about symbolism. We are dealing in Proust with specific processes of symbolism (using the word in the psychoanalytic sense, not its artistic connotation, or in relation to the Symbolist movement). Proust's symbols are latently and potentially universal, at least for our culture, and yet his symbolism also has the stamp of its particular history and highly individual meaning.

In *The Arabian Nights' Entertainment,* Proust's favorite book, the great charm of the Oriental fantasies is once more a matter of highly imaginative symbolism as well as a representation of the unconscious, more free of super-ego restrictions than most of our Western literature. It is unnecessary to mention the Greek and Roman myths, with their strict talion laws which have influenced us deeply, particularly *Oedipus Rex,* Narcissus, and so forth, on which some of the terminology of psychoanalysis rests. Symbolism, as we know, reaches from the universally human to such minute particularization that special words are often invented by individuals (for example, to cattleya, to Proustify).

It would be interesting to check still further the various uses of water, fire, and ice, and other symbolisms such as grasping, walking, in Proust and in other writers of great imagination, and check all this further against symbolism in other types of recorded psychoanalytic case histories.

In Proust's stories, we are given the impression that in trying to retain the love of women, one has to become depleted of money. To obtain love, one gives gifts. Proust was noted for his generosity, but actually there were two conflicting elements: the need to give, and the need to hold on to the substance that made him feel independent or capable of gaining love through gifts.

The need for funds is linked in most of us with the need for social prestige; one begets the other, so we see Charlus capable of purchasing a title and husband for Jupien's niece. Proust had an ambivalent attitude toward money and possessions as he did toward people. In his stories and his life, one purchased love, one clung to money for independence, but still there was a masochistic need to get rid of money, to be dependent again.

This masochistic attitude toward money, children, possessions, and gifts is Proust's way of punishing himself, because the beloved woman of his fantasies, and the child within her, emblem of her betrayal of him, must both die — this is the repressed wish. But immediately it is translated to the riddance, not of a child, but of mere body-content which is only excrement, and its sublimation: money.

Proust himself explained all his difficulties in love by saying jealousy always interfered. Without jealousy, love could not exist for him. But when flagrant jealousy appeared, the torments of jealousy could end only with death: his aggression had to be turned against himself.

At the end, he reversed the aggression toward the mother who betrays the firstborn by her pregnancies, and showed how children betray their mothers. In his book, the young men die in the war, they become homosexuals — and the girls are the betrayers. To this extent, the girls repeat the mother's pattern. The girls mistreat their mothers; and Marcel's fecund state, his identification with pregnancy, after his mistreatment by Albertine, leaves him greatly tortured in the last volume. His creative ability is a race with death. (He identifies with the daughters, and the mothers, even more than with the sons.)

As Proust's patterns revolve, we see how he always emphasizes forgiveness and the overcoming of rejections, retention of love, fear of separation, avoiding his constantly burgeoning aggression and despising it. Instead of chaos, there is order, control, aesthetic pleasure, in this organization of pattern. There is what may be an excess of symmetry, such as Proust recognized when he described the idolatry of imagery which takes place as the imaginative artist evolves his own personal forms of imagery, and then through habit and lack of energy begins to seek safety in repetition of the same images.

The great length of *Remembrance of Things Past* allows scope for the demonstration of many changing aspects of his ego [4] which particularly fascinated Proust. The novel seems to cover every sort of variation of the themes which unconscious insight into Proust's conflicts provided for him. Apparently he found it necessary to elaborate profusely the patterns [5] that were summoned from his unconscious. In his

[4] Proust's dissertations on the temporal variations in his own ego recall once more the dream of Mr. X, in which Mr. X. projected such a change. It is the dream of two generations which was mentioned on page 119, in our chapter on Hardy.

Quoting now from French's *Integration of Behavior*, Vol. I, p. 167: Dream 19 a ". . . I was walking on street. Lot of people digging up surface of street. I got to corner. There was a girl who was like child at first, had big milk can full of water. She was standing at fire-plug and asked me to help carry can home. She turned into grown woman. I carried one side, carried it to her home. She thanked me and offered me a kiss. I kissed and embraced her. Then I woke up."

[5] *Group Processes* (1955), Josiah Macy Jr. Foundation, Madison, N. Y. Modern biologists such as Konrad Lorenz and Niko Tinbergen have, in

novel, ego-syntonic and ego-alien roles tend to be reconciled
and bound together, lines of cleavage shift positions, and in
the course of time disharmonies tend to be erased, or counterbalanced. All the patterns are reorganized, sexual and hostile
wishes are atoned and forgiven and brought under control.
The aesthetic whole is such that Proust's own parents — and
the critics, he hoped — would necessarily approve of his un-
precedented self-revelations and forgive all his too human
impulses. His mother's aesthetic principles, his father's admiration for success, are part of what he demands of himself.
(Perhaps we might, reminiscing about all we have said of
Proust, compare the role of the super-ego in dreams, hypnotism, and in genius.)

In evoking pattern-formations related to the unconscious,
Proust has crossed the boundaries between purely "aesthetic,"
"psychological," and "biological" observation. Proust himself
considered the understanding of the relationship between
cause and effect, the discovery of a truth — the highest
aesthetic achievement.

---

their research, called our attention to the importance of the study of the
morphology of behavior patterns in animals. In their studies of hereditary
behavior patterns, they have pointed out how environmental factors can
affect the development of instinctive patterns in many of their experi-
mental animals. They demonstrate how these behavior patterns are actually
altered by the environment, for example in the behavior of gulls. They
observe group interactions in gulls, chicks, and so forth. It takes both the
environment and the hereditary pattern to release instinctive behavior
patterns. In other words, instinctive behavior appears to be related to
inherited patterns that are influenced also by environment. Therefore any
study of pattern formations in emotional expression, in the most highly
developed, sublimated form, in man, is of biological interest as well, and
is related to the entire biological field of communication. Von Uexkull's
"Bauplan" underlying structures of each organism has been likened to Plato's
philosophical concepts because of the teleological implications, and are
criticized by many as too teleological. Leppik's discovery that honeybees
prefer certain patterns, for example flowers with five petals (mentioned
by Schneirla) is likewise an example of how patterns of instinctive drives
run through all of nature.

Bibliography
and Index

Bibliography

ABRAHAM, KARL: *Selected Papers on Psychoanalysis*, London, Hogarth, 1927.

Bibesco, Martha Lucie: *Au Bal avec Marcel Proust*, Paris, Gallimard, 1929.

Bois, Elie–J.: "À la recherche du temps perdu, Variété littéraire" (Interview accordée à Elie–Joseph Bois) *Le Temps*, Nov. 12, 1913.

Cattaui, Georges: *L'Amitié de Proust* (Préface de Paul Morand), Paris, Gallimard, 1935.

Chernowitz, Maurice E.: *Proust and Painting*, New York, International University Press, 1945.

Cobb, Stanley: "On the Nature and Locus of Mind," *Neurology and Psychiatry* (Feb. 1952), Vol. 67, No. 2, pp. 176–77.

Curtiss, Mina: *Letters of Marcel Proust*, Transl. and ed. with notes by Mina Curtiss, Introduction by Harry Levin, New York, Random House, 1949.

Dandieu, Arnaud: *Marcel Proust: sa revelation psychologique*, Paris, 1936.

Dreyfus, Robert: *Souvenirs sur Marcel Proust*, Paris, Grasset, 1926.

Dubois, Paul: *Psychic Treatment of Nervous Disorders,* transl. Smith E. Jelliffe and William A. White, New York and London, Funk and Wagnalls, 1905.

Erikson, Erik H.: *Childhood and Society,* New York, W. W. Norton, 1950.

Frazer, James G.: *Myths of the Origin of Fire,* London, Mac-Millan, 1930.

French, Thomas M.: *The Integration of Behavior,* Chicago, University of Chicago Press, Vol. I, 1952; Vol. II, 1954.

French, Thomas M., and Franz Alexander: *Psychogenic Factors in Bronchial Asthma,* Parts I and II, Washington, D.C., National Research Council, 1941.

Freud, Sigmund: *The Basic Writings of Sigmund Freud,* transl. and ed. A. A. Brill, New York, Mod. Libr. Ed., 1938.

—— *Beyond the Pleasure Principle,* London, Hogarth, 1922.

—— *Civilization and its Discontents,* London and New York, Hogarth, 1930.

—— *Collected Papers,* London, Hogarth, 1924–1950.

—— "Dostoevsky and Parricide," in *Stavrogin's Confession,* transl. Virginia Woolf, and S. S. Koteliansky, New York, Lear Publishers, 1947. (Originally published in German 1928.) Also contained in *Collected Papers,* Vol. V, p. 222.

—— *Interpretation of Dreams,* New York, Basic Books, Inc., 1955.

—— *New Introductory Lectures on Psychoanalysis,* New York, W. W. Norton, 1933.

—— *The Origins of Psychoanalysis, Letters to Wilhem Fliess, Drafts and Notes: 1887–1902,* ed. Marie Bonaparte, Anna Freud, Ernst Kris, transl. Eric Mosbacher and James Strachey, with introduction by Ernst Kris, New York, Basic Books, Inc., 1954.

Galland, Antoine: *Mille et une Nuits,* Paris, Garnier, 1825.

Gide, André: *Thesée,* Paris (1869); New York, Pantheon, 1946; also in English translation by John Russell, *Oedipus and Theseus.* New York, Alfred A. Knopf, Inc., 1950.

Group Processes, Josiah Macy Jr. Foundation, Madison, N. Y., 1955.

Hardy, Thomas: *The Well-Beloved* (reprinted from a story printed in *The Illustrated London News* in 1892), first published as a novel, New York, Harper & Bros., 1897.

Jones, Ernest: *The Life and Work of Sigmund Freud,* New York, Basic Books, Inc., Vol. I (1953); Vol II (1955).

Kolb, Philip: *Marcel Proust, Correspondance avec sa Mère,* Paris, Plon, 1953.

—— *Marcel Proust et Jacques Rivière, Correspondance 1914–1922,* Paris, Plon, 1955.

——*Marcel Proust, Lettres à Reynaldo Hahn,* Paris Gallimard, 1956.

Krutch, Joseph Wood: *Five Masters, A Study in the Mutations of the Novel,* New York, Cape and Smith, 1930.

Kubie, Lawrence S.: "The Central Representation of the Symbolic Process in Psychosomatic Disorders," *Psychosomatic Med.* (Jan. 1953), Vol. XV, No. 1, pp. 1–7.

Kubie, Lawrence S.: "The Distortion of the Symbolic Process in Neurosis and Psychosis," *Journal of the American Psychoanalytic Ass'n,* Vol. I (Jan. 1953), No. 1, pp. 59–86.

Lewin, Bertram: "Reconsideration of the Dream Screen," *Psychoanalytic Quarterly* (1953) Vol. XXII, No. 2, p. 197.

Lindner, Gladys Dudley (compiler): *Marcel Proust — Reviews and Estimates in English,* Palo Alto, Stanford University Press, 1942.

March, Harold: *The Two Worlds of Marcel Proust,* Philadelphia, University of Pennsylvania Press, 1948.

Maurois, André: *Proust: Portrait of a Genius,* transl. Gerard Hopkins, New York, Harper & Bros., 1950.

Miller, Milton L.: "Ego Functioning in Two Types of Dreams: Mirror Dreams," *Psychoanalytic Quarterly* (Dec. 4, 1948), Vol. 17, pp. 346–55.

—— "On Street Fear," *"International Journal of Psychoanalysis* (1953), Vol. XXXIV, Pt. III, pp. 232–40.

Morand, Paul: *Tendres Stocks* (Préface de Marcel Proust), Paris, Gallimard, 1921.

Morand, Paul: *Le Visiteur du Soir*, Geneva, La Palatine, 1929.

Penfield, Wilder: Memory Mechanisms, *Arch. of Neurology and Psychiatry* (Feb. 1952), Vol. 67, pp. 178–91.

Pierre-Quint, Léon: *Marcel Proust, sa vie, son oeuvre*, Paris, Kra (1925), 1928.

—— *Proust et la Stratégie Littéraire*, Paris, Editions Correa, Buchet/Chastel, 1954.

Proust, Achilles Adrien, and Gilbert Ballet: *The Treatment of Neurasthenia*, transl. Peter C. Smith, London, Henry Kimpton, 1902.

Proust, Marcel: *A un Ami* (Préface de Georges de Lauris), Paris, Amiot-Dumont, 1948.

—— *The Captive*, Mod. Libr. Ed., New York, Random House, 1929.

—— *Cities of the Plain*, Mod. Libr. Ed., New York, Random House, 1927.

—— *Chroniques*, Paris, Gallimard, 1927.

—— *The Guermantes Way*, Mod. Libr. Ed., New York, Random House, 1935.

—— *Jean Santeuil*, Preface by André Maurois, Paris, Librairie Gallimard, 1952.

—— *Contre Saint-Beuve*, Paris, Gallimard, 1954.

—— *The Past Recaptured*, Mod. Libr. Ed., New York, Random House, 1951.

—— *Pastiches et Mélanges*, Paris, Gallimard (1927), 1919.

—— *Les Plaisirs et les Jours* (new edition), Paris, Gallimard, 1921.

—— *Swann's Way*, Mod. Libr. Ed. New York, Random House, 1928.

—— *The Sweet Cheat Gone*, Mod. Libr. Ed., New York, Random House, 1948.

—— *Within a Budding Grove*, Mod. Libr. Ed., New York, Random House, 1951.

Ruskin, John: "Les Pierres de Venise," *Chronique des Arts et de la curiosité* (supplément de *La Gazette des Beaux-Arts*) May 5, 1906.

—— *Sésame et les Lys* (Traduction, Préface et Notes de Marcel Proust) Paris (1906), Mercure de France, 1935.

Saul, Leon J.: "The Relations to the Mother as Seen in Cases of Allergy," in *The Nervous Child*, 1946.

Scheikévitch, Marie: *Time Past*, Boston, Houghton Mifflin Co., 1935.

Simmons, Ernest J.: *Dostoevsky, The Making of a Novelist*, London, Lehmann, 1950.

Wheeler, William Morton: *Essays on Philosophical Biology*, Cambridge, Mass., Harvard University Press, 1939.

Wiener, Norbert: *The Human Use of Human Beings*, Boston, Houghton Mifflin Co., 1954.

Wilson, Edmund: *Axel's Castle*, New York, Scribner & Sons, 1931.

Young, J. Z.: *Doubt and Certainty in Science*, Oxford, Clarendon Press, 1951.

Zilboorg, Gregory: "The Discovery of the Oedipus Complex," *Psychoanalytic Quarterly* (1939), Vol. VIII, pp. 279–302.

Index